REDRESS

REDRESS

THE INSIDE STORY OF THE SUCCESSFUL CAMPAIGN FOR JAPANESE AMERICAN REPARATIONS

JOHN TATEISHI

HEYDAY
50

BERKELEY, CALIFORNIA

Funding made possible by the Henri and Tomoye Takahashi Charitable Foundation.

The Library of Congress has cataloged the hardcover edition as follows:
Names: Tateishi, John, 1939- author.
Title: Redress : the inside story of the successful campaign for Japanese
    American reparations / by John Tateishi.
Other titles: Inside story of the successful campaign for Japanese
    American reparations
Description: Berkeley, California : Heyday, [2020] | Includes index.
Identifiers: LCCN 2019045837 (print) | LCCN 2019045838 (ebook) | ISBN
    9781597144988 (cloth) | ISBN 9781597145053 (epub)
Subjects: LCSH: Japanese Americans--Evacuation and relocation, 1942-1945. |
    Japanese Americans--Reparations. | Japanese Americans--Civil rights. |
    Japanese American Citizens' League. National Committee for
    Redress--History. | Tateishi, John, 1939-
Classification: LCC D769.8.A6 T383 2020 (print) | LCC D769.8.A6 (ebook) |
    DDC 940.53/1773089956--dc23
LC record available at https://lccn.loc.gov/2019045837
LC ebook record available at https://lccn.loc.gov/2019045838

Cover Photo: Audience photograph taken by Roy Nakano at the 1981 Commission on
    Wartime Relocation and Internment of Civilians, Los Angeles hearings, CA. Courtesy
    of Visual Communications
Cover Design: Archie Ferguson
Interior Design/Typesetting: Ashley Ingram and Marlon Rigel

Published by Heyday
P.O. Box 9145, Berkeley, CA 94709
(510) 549-3564
heydaybooks.com

Printed in East Peoria, Illinois, by Versa Press, Inc.

10 9 8 7 6 5 4 3 2 1

CONTENTS

6 THE FINAL STAGE (1983–1988)

7 9/11: LESSONS FROM THE PAST (2001–2007)

PREFACE TO THE 2024 EDITION

If timing is everything, mine with *Redress* was disastrous, or so I thought at first. The original edition of this book appeared in March 2020, within days of the official announcement that COVID-19 had reached American shores and was evolving into a worldwide pandemic. The one bookstore event I did before stores closed was in Brentwood, in the Los Angeles area. I found the normally packed flight from San Francisco to Los Angeles nearly empty, and the bookstore, its display window stacked with copies of my book, had only five or six people inside, three of whom were friends of mine who had driven across town to attend.

Shortly thereafter, virtually all stores and public venues shuttered their doors as fear of the virus grew, and the speaking engagements I had planned to promote the book were cancelled. But that's when *Redress* took on a life I could never have predicted.

Although the deadly spread of the virus seemingly brought everything to a standstill, many people made heroic efforts to create some sense of normalcy. Within two months I had learned to navigate Zoom, and soon many of the venues where we had mutually called off in-person appearances contacted me to do talks online. Book events and interviews were no longer limited by my ability to travel to physical venues, or by the ability of interested people to join an in-person audience sitting before me. Internet platforms created accessibility from any location across the country. It was also now possible for community groups and institutions to host interviews especially for their members and constituencies. My audience broadened.

I took it as a given that my primary audience would be Japanese and other Asian Americans, and I imagined readers of this book beyond that would be people interested in history and politics but who might not know much about the Japanese American redress campaign in the 1970s and '80s. I have been surprised, however, that the readers for whom this book seems to have resonated most have been proponents of the Black reparations movement. The conversations I had in 2020 made me reflect on the greater significance of the Japanese American redress campaign and on what the campaign's achievements have meant to others who have faced injustice. It's *that* story I want to tell here.

I began receiving invitations from people who were focused on the philosophical notions of reparations and reconciliation. One group exploring the idea of reparations as redemption wondered if reparations truly could lead the way to remedying injustice. Another was studying the global reparations movement and included not just Americans but also attendees from the Netherlands and Africa. There were also telephone calls and Zoom sessions with individuals who had personal interest in issues of collective guilt and healing. Many who contacted me were primarily curious about our initial strategy of creating a federal commission to examine our wartime treatment. In particular, they wanted to know more about the commission's public hearings: their impact, their redemptive nature, and whether the hearing process led to some sort of reconciliation. And ultimately, they asked, who are the beneficiaries of such a reconciliation?

The subject of Black reparations invariably came up—not surprising since this was a topic that had gained particular political and social gravitas following the compelling 2014 *Atlantic* article "The Case for Reparations," by Ta-Nehisi Coates, who describes past and continuing injustices against Black Americans and presents a case for Black reparations. The brutal killing of George Floyd in May 2020 also created a tectonic shift in the consciousness of America, with protests across the country and the Black Lives Matter movement bringing focused attention to the injustices Black Americans face. For a moment, the social momentum in this country seemed to make passage of H.R. 40—the congressional Black reparations bill that had languished in the House of Representatives for more than three decades—a possibility.

As all this was happening, I was contacted by a woman who identified herself as a member of American Descendants of Slavery (ADOS), one of several Black reparations groups. Many in her organization had read my book and were interested in hearing about our strategies for redress. I was invited to participate in a virtual ADOS conference to discuss the topic "Is Japanese Internment a Model for ADOS Reparations?"

The following month, I was sharing the Zoom airwaves with William A. Darity, Jr., and A. Kirsten Mullen, authors of *From Here to Equality: Reparations for Black Americans in the Twenty-First Century* (2020), one of the most interesting publications I've read on the subject. On a broadcast hosted by the Regulator Bookshop in Durham, North Carolina, together we explored what Darity and Mullen have put forth as some of the most convincing arguments for Black reparations. Later that same day, I participated in a *San Diego Tribune*–sponsored panel on Black reparations that included then–California assemblywoman Shirley Weber (now California's secretary of state), author of A.B. 3121, the legislation that in fall 2020 created California's Task Force to Study and Develop Reparation Proposals for African Americans. The task force examined California's past as an anti-slave state and, three years later, produced a five-hundred-page indictment of the state's tolerance of slavery and its lasting legacy of racism against Black Americans. From Durham, North Carolina, to San Diego, California, in a span of two hours: online conference platforms had indeed expanded my world.

From that point onward and with only a few exceptions, Black reparations became the central interest of invitations I received to discuss my book. I eventually reunited with Mullen and Darity for a conversation hosted by the University of Southern California titled "From Japanese American Redress to Black Reparations." And the Asian American Research Center at UC Berkeley hosted "The Politics of Racial Reparations: Japanese American and Black American Intersections," giving me a chance to talk with Charles P. Henry, author of the fascinating book *Long Overdue: The Politics of Racial Reparations* (2007). Regardless of the starting point of those conversations, one could not talk about the Japanese American redress campaign without wondering how it could inform the Black reparations movement as it navigates the obstacles that lie ahead.

In September 2022, I went to Atlanta to speak at the inaugural Reparations Summit of the National Assembly of American Slavery Descendants (NAASD). Titled "Where Do We Go from Here: Imagining Our Future," the conference drew participants from across the United States, all activists in their local areas coming together as members of an organization that was part of the national Black reparations movement. At one point, when I was outside to eat my lunch and take advantage of the beautiful weather, I began talking with one of the participants. She had read my book and was intrigued by the strategies we had employed to overcome both the public's hostility to our arguments for reparations and our own community's resistance to our campaign. Reading about those strategies' success, she said, gave her a sense of hope.

Until that moment, I had wondered why my book seemed to resonate at all within the Black reparations movement. From my personal experience of twenty years in the civil rights world, I know that Black advocates and leaders are politically far more sophisticated and better connected than we ever were during our fight for redress. I've always felt there was little I could offer as wisdom based on my experience. What, after all, could I tell them about injustice and suffering, or about the anger and hatred they would face simply because theirs was a just cause? The collective experiences of our communities are so vastly different in magnitude, and, by extension, the challenges in the fight for Black reparations are much more complex and difficult. Yet once my book began making its way among those involved in the movement, something about it stayed with them.

I realized as we sat there in the warm Atlanta sun that what I offered, what this book offered, was the story of my life inside the campaign: how I had evolved with it, had been at the heart of it, and had been the compass providing its direction. As Chad Brown of the podcast *Politics in Black* said to me, I'd been there and I had figured it out. People are interested in this book, I think, because of everything I'd needed to figure out while navigating the many obstacles we faced. Any one of those obstacles could have brought the campaign to an end. I'd made so many strategic calculations, sometimes on a daily basis, and those calculations were never about monetary compensation but about the challenges of directing a national campaign. Once we'd determined the amount of reparations we would demand, the compensation issue became mostly a symbolic objective upon which we built our campaign.

In all the conversations I have had with advocates of the Black reparations movement, only rarely have we talked about finding justifications for compensation. There have always been enough facts and reasons to support compensation, and for those who still need convincing, both

Darity / Mullen and Henry provide compelling arguments for compensation as a means of addressing the legacy of injustice. Instead, the focus of our connection has been on process, on the commission, on the hearings. In the 1970s and '80s, we had chosen what many considered a tiresome political procedure, but we used it to our advantage and transformed the way the public viewed our issue. The compensation we ultimately received was important, but the change, the healing, was evident long before we began the final push for legislation that would make monetary compensation a reality. This is what advocates for Black reparations have focused on in my conversations with them: the healing power of the hearings, or what many of them refer to as truth and reconciliation.

Every time I hear someone use those terms—truth and reconciliation—to refer to the process we chose, I am taken aback because, while the parallel is there, the profundity is, in my mind, not comparable. And yet I hear that phrase used regularly by many people I've talked with about Black reparations. I am not so naïve as to suppose the model we undertook had any influence at all on the Truth and Reconciliation Commission that assembled in post-apartheid South Africa in 1996, but hearing the comparison so often has made me reflect on the larger scope of what we had accomplished in our long battle for redress. I realized that the hearings in South Africa gave new meaning to the process we had adopted to reach our goal of reconciliation—both with our internment experiences and with ourselves.

I had never referred to our hearing process as truth and reconciliation, but that's exactly what it was for us. The hearings gave us an opportunity to unburden ourselves of the truths of our victimization, and by doing so, they expiated our sense of guilt for that victimization. If there was reconciliation in the process, it was with our past and our previous inability to accept or demand our place in this country. And yet telling our stories to the commission, an agent of the government, was significant because it revealed for us the pathway to our own truths.

Through the conversations I've had with those involved in the fight for Black reparations, I've been enormously impressed with how undaunted they are, especially considering the fight that lies ahead for them. I'd been told many times over that the Japanese American redress campaign was doomed to failure and utterly impossible to achieve. But we persisted and we succeeded. Those fighting for Black reparations understand that the achievement of one group in no way assures similar outcomes for others and that the road to reconciliation may also be radically different for those who follow, and yet it helps to know that the redress campaign opened a door that heretofore had been sealed shut.

Recognizing the sliver of an opening that the Japanese American redress campaign once had can offer hope for what may come through the sliver of an opening that the campaign for Black reparations has now. Japanese American redress concluded successfully in so many ways. Although we still face racism and hatred, we learned that injustice, like wounds, festers until given a chance to heal. And maybe reparations advocates today can draw inspiration from our healing as a community.

Our histories—as Japanese Americans, as Black Americans—may be distinct, but our paths have intersected in meaningful ways, and perhaps never more than in this moment.

The four years since the publication of this book have taken me on a long journey, brought me new friends, and given me a fresh perspective on an issue to which I had devoted much of my life. I could not have anticipated the trajectory of this book from its inauspicious beginning to the place it found in one of the most significant social and political movements in our nation's history. I'm thankful for having had the opportunity to walk on the same path.

PREFACE TO THE FIRST EDITION

When my son, Stephen, was in kindergarten, his teacher was reading a story to the class in which some kind of miracle occurs. She stopped and asked the students if anyone could explain what a miracle was. Stephen raised his hand and answered, "It's something that can't happen, but does."

Five years later, in 1980, I was doing an interview with Bernard Goldberg, who was at that time the West Coast reporter for the *CBS Evening News*. Earlier that week, he had watched a news item about the World War II incarceration of Japanese Americans on KPIX, the local San Francisco CBS affiliate, and he called me to talk about our seeking redress for the injustice of our treatment during the war. I was then the chairman of the National Committee for Redress for a national civil rights organization called the Japanese American Citizens League (JACL). My responsibility was to continue to develop the framework of the issue, but I had decided instead to launch a campaign that would seek an apology and monetary compensation from the United States government for the forced removal and imprisonment of the entire West Coast Japanese American population during World War II. What interested Goldberg was that the JACL's redress campaign went far beyond a demand for monetary reparations. In pushing for an official apology, it sought to prevent the United States from ever repeating the treatment we had experienced in wartime.

The story that aired on KPIX was the first time the topic of incarceration and redress had aired as a major news story anywhere in the country. Goldberg wanted to interview me about the JACL's redress campaign, which by then had begun to gain public attention. At that time, hardly anyone outside the Japanese American community knew anything about the internment, and I knew that we could not even consider a legislative battle until we educated the American public about the wartime experiences of Japanese Americans and convinced the majority that a grave injustice had occurred. I knew that our most effective tool toward achieving this goal was to use and exploit the media, so when Goldberg called to ask for an interview, I welcomed the opportunity.

As we sat chatting at the JACL national headquarters building in San Francisco while his crew set up their equipment, he asked me what odds I gave to the campaign's success.

"Optimistically, maybe about a thousand to one," I said.

Goldberg looked at me and told me he had talked to colleagues and to political contacts in Washington to ask what they thought, and not a single person believed it was possible. They all agreed it would take a miracle for us to succeed.

So there it was, that word: miracle. Something that can't happen, but does.

———

As it turned out, there was no miracle that led to the success of the Japanese American redress campaign. No one person stepped onto the scene, and no single action turned the tide in our favor. Did we have luck? Yes, there was plenty of luck and good fortune, but mostly it was hard work and perseverance and an undaunted belief in American idealism that allowed us to conquer a Sisyphean task that no one thought was possible.

In the decades since, a few books and several articles have been written about the Japanese American redress campaign, each with different perspectives, each with different heroes. I've not read them all— only a couple, to be honest, because I pretty much know the story they tell about the separate pieces of the campaign as their authors understand it. You put those separate pieces together and what you get are the different parts of a puzzle that forms a larger picture of an extraordinary campaign. It's much like Henry James's comment in his preface to *The Portrait of a Lady*, about seeing a figure in a house through different windows: the image varies in shape and form depending on the window through which one observes the figure. I learned as a student at UC Berkeley that historical narratives are like that, a reflection of the multitude of factors and influences that shape the narratives of any factual account.

I've found this to be true about the WWII internment and the redress campaign, both of which I experienced firsthand: one as a child and the other as a person at the helm of an often acrimonious and always volatile national effort to set the historical record straight.

I first wrote the manuscript for this book in 2007, with the intent to record the history of the Japanese American redress campaign from my perspective, beginning with my earliest involvement until I left the campaign, and then my subsequent involvement in events following the terrorist attacks on September 11, 2001. The parallels between the strikes on Pearl Harbor and the World Trade Center towers were obvious; the moral imperative for us to do whatever we could to prevent a repetition of our wartime experience was compelling.

For years I was prompted to write the history of the redress campaign at the urging of Senator Daniel Inouye (D-Hawaii), who kept telling me I was the only one who knew the real story and the immense obstacles we faced from the earliest stages of the endeavor through to the very last effort. My response to him always was that I couldn't write an accurate history of the campaign without airing the dirty—the sometimes disgustingly dirty—laundry that would need to get hung out on the line with the rest of the facts. Too many people had already been hurt, I told him, and I had no desire to expose those who had forgotten who we were as a community.

"Just tell the truth—tell it all," he would say. "Someone needs to write the honest history, and you're the only one who really knows what happened from the beginning."

I wondered out loud if he would be bothered by some of the criticism even he himself would suffer if I told my story. He had been, in my view, a noble figure throughout the campaign, but I also remembered moments that had shown me why he had lasted so long in Washington— the place I think of as the meanest little town in America. I reminded him of a few things that had happened in D.C. among the congressional members, things that would expose certain truths he might rather not examine. There were also cringeworthy details I hesitated to share about members of our Japanese American community.

"Tell it all," was his response. "No one is immune from the truth."

So tell the truth I did…in that original manuscript, which will not see the light of day for a long time—certainly long after I and those who are part of the history are gone. As the saying goes, those stories are for me to know and you to find out.

I revisited that manuscript in 2016, nine years after I had written it, and in reading with the perspective of time and distance—both from the events and from my writing about them—I confirmed my resolve to let scholars of the future discover that original, more complete version of the story later, if anyone's even interested by then. But what I also did was see if I could edit out the parts of the manuscript not intended for the public's eyes—at least not yet—and produce a work for publication. That effort eventually led to the book you now hold. With editing, a good deal of additional research, and some rewriting, that original narrative still comes forth on these pages and tells the story of the decade-long campaign (of which I was the director for nearly eight years) to seek redress for Japanese Americans who had been incarcerated during World War II.

Much has changed in the three decades since the days of the redress campaign, and we as a community have evolved in the ways we view our wartime experiences, in part as a result of that campaign. The language we use to speak about these events has played an important part in our being able to comprehend the psychology of our own imprisonment, and our insistence on honesty has been vital to that understanding. After the war, we Japanese Americans referred to the U.S. government's order to remove us from our homes as "evacuation," to our forced imprisonment as "relocation" and "camp." But the redress campaign, as a reckoning with the truth of our experience, demanded a more candid vocabulary, and we thus described our experience using the terms "forced exclusion," "expulsion," "internment," "incarceration," "prisons," and "concentration camps."

And finally, the term "Japanese Americans" is used throughout my narrative to describe American citizens born in the United States to parents of Japanese descent. The Japanese immigrants who arrived to our shores around the turn of the century were prohibited by federal statute from becoming naturalized citizens but were granted the status of legal resident aliens. It was these groups, Japanese Americans born here and their immigrant parents, who were directly affected by the government's wartime policies of exclusion and detention. A third group brought to the United States from Central and South American countries became victims of a separate action by the United States government.

As the director of the redress campaign, I used the word "internment," which I felt best described our wartime situation as political prisoners: we were the victims of racial politics. Today, the word "incarceration" has been generally accepted by Japanese Americans as a term that better describes our imprisonment. I have no argument with that position but have chosen to use "internment" in my narrative to try to give a sense of how, in the 1980s, we navigated the tricky political and social landscapes that then lay ahead of us.

This book is my story. It's the story of the Japanese American redress campaign from my perspective and experience as the person who formulated the public affairs and initial legislative strategies for the campaign and who led the effort from its inception as a national campaign and into the legislative battles in Washington.

It's a story of something that never should have succeeded—something that couldn't happen, but did. It's a story of an organization that was the only vehicle in our community capable of carrying such an endeavor and yet was in many ways ill equipped to handle the demands of a national campaign, the magnitude and profundity of which were far beyond its capabilities.

It's a story of a campaign that depended on a unified effort but began within an acutely divided community—some members of which viewed the cause as a violation of deeply held cultural values—and an organization equally torn between those who believed we dishonored ourselves by demanding restitution and those who believed we owed this fight not just to ourselves but to the nation, to prevent such horrors from ever happening again.

Our success couldn't have been predicted, and even I myself had doubted it. But we won. We beat the thousand-to-one odds. It was, in its way, a miracle.

1

BEGINNINGS

(1970 - 1976)

THE BIRTH OF THE MOVEMENT

"There's more about Chinese checkers in the Encyclopaedia Britannica *than there is about the internment of Japanese Americans."*

That comment was made during a heated debate at the 1978 convention of the Japanese American Citizens League. Established in 1929, the JACL was the nation's oldest and largest—and, at the time, the only— Asian American civil rights organization. The topic was redress: Would the JACL pursue a more altruistic goal than simply reparations—the demand for monetary compensation—and, if so, what were the parameters of its broader demands? In the heat of the discussion, convention delegate Charles Kubokawa, a NASA psychologist, made the statement about Chinese checkers, which, apart from implying how successfully the government had buried one of the most shameful episodes in U.S. history, revealed the immense difficulties the JACL faced not only in executing a national campaign for an issue familiar to almost no one but also in navigating what promised to be a hostile and treacherous landscape as the public and Congress learned the full truth of our wartime experiences.

I was one of the two hundred delegates who heard Kubokawa's statement. I don't know how others reacted to it at the time, but I was astounded. If true—and I had no reason to question the veracity of Chuck's comment—it meant that the forced removal and imprisonment of an entire segment of the U.S. population during World War II was little more than a footnote in our nation's story, even to scholars and historians. It also meant that those same scholars and historians found it unremarkable that Franklin Delano Roosevelt, much revered as one of the nation's greatest presidents, had knowingly signed an executive order whose intent was to single out American citizens of Japanese ancestry and force their removal and imprisonment without any evidence to warrant such action. And he did this without concern that his order would result in the total abrogation of constitutional protections guaranteed to all citizens and legal residents of this nation.

It was, at its worst, a racist action and an arrogance of power.

Given that FDR's orders had had a direct impact on the lives of every delegate at that 1978 JACL convention, one would expect that the issue of ethnicity and race would have guided the debate. But while addressing racism was the impetus, it turned out to be almost incidental to the focus. The discussion on the convention floor was driven not by the issue of race but by a sense of obligation to do what we could to prevent a recurrence of the kind of victimization we had experienced during the war. The discussion focused on the Bill of Rights and the Constitution and the guarantees of the rights of all people as enumerated in those founding documents. The talk was about American idealism and the belief in democracy and individual freedom.

The conversation that day was also an interesting window into the various minds within one particular group of Japanese Americans, the *Nisei*, the second-generation Americans who were born generally between the years 1910 and 1930 to immigrant Japanese parents, part of the *Issei* generation. It was the Nisei who continued throughout the 1970s and '80s to constitute the majority of the JACL, and to be the organization's most influential members. One perhaps surprising detail about this group was that where one might expect bitterness and anger from people who had been dealt such extraordinary injustice at the hands of their own government, instead their position was dominated by a deep concern for the future of the country and a resolved determination that our wartime experience would not be repeated, not toward our community or any others. While the convention discussion addressed indemnification for our losses and reparations for the injustices we suffered, the ultimate focus was toward a higher, more altruistic purpose: to strengthen the foundations of American democracy.

To my generation, the *Sansei*—or third-generation Japanese Americans, offspring of the Nisei—the generation whose political sensibilities were hewn by the rebelliousness of the 1960s and the civil rights movement, such thinking was viewed as weak and obsequious, so kiss-ass. For the younger Sansei, those who had been born after the war and had not experienced the internment firsthand, it was easy to dismiss the members of the older generation. But I was part of the Sansei generation that was born before the war and shaped by both the wartime experience and the virulent racism and antipathy of the immediate postwar years, and I therefore felt I understood something of the Nisei commitment to make our country better. I didn't necessarily buy into it, but I understood the faith expressed in the JACL motto "Better Americans in a Greater America." Pollyannaish? Perhaps. Idealistic? Certainly. And yet I understood why the Nisei believed deeply in the meaning of that motto.

As a group, the Nisei harbored a complicated and complex need to have their fellow Americans understand just how much Japanese Americans believed in this country and how their loyalty to this country was unwavering, even as their freedom and rights as Americans were stripped from them during the war. They wanted it to be known that their values were founded in the idealistic belief in American democracy, and this was especially true for those Nisei who were JACL members, for it was this organization that had cooperated with, and even assisted, the government when it ordered our removal from the West Coast. I know personally that many of those who were involved in the debate on that day of the 1978 convention were WWII veterans, all of them having volunteered from the concentration camps in which they were imprisoned to join the U.S. Army, the very authority that had stolen our freedom.

While many mainstream Americans claimed that our demands for restitution for the injustice we experienced were unpatriotic and un-American, the Nisei and the JACL saw the effort as a way to ensure that the mistakes of the past would never threaten other citizens.

By 1978, the JACL's discussions about redress had progressed significantly further than those of the Japanese American community in general, and it had become apparent that the JACL would lead any coordinated effort to seek redress, even if only by default, since there was no other organization in the community that had a comparable infrastructure and broad national network of chapters. Notwithstanding the controversies that surrounded the JACL when it came to anything related to the internment, it was still the best group for the job, as it was also the only Japanese American organization that had a foothold in Washington, D.C.

While the JACL may have taken the lead on redress, however, the organization by no means "owned" the issue. In fact, the JACL was not an early driving force in promoting the significance of redress. That claim belonged to a group of mostly Sansei social activists in Los Angeles in the mid-1960s. In the shadow of the civil rights movement, the younger part of the Sansei generation, those born after the war, embraced the spirit of the social movement and its demand for an honest assessment of past injustices and a recognition of the inequalities imposed on all ethnic minorities.

One obstacle for the postwar Sansei was that they generally knew little, if anything, about the community's wartime experience because their parents and the community in general had built a wall of silence behind which the truths about their WWII incarceration lay concealed. The silence did not derive from a need to keep the past hidden or secret but, more than anything, reflected the inability of the Nisei to reconcile what they considered a betrayal by their own government and a rejection by their fellow American citizens. They could not bear to explain their own imprisonment and the shame it cast on them.

And if Japanese Americans could not talk about their own wartime experiences, mainstream America certainly was not going to concern itself with the issue. After all, these were not the death camps of WWII Germany; the few people who spoke or wrote anything about the internment were nothing but voices in the wind. As significant as the internment experience was in terms of the constitutional and legal history of the nation, the victims of this injustice were a small and quiet segment of the American population, one easily brushed aside. Even during the height of the civil rights movement, Japanese Americans (the most politically prominent group among Asian Americans at the time) simply did not exist as part of the nation's social conscience. They were not on anyone's radar, not during the war and not after it. Just as mainstream Americans had been indifferent as their fellow citizens were being led into America's concentration camps, so were they equally indifferent to the racism Japanese Americans encountered as they quietly struggled to rebuild their lives and find their place in American society after the war. For Japanese Americans, it was easier and less painful to bury the past and to forge ahead into the future without protests or complaints.

Rather than invest their efforts in trying to prove their victimization by exposing the truth about their wartime treatment, Japanese Americans did what they did so often and so well: they remained silent and rarely complained about their circumstances, making the best of a difficult situation as they started from scratch to rebuild their lives and their communities. *Shikataganai* ("It can't be helped; don't dwell on what cannot be undone"), a deeply rooted cultural value that urges looking forward rather than to the past, had helped Japanese Americans endure the hardships and intolerable injustices of the war years, and after the war it continued to guide their lives as they sought to put their wartime experiences behind them and focus on securing their place in America once again.

Consequently, even twenty years after the war, many Japanese Americans knew little of how it happened that their fates had been placed in the hands of authorities who wanted nothing less than their total and permanent banishment. For many years following the war, no one wrote about the internment, and no one seemed to care. Journalists had no interest in exposing the government's racist policies, in part because their own newspapers were often complicit, even joining the chorus of bigots who called for the ousting of Japanese Americans. And academicians, rather than examine the profound social, political, and constitutional implications of the internment—all fecund fields for academic research—turned their attention to other areas of interest.

The earliest efforts to reconcile the past began in Los Angeles in the late 1960s with organized pilgrimages to the first of the ten concentration camps to become operational: the so-called Manzanar War Relocation Center, located in the Owens Valley, a little more than two hundred miles east of Los Angeles. The majority population at Manzanar were those who had been forcibly removed from Los Angeles. The Manzanar pilgrimage, which would become an annual event and continues to this day, was organized primarily by Sue Embrey, a former incarceree at Manzanar, and community leaders including Warren Furutani, one of the early activists who demanded the truth about our wartime experiences, and Rose Ochi, pro bono counsel to the organizing group, which would eventually come to be known as the Manzanar Committee. It quickly attracted the attention of the younger Sansei, who by then were hungry for information about the camps and our wartime experiences.

It was talk of the pilgrimage and "camp" that led many postwar Sansei to begin demanding answers from their parents. Now in their twenties, some of them had heard nothing about internment growing up, and some only knew about it because a professor happened to mention it in passing during a college history course. Even then, these younger Sansei had no idea if their own families had been involved. For some, their initial curiosity often turned to anger at their parents, first for keeping such a monumental truth from them and for allowing themselves to have been so ignominiously herded into concentration camps, and then at the government for the injustice of imposing such a racist policy upon their families and community.

But from that anger, the seeds of a new movement were sown. From the lessons of the social revolution they saw taking shape around them in the civil rights movement, it was primarily the Sansei who demanded a true reckoning with history and truth and ultimately forged the movement to seek reparations.

———

Within the Japanese American community itself, the demand for reparations by younger Sansei often met with resistance from many of the Nisei elders, who thought it shameful and a denigration of our proud cultural traditions. It was, however, the beginning of a movement that would gain traction within the community when Japanese Americans began to understand the degree to which their lives had been so callously manipulated by leaders in Washington and by General John L.

DeWitt, commander of the Western Defense Command, responsible for West Coast security. At a time and place in which Japanese Americans were already hated by many of their fellow citizens, Executive Order 9066 brought everything crashing down around them.

When the postwar Sansei demanded the truth from their parents and took their protest about the incarceration of Japanese Americans public, they were ignored by mainstream media outlets, even in California, where the majority of the nation's Japanese Americans resided. It didn't help that most of those who had been incarcerated were unwilling to talk about their wartime experiences in public. Many of them could not even talk about those experiences in the privacy of their own homes, leaving an enormous void in the history of family legacies. The internment was not talked about anywhere: not in the community, certainly not in public schools, and not even at universities, where, with a few exceptions, history, political science, and sociology professors remained silent about this shameful episode in America's past. They knew *something* about the internment, but they ignored it, perhaps considering it an unimportant lapse in the integrity of the U.S. government, or perhaps just inconsequential within the larger context of World War II. They lacked either an understanding of the significance of the internment or the courage to point out the callous, racist policies of the government. In the 1960s, the focus of injustice in America turned to the country's history of slavery and its continued oppression of black people, while other issues like the plight of Native Americans and disadvantaged farmworkers, and the struggle for gender equality, seemed addenda to the larger and more pressing social problems of black Americans. Within the ocean of what was happening in America in the 1960s, the catastrophic breach of the constitutional rights of Japanese Americans barely made a ripple.

As the awareness of younger Sanseis was growing, and with it the demand for more information, two publications by Japanese Americans had a major effect on shaping views of both Japanese Americans and mainstream audiences. The publication of Jeanne Wakatsuki Houston's internment memoir *Farewell to Manzanar* in 1973, and a subsequent made-for-television movie based on the book, was for many Americans their first exposure to the story of the wartime imprisonment of

Japanese Americans. Michi Weglyn's *Years of Infamy: The Untold Story of America's Concentration Camps* (1976) garnered a wide audience among Japanese Americans and was one of the earliest exposés to reveal the extent to which the Roosevelt administration knowingly ignored the constitutional rights of Japanese Americans, as well as the duplicitous manner in which the army skirted constitutional concerns as those in charge prided themselves on their cleverness in finding ways to implement racist policies on a massive scale.

Weglyn's *Years of Infamy* introduced Japanese Americans to FDR's infamous Executive Order 9066 and to names like John DeWitt and Karl Bendetsen and a host of others who played important roles in the series of events that resulted in the imprisonment of Japanese Americans, and perhaps more significantly, it awakened Japanese Americans to the fact that their removal and incarceration were not the inevitable consequence of the attack at Pearl Harbor but were the results of the racist policies of Franklin Roosevelt's administration. Many Japanese American activists and leaders credit Weglyn with being a spark that helped ignite the fires of the redress movement, and I, for one, concur with that view. There was symbiosis between the activists who sought the truths about the World War II treatment of Japanese Americans and Weglyn, herself eager to find those truths. She played an important part in opening doors that led to the uncovering of facts long hidden.

By the mid- to late 1960s, two conversations began to take place within the Japanese American community simultaneously: First, the facts were coming to light, piece by piece, revealing how the Roosevelt administration and the army's Western Defense Command had plotted to remove and imprison the entire Japanese American population of 120,000 individuals, two-thirds of whom were American citizens and the remaining one-third legal resident aliens. Second, the Sansei were demanding not only the truth about the internment but justice for what had happened. In the major Japanese American population areas on the West Coast—Los Angeles, San Francisco, and Seattle—as well as in other locations with significant Japanese American populations, like Chicago and Denver, the uncomfortable subject of "camp" (a generic term used by Japanese Americans to describe the wartime experience) was becoming the focus of community discussions.

It was uncomfortable, but it was necessary. Once the demand for truth and justice came from the postwar Sansei, it would not go away; a reckoning with the past was inevitable, and that reckoning would lead invariably to a fateful decision the JACL had made back in the early months of the war.

Following the attack at Pearl Harbor and America's entry into World War II, an overwhelming sentiment of patriotism spread across the land; if ever citizens took pride in being American, it was in the days of World War II. Japanese Americans felt no different about the nation than their fellow citizens, especially in their animosity toward the imperialist Japanese war machine. In the midst of this fervor of patriotism and growing fear, Japanese Americans felt especially self-conscious because the land of their ancestors had attacked the United States, the country of their birth. If most Americans felt the surge of patriotism in their hearts, many Nisei felt the need to demonstrate their national pride even more. Given the general anti-Asian, anti-Japanese environment in which they had grown up, the Nisei felt they had to constantly prove their worthiness as Americans, and now with the added distrust following the attacks at Pearl Harbor, the Nisei grew even more determined to prove that they were as loyal as, or even more loyal than, anyone else. But in doing so, the Nisei put themselves in a "damned if you do and damned if you don't" situation. Should they demonstrate their loyalty by acquiescing to whatever was demanded of them, or should they simply ask that their fellow citizens accept them for the loyal Americans they were?

This was the climate in which Saburo Kido, as the JACL's president, found himself as the anti-Japanese rhetoric grew. The JACL had been formed a little more than a decade earlier (1929) by young men in their late teens and early twenties to protect the civil rights of Japanese Americans and other Asians in the face of discriminatory laws and ordinances in the western states. In many ways, it was audacious and perhaps even arrogant that this group of young people, inexperienced in politics and life in general, imagined they could take on the power structure in their local cities and states, and even the federal government, to wipe out decades of what had become institutional bigotry against both Japanese Americans and those of Chinese ancestry who had come to this country before them. Surprisingly, however, that's exactly what they accomplished. They began by challenging the discriminatory ordinances of local governing authorities in Seattle, San Francisco, and Los Angeles, and they launched legal challenges against racist statutes. Most were small victories, but they were victories nonetheless. The effect of these experiences didn't embolden the leaders of the JACL, however; curiously, they made them feel an even stronger connection to the American scene. They adopted the motto "Better Americans in a Greater America," and like everyone else, they joined in the swelling sense of patriotism that the war inspired, believing, perhaps naïvely, that others would recognize that their efforts were clear contributions to the betterment of American society.

Along with showing great pride in their country, Japanese Americans also shared the concerns and fears of other citizens when the nation went to war, and these feelings took on new gravity when the government turned against them. On February 19, 1942, two and a half months after the attack at Pearl Harbor, President Franklin Roosevelt signed Executive Order 9066, which placed responsibility in the hands of both East and West Coast military commanders to secure their respective areas against possible sabotage and other hostile activities. Under the supervision of Assistant Secretary of War John J. McCloy—one of the key architects of the policy, and the person who would oversee the execution of the president's order—General John L. DeWitt, assigned in 1939 to be the military commander of the Western Defense Command, now had a major role in securing the western region of the country. A product of the Quartermaster Corps and hardly competent enough to meet the challenges of the job before him in this new crisis, DeWitt became a puppet of army colleagues and of California's bigoted politicians who had clamored for decades to rid the state of its Japanese population. While DeWitt himself created and implemented the military policies that led to the imprisonment of the entire West Coast Japanese population, two people in particular encouraged his extremist views. Major Karl Bendetsen, Office of Provost Marshal, was assigned to assist

DeWitt in the planning and execution of the military policies but was in fact one of the creators of those policies. Bendetsen was a subordinate to General Allen Gullion, Army Provost, whose name does not often come up in discussions about the WWII treatment of Japanese Americans, although I have long considered him one of the evil forces behind the internment.

Under the president's order, and with no reason to doubt the loyalty of the Japanese American population on the West Coast, DeWitt began issuing proclamations aimed solely at individuals of Japanese ancestry. The first action was a restrictive curfew that singled out Japanese Americans in the western states, and that was soon followed by their forced exclusion from the entire West Coast region. The Japanese American community found itself reeling, betrayed not only by their government but by their white neighbors, who, with rare exceptions, turned their backs and left their fellow citizens to defend themselves, isolated from any outside help.

To spread news throughout the Japanese American communities along the Pacific, the government chose the JACL as their communication link, not for its stature or experience but simply because it had a robust network of chapters that reached into practically every Japanese American community up and down the West Coast. Two of its leaders—twenty-seven-year-old Mike Masaoka, the JACL's National Secretary, and President Kido, age forty—met with federal authorities to call out what was taking place as nothing more than a charade of racist policies based on the demands of white supremacist groups like the Asiatic Exclusion League, which had for years sought the expulsion of the Japanese population and now advocated that all Japanese Americans be stripped of their American citizenship. The outcome of that encounter was that Kido and Masaoka returned to an emergency meeting of their delegates and warned, as they had been told, that there would be violence if the community resisted the orders. The delegates representing the JACL's sixty chapters (most of whom were at the meeting) ultimately decided to advise Japanese Americans to cooperate with the so-called evacuation orders lest there be bloodshed. Untested in national politics and many still in their twenties, the JACL leadership was hardly equipped to deal with the demands being placed on them.

They emerged from the meeting bewildered and not at all certain about their decision and its potential impact on the Japanese American community. But it wouldn't be long before they found out how their actions were received. Almost immediately, the wrath of many in the community turned against the JACL leadership, and in particular against Masaoka and Kido.

It was a defining moment for the JACL, this tragic decision made by an untested leadership who did not really know how else to respond when they saw the odds stacked so forcefully against them. However sympathetically one may look at the episode in hindsight, though, the majority of Japanese Americans blamed the JACL for calling on the community to cooperate with the government's policies, a decision that would hang over the JACL like a dark cloud for decades, and even to this day.

In San Francisco, a quiet and unassuming man named Edison Uno had, by the late 1960s, forged a reputation as a tireless social activist. An administrator at the University of California, San Francisco, Uno was a strong advocate for the Bay Area's minority populations. Looking younger than his age with his signature horn-rimmed glasses and turtleneck tops, Uno became one of the leading voices in the Bay Area on social justice issues, and he was undaunted by criticisms from within his own community of being the nail that stuck up above the rest. He was a role model for many younger Japanese Americans and was also arguably the most radical Asian American in the Bay Area, even while being an active and highly respected member of the JACL, an organization that many of his young admirers scoffed at as a conservative organization that had sold out its own people.

Within the JACL, Uno was considered a provocateur, a gadfly. For many, he was an enigma. As a member of the JACL, he was also one of the organization's most outspoken critics and would have been ostracized by the old guard except for the fact that he was married to Rosalyn Kido, daughter of the JACL's highly respected but embattled wartime president, Saburo Kido, a San Francisco civil rights attorney. Uno could hold his own, certainly, but being the son-in-law of the legendary Sab Kido kept the dogs at bay. Uno often seemed out of step with the rest of the JACL's thinking and politics, but he believed the JACL was capable of being the standard-bearer when it came to Asian American civil rights and quietly plotted a course that would lead the JACL toward the issue of reparations, ever mindful of the tightrope he had to walk because of Kido's controversial leadership and the JACL's fateful decision to urge cooperation.

However, Uno had the respect of those who knew him personally or knew of him through his reputation as a fearless advocate who fought tirelessly for equality and social justice. In his day, there were very few like him in the Japanese American and Asian American communities anywhere in the country. Especially in the 1960s and '70s, the young radicals—both Japanese Americans and, to a lesser degree, Chinese Americans—were mercilessly critical of the JACL and its actions during the war, but none of them would dare criticize Uno publicly because none could come close to equaling his achievements as a social advocate or a social critic, and even as a critic of the JACL. He acted and accomplished where many others criticized but did little to change things.

As the JACL approached its biennial convention in Chicago in 1970, Uno had been working with a Bay Area colleague, Raymond Okamura, a chemist from Berkeley with whom Uno was involved in the campaign to repeal Title II of the Internal Security Act, which allowed the use of former concentration camp sites to detain civil rights activists and antiwar protestors. Uno cochaired that effort and worked closely with Okamura, who was himself an enigmatic figure within the JACL. He was well informed when it came to issues like the internment, the war in Vietnam, and other controversial issues, and he certainly thought outside the proverbial box of conventional views. Okamura was also fearless and never seemed to hesitate in his criticisms of the JACL, both past and present. A virtual walking encyclopedia on the internment, Okamura was always a credible and reliable source of information, and what he didn't personally know, he would find out.

Uno and Okamura drafted a proposal for the JACL's 1970 convention with the intent to place reparations on the organization's action agenda for the next two years. On the floor of the convention at the Chicago Hilton, Okamura, a convention delegate, introduced Edison Uno as the cochair of the Title II committee and yielded his time to Uno, who began his statement with, "What I'm going to propose this afternoon is a new direction for the JACL." That new direction was reparations. The resolution was couched in language that sought altruistic ideals and the paving of a road to social equality through both America's and the JACL's examination of the injustices of black slavery and the treatment of Native tribes in America. It naturally included among its concerns the injustices visited upon Japanese Americans. The resolution went far beyond the parochial concerns of the JACL and the Japanese American community, but it was clear that one intended outcome of the effort was to start the debate about whether the JACL should undertake a reparations campaign. Uno understood that Japanese Americans would be reluctant to talk about reparations and the camp experience and that the JACL would have to move slowly into the issue, but he also felt, more than two decades after the war had ended, that it was time for the community to face the hard truths about the camps and about themselves, and he hoped the starting point of that difficult journey would be the JACL.

There are some who say that Uno was the father of the redress campaign, but that would not be fair to him or to those who began the effort much earlier. What *is* important about the 1970 resolution is that it gave a structural form to the issue for the first time and set the stage for what would become intense debates within the JACL, and eventually within the larger Japanese American community, about the issues surrounding the entire camp experience. In some ways, Uno knew that the debate would be destructive and hurtful, and he knew better than most that the reputation of his father-in-law was especially vulnerable, but he was convinced that the only way the Japanese American community could begin to heal itself from the traumatic experiences of the war was by facing the issue head on. His and Okamura's resolution was the first step in that direction.

MY JOURNEY TO THE JACL

My life was not unlike the lives of other Sanseis who had been children in camp and then grown up in the years following the war, but although it took a dramatic turn when I found myself in the army at the age of nineteen, there was nothing that impacted my worldview more than my years as a student during the 1960s at UC Berkeley, where some of my political views were shaped. Two previous years in the army had introduced me to the disciplined culture that demands one place duty before self, sometimes requiring that its members not question certain realities, or even their own logic, and indeed that is the necessary moral ethic of the military.

The contrast between life in the military and life on the campus of UC Berkeley in the 1960s, however, could not have been greater: I went from an atmosphere in which I was forced to accept discipline and certain truths as they were handed down to me into an atmosphere in which I was encouraged to question everything. Berkeley opened up a whole new world to me, where the only limitations were those of intellect and critical thinking. Berkeley offered a kind of education I hadn't anticipated when I'd headed north from Los Angeles after spending some time at home following my discharge from the army.

It was in the midst of that education that the campus became the center of the student demonstrations fueled by the free speech movement (FSM), a force for radical political change that altered forever the link between politics and college education. In a three-month-long sit-in protest, FSM brought awareness to the rights of students to free speech and academic freedom at their universities and beyond. The Berkeley student population was split on FSM; the conservative students, backed by fraternities and sororities, joined the media, which characterized those who took part in the protests as left-wing radicals, while the students who supported the cause were convinced there were important principles at stake, including matters of civil rights, America's participation in foreign conflicts, and other pressing social concerns. FSM was a real lesson for those of us who participated, whether we were on the periphery or at the center of the action. For us, the movement spoke to the very heart of what American democracy was all about, and it changed many of us forever.

At around the same time, and encouraged by the success of FSM, Berkeley also became an important part of the movement protesting the United States' involvement in the Vietnam War. What began as three or four students setting up a stand with posters and talking about America's incursion into an Asian country then little known to mainstream Americans gradually grew into a larger and larger force until, eventually, similar protests were springing up on campuses across the country.

My education in street politics in America took place in this environment, and I watched as efforts that started with just a few students demanding truth grew into demonstrations and marches of thousands. Unfortunately, some of the actions turned ugly and violent, as with the 1965 anti–Vietnam War marches that spilled off campus onto Berkeley's city streets and met with a phalanx of police with helmets and batons. The real lesson for me, though—and the lesson that would serve me later—was witnessing how these events evolved. What the most successful actions had in common was that the principles were at the forefront of the effort, and it was the unequivocal and even idealized belief in those principles that gave life to a movement.

The media characterized both the FSM and antiwar protests as manifestations of rebellious youth challenging authority, but that description was far from accurate. In both instances, the students understood the profound principles at stake—the First Amendment and the immorality of an unjust war—and were unwavering in the belief that they were on the right side of history, despite harsh criticism from politicians and administration officials, despite their negative characterization by the media, despite the bloody beatings that occurred in clashes with the police in what were *peace* marches against the war, and despite the ugly public sentiment growing against them. They—*we*—knew we were right. That was what was so important in both movements: determination borne of a strong conviction in an important principle. This was ultimately what brought victory. And that was the lesson I would remember fifteen years later when I, as the redress campaign's director for the JACL, calculated the strategies for the redress effort.

————

In 1964, I married Carol Shinoda as we finished our studies at Berkeley (we both majored in English literature), and the next year I began my graduate work at the UC campus in the bucolic town of Davis, about an hour to the northeast. By 1967, I had had enough of graduate school and so we set off for London, with the idea that we would stay for a year and then return to resume our lives. We both secured teaching positions, and a year turned into two and then three, all thoughts of returning to the States having faded quickly for both of us.

During non-teaching holidays, we would don backpacks and, boarding the ferry at Dover, set off for the Continent, where we hitch-hiked through much of Europe and found ourselves living a life most people only dreamed about. The net effect of our years in Europe—living in London, traveling in the fashion we did, meeting all kinds of people, and seeing how social safety nets like national health programs enhanced democracies rather than weakened them—imbued in me a greater affinity for life in Europe than in the United States, where capitalism brought about so many disparities. As my thinking became more progressive, I found myself more at home in Europe.

With so much going on in the States in the latter half of the 1960s—the continuing struggles for civil rights turning uglier and more violent in the South, the assassination first of Martin Luther King, Jr., and then Bobby Kennedy, the escalation of the war in Vietnam and the subsequent increase in antiwar protests and their concomitant violence—we came to appreciate even more our lives abroad. I remember thinking one day as I walked on the High Street in Hampstead Village, where we lived, that life would never again be as good as it was right then; this was a moment in my life I would remember forever as among the best I'd ever experienced. I talked to Carol later that evening, and we realized that we had each come to the decision that our lives were better outside of the United States, that this was where we wanted to spend our future, whether in

London or somewhere in mainland Europe, probably the south of France.

And we surely would have stayed in Europe, perhaps not forever but certainly for several decades, had we not had children. We had talked about the idea in the abstract, and it was fine to think of raising a family in London or France, but the reality struck us both deeply when we learned we were going to have our first child. We looked forward to our life in London with a family until we started talking about how our children would never understand what it means to be Japanese American. The concept of a hyphenated minority had no meaning in England because, in those days, one was either British/European, meaning white, or one was "colored," which included anyone who was nonwhite, regardless of nationality. As much as we cherished the idea of living abroad, it was important to us that our children understand instinctively the significance of being Japanese American. We wanted them to be around other Japanese Americans and feel the sense of community, to understand something of our history in America, the wartime imprisonment, the struggle to rebuild our lives, all of it. We wanted them to experience for themselves why we felt such pride in being Japanese American, a feeling that would be denied them if they were raised outside of the United States and, specifically for us, outside of California. We were resolved that our child would be Japanese American.

Not long after Stephen was born in 1969, we packed our belongings and flew home to the United States after being gone for what felt like half a lifetime. Returning to America was a bigger cultural shock for us than it had been when we'd first arrived in London. Los Angeles was jarring compared to the life we'd known in Hampstead Village, with its odd, crooked, narrow streets, a local greengrocer and butcher, the quaint little village shops, the quiet gentility…it was like walking into the past. Los Angeles had wide, straight streets where huge cars sped past, and supermarkets with wide aisles that seemed to go on forever, stacked full with every kind of product. It was the materialism and commercialism of America that we found so disturbing, the opposite of everything we had loved about life abroad. But California was now home for us. This was where we had decided to raise our family and to become part of what America was all about in the 1970s.

That one decision—to return to the States—and all the circumstances that evolved from it would lead me inevitably to the JACL. In retro-spect, it was as if everything, each step we took as we readied our lives for the future—my service in the army, our both being at UC Berkeley and experiencing FSM and anti–Vietnam War protests, our decision to live and travel in Europe—was forging a path that had its own inevita-bility toward something unexpected, toward something, I would have said at one time, totally out of character for me. I had grown up feeling so encumbered by the Japanese American community that at times I wanted nothing more than to escape it. But I am who I am, and the com-munity was always an important part of my life, even as, and maybe especially when, I found my way outside it.

———————

We returned to the United States in early 1970 and by August had moved to the Bay Area, where I had been hired for a teaching position in the English Department at City College of San Francisco. We settled across the Golden Gate Bridge, in Marin County, which we soon real-ized was homogenously white. We were disappointed that our search for community with other Japanese Americans—a major factor in our return to California—would have to be delayed for a while, but by 1975, Marin was forming its own local chapter of the JACL, and Carol and I became founding members.

Accepting that I had joined what I considered to be a conservative organization, I was happy to discover that the JACL, with its strong com-mitment to social justice issues, was much more progressive than I had thought. The organizational *raison d'être* was demanding social equality and challenging any forms of racial discrimination to ensure our place in the social transformations that were then occurring in America. By that time, the push for reparations was at the heart of the JACL's social/political agenda.

The Marin chapter of the JACL was part of the organization's pro-gressive Northern California / Western Nevada district and a signifi-cant part of the reparations effort. As with the other seven districts, the NorCal region had a reparations committee in place, but as it turned out, the chairman announced his resignation at the first district meeting I attended. Since I had shown a keen interest in the issue (I had contributed a lot of questions and comments during the committee chair's report), I was offered the chairmanship of the committee, an opportunity I accepted gladly but at the same time insisting that I share the position with a Nisei who already had credibility in the district. Ben Takeshita, a member of the district's executive board, agreed to cochair with me, but, as he put it, he was doing so primarily as my wingman and not to share responsibilities equally.

It was remarkable to have been offered the chairmanship of a district committee with such high priority in the JACL, but it was perhaps even more remarkable that I was a member of this organization at all, given my family history. I had grown up under a *Kibei* father who, typical of the Kibei, had little use for the JACL. The Kibei, American born but educated at least partially in Japan, were a strong voice in the Japanese American community but were considered an outlier minority because they were only a very small subset of the Nisei generation and were also disadvantaged by having limited English-speaking skills. Thus, while they may have had strong objections to the discriminatory restrictions imposed on the community after the outbreak of war, they were often dependent on the Nisei, who were generally less willing to speak out against the U.S. government. The Kibei felt no less American than the Nisei, who honored their Japanese cultural heritage but identified completely as American, but because the Kibei had grown up in a homogenous Japanese society, they were more comfortable with their Japanese cultural identity. Given this connection to their ancestral homeland, it was no surprise that the Kibei were harshly critical of the JACL's decision to cooperate with a government that had systematically stripped Japanese Americans of their constitutional rights as citizens.

The Kibei and JACL had also clashed in the camps. Incarcerated JACL leaders were given the responsibility of organizing governance infrastructures within the camps themselves, and they often assigned the least desirable jobs to the Kibei who openly criticized the government and questioned the authority of the JACL, going so far as to accuse JACL leaders of collaborating with camp authorities and even being informants. Some Kibei suspected there were even fellow Kibei incarcerees among the "traitors." Groups of Kibei sought retaliation against the JACL, vowing, in some cases, to kill the leaders. As a precaution, the camp administrators removed those JACL leaders whose lives were threatened, and they sent suspect Kibei to what were called Citizen Isolation Centers and to the facility at Tule Lake, which had originally been one of the ten concentration camps for the general Japanese American population but was eventually converted into a high-security facility to hold those considered troublemakers. That uneasy relationship during imprisonment lasted far beyond the years in the concentration camps and spilled over into the postwar community. At the very least, both sides learned to coexist after the war primarily by ignoring each other.

My views of the JACL were of course shaped to a large extent by my Kibei father, but over time I came to learn that he did not dislike the organization so much as he wondered at what he considered the JACL's obsequious need to prove that Japanese Americans were loyal to the nation. As for me, there was still some personal conflict in accepting the chairmanship of the Northern California district's reparations committee. I was impressed by its strong commitment to social justice issues, as exemplified by the frequent heated debates, but I soon realized that I would have to reconcile for myself the inescapable fact of the JACL's wartime decision to cooperate with the government, or, as many in the community expressed it, the decision to sell out, to kowtow to the racists and bigots and those who turned their backs on Japanese Americans. I marveled at what felt like a colossal hypocrisy, to argue so passionately about equality and fair play and doing what's right, even as the proverbial elephant was there in the room. Or was this effort to put things right maybe a crucial part of a larger plan to overcome and compensate for that fateful decision of 1942?

Cooperation. That one word still hung over the JACL, and in 1975, as I listened to the debates about various equity issues, the memories were still fresh and raw. Only thirty years previously, the same men and women now sitting before me had been in concentration camps under the watchful eyes of armed guards. I was in my mid-thirties by the time I joined the JACL, and I still had strong memories of my time in camp, even though I had only been a child. Many of those debating issues on the floor of these meetings, however, were old enough to remember "evacuation day," were in fact old enough to have been at that historic meeting in San Francisco when the JACL made the decision to cooperate with the U.S. government.

Many of those I came to know as friends in the JACL were what I'd call, for lack of a better term, true "loyalists." They had been in the war—mostly veterans of the 442nd Regimental Combat Team, but also a handful from some mysterious branch of Military Intelligence they only mumbled about or mentioned vaguely—and they had followed the JACL leaders from the camps into the military, along with thousands of non-JACLers who either enlisted or were drafted into the army, expressly to make a point about the loyalty of Japanese Americans. I admired them for their courage and sacrifices, but now, as part of the organization, the question continued to gnaw at the back of my mind: What about cooperation? I decided that, if I ever had the opportunity, I would ask the question directly of anyone who might have been at the 1942 meeting, although I would do it privately.

Given the diversity of opinions within the postwar JACL, I was able to connect with and learn about the different perspectives within the organization. Although I was a Sansei with progressive political views, I nevertheless felt a kinship, an empathy, with the more conservative Nisei, in part because we had shared the incarceration experience. The concept of "camp" for me was not an abstract idea learned from history books; it was very real. It was a visceral memory for me, and I felt a need to come to terms with what the internment meant to Japanese Americans both as individuals and as a community. Having been a child of the camps, I didn't believe, as some of the younger Sansei did in those days, that the Nisei lacked backbone for having allowed themselves to become victims of the government. Quite the opposite. I had always thought of the Nisei as heroes, *all* of them: the young men who went off to war to fight for this country; those who in one form or another resisted the government during our imprisonment; the women who stayed behind to maintain families under intolerable conditions and to protect the children; the men who never stopped insisting that the internment was wrong and unjust; and the Nisei who endured their fate without complaining after the war, resolving to rebuild our community and make a life for us Sansei. I understood all of this about the Nisei and felt that my generation owed them a debt of gratitude.

And decades later, here we all were, talking about the most radical issue ever discussed in the Japanese American community. Now that I had accepted responsibility for the district's reparations program, my entire perception of the JACL and its membership began to change. Here was an organization that developed the courage to channel its outrage into action. The JACL wanted to rectify the injustices of the internment, and although some may have called it hypocrisy, I saw something different going on. As I listened to the debates, what I found remarkable (and maybe even a little corny for a left-winger like me) was the simple but profound fact that the Nisei in the JACL wanted to forge ahead with the redress effort not for themselves but for the country. They wanted their legacy to last beyond current generations, to change forever the way the nation treated its citizens. Even after all they had already contributed and sacrificed for the country during the war years, they wanted to press on and confront the government about its treatment of Japanese Americans in hopes that they could prevent something similar recurring in the future.

GAMAN

As I contemplated the many challenges of the reparations issue from my role as the chair of my district's reparations committee, I knew that none would be more difficult than the division in our community. One of the main objections to the reparations movement was that it challenged some deeply held attitudes of Japanese Americans. The concept of *gaman*, which teaches us to endure or persevere with dignity, had guided us for generations to be strong in the face of adversities and crises; as a proud and strong people, we don't ask for handouts, and we don't disgrace our own traditions. In a similar vein, the phrase *shikataganai*, "it can't be helped" or "it can't be undone," urges us to not dwell on the past but focus on the future, to make life better for our children, for future generations. The act of seeking reparations felt to some like a betrayal of these values.

While *shikataganai* helped us endure the war years in the camps and our postwar travails, there also was a fundamental need to restore our sense of honor, both individually and as a community. In the days, months, and years following the war, everything we did was relative to the community, and just as it was important never to dishonor the family, it was equally important never to dishonor the community. As a people considered a second-class minority in the eyes of others, we learned from experience that while we never had complete control of our fates, our strength came from within. Just as we had proven loyalty by enduring the hardships of the internment, we would prove our worth by our accomplishments. We had survived mistreatment before, and we would do so again if we had to.

Within this framework, it is easy to see why the very concept of redress was totally anathema to such thinking. Japanese Americans who opposed the campaign saw it as a political move that dishonored the community. Some Nisei argued that while "others" sought government handouts and welfare, Japanese Americans, regardless of how poorly we fared in the face of hardships, were too proud and too good to beg. We had lost everything in the war, having given up our way of life and accepted imprisonment and shame to prove our loyalty, but we had ultimately come back from those prisons and rebuilt our lives and communities. We never sought help from outside sources because we always took care of ourselves and our own. To ask for money now for something that had happened so long ago in the past was to demean who we were. It was like a *samurai* turning *ronin,* turning beggar. The very thought was objectionable, if not wholly foreign, to the Japanese sense of honor.

Whatever the objections may have been for the Nisei to maintain a silence about their wartime experiences, it seemed to me that underlying the fervor of the opposition was, for many if not most, a complex psychology they might not have even recognized at the time. The debates about reparations in the JACL had already breached a thirty-year wall of silence following the war, but the discussion still conjured up the helplessness and shame they had felt about their wartime imprisonment and the humiliation and degradation they had endured in the postwar years as they sought to rebuild their lives and find a place once again in American society. I realized that this was a source of resistance to pressing the issue all these years later.

The pain and shame were so deep within the Nisei that many still would not or could not talk about the war years, with some even hiding the truth from their children born after the war. This inability to acknowledge and speak about what had happened, and about how much we had lost and sacrificed, not only created a huge void in our history but suggested that, on some level, the Nisei considered their lives to be inconsequential. They had been rendered powerless against the racists who sought their expulsion and had been used as political pawns at the hands of the government. The Nisei felt they were as good as any American, but our wartime imprisonment and the implications of betrayal left them with a sense of shame and guilt. In the long shadow that cast upon them, the Nisei turned to *gaman* and sought to heal themselves in silence.

But true healing never took place—how could it when we weren't able to talk even among ourselves about what we had experienced, when the trauma that results from such an experience is so disabling that we hide in silence, build walls to protect our psyches from the truths of who and what we had become and what we had endured? We were not technically casualties of war, and yet we were wounded; and as a community, we were disabled by our inability to articulate the experience and by our need to hide behind silence.

DEFINING THE ISSUE

In the early 1970s, the JACL's discussions focused on the idea of reparations, the effort to gain monetary compensation for the injustices of our wartime incarceration. But in 1977, in a strategic move to more accurately describe the JACL's effort, the organization redefined its program as redress, with its broader goal of vindicating Japanese Americans of the implied charge of having been traitors, and setting the historical record straight to lift the veil of guilt that Japanese Americans had had to endure. The mechanism of redress would be to demand both monetary reparations and an apology for the injustice done not only to Japanese Americans but to the nation as well. While monetary restitution would be a centerpiece of the campaign, the ultimate goal of redress for Japanese Americans would be to seek measures ensuring that what we experienced during World War II would never occur again in this country.

It was hoped that a clearer and more altruistic explanation of our effort would appease those within our community who opposed the campaign. However, that strategy did little to establish consensus on the issue of compensation among organization and community members. Compensation had been the primary issue at prior JACL biennial conventions. It began with the introduction of the Uno-Okamura resolution in 1970, and it was the priority issue at the following 1972 convention in Washington, D.C., and then again in 1974 in Portland, Oregon, where a heated debate on compensation widened the chasm among the delegates. While the JACL was committed to some form of monetary compensation for former incarcerees, it could not decide whether it should come in the form of individual payments or a single trust fund. Following the Portland convention, the debate continued at the JACL's eight district council meetings and at chapter gatherings, and the more it was discussed, the more it seemed to divide the membership.

Even among the pro-reparations group there was little agreement about what the remedies should be. Then there were those who argued against any kind of monetary compensation because, they insisted, you could not put a price on freedom and to do so would only cheapen it.

We had not at that point defined what would constitute "success" for us in this effort, but it was clear to me that we should start with one important element: educating the public. Most Americans knew nothing about the treatment of Japanese Americans during the war, and many of those who did thought we had gotten what we deserved. Putting the facts before the public and getting the record straight would be the necessary first step to achieving our larger goal. And yet even that seemed an impossible task. We would have to find a way to erase decades of deeply felt bigotry and hatred against us and then convince the public that the nation's leaders had not only contributed to spreading racist misinformation about our community but also failed in their sacred trust to protect our constitutional rights as U.S. citizens. And that was only the first stage of a long process.

To get some perspective of the enormity of the challenge, consider that the JACL's 25,000 members represented a mere 3.8 percent of the 650,000 Japanese Americans in the United States. Despite the fact that a majority of the larger group registered as Democrats (interestingly, the party of FDR, who had signed the order that led to our imprisonment), they were what I described as politically cautious moderates. The community on the whole was reluctant to discuss the wartime experience, preferring to continue life without any further disruptions and controversies, and to make matters even tougher, the most active voices in the West Coast communities were themselves critical of the JACL, voicing their distrust of, and many misgivings about, the organization. Worse still, most Japanese American academics—and it was they who strongly influenced younger Japanese Americans at the time—were also critics of the JACL leadership and questioned the organization's legitimacy in attempting to rectify any kind of injustice; they ignored, or at least overlooked, the organization's rich history of combating anti-Asian racism, both institutional and individual, including its successful challenges of racist policies and statutes (for example, alien land laws, anti-miscegenation laws, restrictive covenants, and discriminatory local ordinances). If the Japanese American community couldn't come together behind the redress movement, what chance did we have of winning over Congress and the American people?

No one said it was going to be easy, but it didn't help to hear so many say it would be impossible.

THE TESTING GROUND

My work as the redress chair of the Northern California/Western Nevada (NCWN) district began more as a seat-of-the-pants effort than anything else. I was operating purely on instinct; I wasn't given any directives from the national committee, and I was not adhering to any kind of broader national strategy because one did not exist. There were other activities going on in other JACL regions, to be sure, but I wasn't aware of them at the time.

Because the Northern California JACL district was so large, and because it was politically progressive, I considered it ideal for testing issues within both the Japanese American community and the local public arena.

I intended to establish a media-focused strategy in the Bay Area, but I soon realized there could be no campaign without the Nisei voice. Because I had no real authority and had not yet, in the short time I had held the chairmanship of the regional reparations committee, established any credibility, I knew it would be futile for me personally to enjoin the Nisei to talk publicly about the internment. On the one hand, I would be viewed as an interloper ("Who is he and who the hell does he think he is?") and, on the other, I knew the Nisei would consider me unqualified to talk about the internment ("He was too young to remember anything, so who the hell does he think he is?"). While I was convinced of the wisdom of using the media, I also knew that our biggest challenge at the outset would be to convince news outlets that ours was a compelling story and that this past injustice was of major magnitude. But first I needed to convince the Nisei to share their personal experiences.

It's one thing to plan a media strategy, but it's quite a different matter to execute it, especially when the media has no interest in what you're offering them. I was new to all of this—I had never worked with the media before, nor had any of my JACL colleagues or anyone I knew in the Japanese American or Asian American communities except for Edison Uno. In those days, the media, like politicians in Washington, seemed beyond the reach of the average citizen. Two years hence I would have enough media savvy to be able to use them, but at this beginning stage, I struggled to get our story on the air.

It was eye-opening to realize just how inconsequential our story was perceived to be, despite its profound and lasting consequences. A story this juicy—a beloved president and his racist policies, bigoted politicians, a major violation of the Constitution, the forced removal of an entire segment of the population into concentration camps—and yet not a single news editor interested enough even to enquire? I was convinced there was a significant and worthwhile story in both the internment and redress issues, but I realized that what we were missing was a proverbial "hook" that would get the right people to take notice. Thus far, the human-interest side of the internment hadn't elicited much reaction, and the JACL's redress campaign was still too new to have any pull.

Those early ventures with the media weren't a total flop, however, because although it wasn't on the scale I'd hoped, I *was* able to get *some* airtime…usually on programs that were devoted to local ethnic community issues and normally aired at pre-dawn hours on Sunday mornings! But I didn't care; it was a start. I used local speaking engagements and those early Sunday-morning television programs to help shape the message, to discover the best sound bites, to test audience responses to different aspects of the issue, and even at times to play the provocateur with less-than-friendly audiences. To rile up an audience, I discovered it took little more than stating we were the innocent victims of a racist policy or declaring that there was no evidence to support the government's claim that our imprisonment was both warranted and justified. The response from the opposition was always swift: "proof" of our guilt and hard "evidence" against us, all of which was easily debunked. One caller claimed to have seen his Japanese neighbor on several occasions sneak out in the middle of the night on some nefarious mission, although he never reported it to the authorities. One of the most memorable encounters was a caller who shared a story about the night he was invited for dinner at the home of a Japanese American coworker. During the evening, the guest sneaked into the host's bedroom to look in his closet, where he saw a Japanese military uniform and what appeared to be a codebook of some kind—unreadable because it was, of course, written in Japanese. It was a bizarre fabrication, and as I began peppering the caller with questions about why he hadn't reported the incident to the authorities at the time, the caller simply hung up. Still others would phone in to argue that because this country is a democracy, by definition the government simply does not imprison anyone without evidence of a crime. When I asked what the evidence was, what crime had occurred in the case of Japanese Americans, there was never an answer except that the information was probably classified.

Regardless of how absurd the calls sometimes became, those talk shows at least gave us a platform to expose and debate the issue. I was especially interested in local radio programs broadcasting to areas that drew more conservative audiences; I thought we should know what that opposition would look like as we prepared to face audiences that were convinced it was we who were undermining the foundations of American democracy.

QUESTIONS 27 AND 28

One of the benefits of testing local audience responses to our issue was learning where we were vulnerable. When I found myself able to provide only vague information based on the sensibilities of the community, I knew I needed to arm myself with provable facts that would hold up to criticism. I had a sense, for example, that the community would support the monetary compensation issue, but I had no evidence of this, nor evidence that, despite objections to the campaign by some in our community, Japanese Americans would unite behind an effort that sought recognition of the injustices of our wartime treatment. The few reporters curious about the subject began to pick up on the undercurrent of drama and began to raise the question of unity among Japanese Americans.

Given that, after five years of debate, the JACL membership was still arguing about critical issues like compensation and whether we should even talk about camp, it stood to reason that the split in the community was even greater. It seemed obvious to me that we needed to know how large that gap was if we intended to pursue the issue of reparations on behalf of the Japanese American community.

The plan for gathering this information was to conduct a community-wide survey, one that, given the reticence of Japanese Americans when it came to the subject of the internment, would have to allow respondents to answer questionnaires anonymously and in the privacy of their own homes. Together with my cochair Ben Takeshita, we put together a committee to write the survey.

My top choices for the committee were Ray Okamura, coauthor of the now-celebrated 1970 Uno resolution, and Cherry Tsutsumida, an astute political thinker from Washington, D.C., and the highest-level Asian American appointee in the Carter administration. Both Tsutsumida and Okamura were already closely tied to the community, which to me was always an important factor for anyone connected to the campaign, since if we expected people to talk to us, we needed them first to trust us.

Our prediction was that the community would support redress, but we needed empirical data that would show conclusively (1) how Japanese Americans felt about their World War II experiences and (2) whether they supported any effort to seek redress. Because we were probing a controversial issue, we found ourselves debating strategy at almost every turn. In the end, no topic was more challenging than whether we should include a question about a group of internees referred to as the No-No Boys.

The No-No Boys was the name used for the group of incarcerees who had been singled out from the ten camps when, in the spring of 1943, the government issued what it called the Application for Leave Clearance Questionnaire, which was administered to every man and woman in camp who was seventeen years of age or older. The infamous Questions 27 and 28, which were originally issued in a different army questionnaire to recruit Nisei for the service, were included as part of the questionnaire and essentially forced the respondents to make a declaration of national loyalty:

Question 27:

Are you willing to serve in the armed forces of the United States on combat duty, wherever ordered? *

Question 28:

Will you swear unqualified allegiance to the United States of America and faithfully defend the United States from any or all attack by foreign or domestic forces, and forswear any form of allegiance or obedience to the Japanese emperor, or any other foreign government, power, or organization?

The respondents to the questionnaire of course knew this was a loyalty test, and these two questions in particular offended everyone's sensibilities.

---

* These two questions varied slightly for respondents who were not eligible to serve in the U.S. military—women and the Issei (Japanese immigrants)—but all versions of the questionnaire asked for similar declarations of loyalty.

Question 27 was an outrageous insult. Having been forced at gun-point from their homes, having lost their businesses and freedom, having been imprisoned behind barbed-wire fences without their right to due process, having been stripped completely of their constitutional rights, *and then* to be asked if they would serve to defend the government and army that had done this to them? "Set my family free and then I will serve," many said. The response to Question 27 was a kind of furious incredulity. It was salt on a festering, searing wound.

Question 28 was like an arrow to the heart. Because of the way in which it was worded—specifically the term "forswear"—answering Yes to Number 28 was essentially admitting at least *former* allegiance to the emperor of Japan, a position that was absurd to the Nisei, who were American-born. Even though they were not loyal to Japan, they were reluctant to answer Yes to Question 28 because it implied they were agreeing to *renounce* their allegiance to a country to which they had no fidelity at all but honored culturally as the land of their ancestors. Fearing that no matter how they answered, they would be providing the army with justification for their exclusion and detention policies, many answered Yes but with qualifying statements written in the margins—statements that were then construed by the authorities as No answers. It was an untenable situation for the Nisei because it was impossible to answer the questionnaire without implicating themselves in one way or another.

For the Issei, who were denied naturalization rights by federal statute, Question 28 posed a different dilemma. A Yes answer was, for these first-generation immigrants, tantamount to renouncing their Japanese citizenship, which would leave them stateless. America was their chosen home and had been, for some, for over fifty years, and yet because they were not allowed to become U.S. citizens, they had thus continued to maintain their Japanese citizenship. If they answered Yes to Question 28, however, what would happen to them? And what about their Nisei children? Would they be abandoning their parents by answering affirmatively to Question 28?

Despite the anger and frustration caused by Questions 27 and 28, the majority of camp prisoners answered Yes to both questions, to yet once again demonstrate their loyalty to the country that had betrayed them. At the same time, those who answered No did so with strong convictions about their rights as American citizens and their obligations to their Issei parents. Passions flared on both sides, often setting brothers against brothers, friends against friends; entire families were destroyed over the issue, and the community was torn apart in a way that was especially cruel and unforgivable. Many family members never spoke to each other again, longtime friends became bitter enemies, and the entire camp population stood by helplessly as the young men who had volunteered for the army as a demonstration of their loyalty were sent off to war, many never to return. The loyalty questionnaire created an emotional breach in the Japanese American community that festered unresolved well into the 1980s.

Those who answered No to both questions were labeled disloyal by government officials and transferred to Tule Lake, a camp in California near the Oregon border that by then had already been converted into a high-security facility for incarcerees considered troublemakers. Some of the JACL's leaders, in an ill-advised and insensitive reaction, took it upon themselves to lash out at the No-No Boys for having made everyone vulnerable to the charge of disloyalty; and at a time when emotions were already running high throughout the ten camps, their intolerance only served to exacerbate the already volatile situation.

Decades later, the loyalty questionnaire still evoked among many in our community the same emotional venom as it did when it was administered in 1943, and our redress committee struggled with the No-No Boy issue, specifically whether to ask survey respondents if No-Nos should be included in any consideration of redress. We wondered if any of the No-Nos would even answer our survey.

"I would," said Ben. His response stunned us to silence. None of us knew that Ben was a No-No, and none of us cared or thought it changed anything, but we were struck speechless because no one ever declared him- or herself a No-No in those days; it was simply too controversial. Ben explained that as a young teenager of elderly Issei parents, he felt an obligation to stay with them and thus ended up a No-No without choosing to be, and thus his experiences helped only partially in resolving the content of our survey. We all agreed it should include the difficult questions, but was it worth unearthing all the worst emotions and memories, or should we leave that territory—and other fraught issues, like those who resisted and refused the draft—for another day...if we ever got that far in our efforts with this campaign? Philosophically, we at least agreed that all of the conflicts and concerns that arose from our imprisonment were the consequence of the unlawful impeachment of our rights as citizens, but there was still so much gray area in the details. Night after night we debated these issues, and we never fully agreed about whether the intended ultimate outcome of our survey—some form of reparations from the U.S. government—would be worth the potential negative consequences of including the controversial questions.

I steered the committee to accept a survey format that would move us as directly as possible to the bottom-line questions: Do you believe Japanese Americans were treated unjustly during World War II, and do you believe Japanese Americans should seek redress from the U.S. government, and, finally, do you favor monetary compensation? As far as I was concerned, these were the most important attitudes we needed to gauge, and, not unexpectedly, Cherry Tsutsumida objected—and she was absolutely right to do so—that the tone of the final question in particular was, as she put it, skewed to reach a specific conclusion. But how, I asked, do you pose questions about the years of lost jobs, homes, education, and, most importantly, lost freedom and your rights as a citizen in a way that doesn't come across as condemning of, and asking for compensation from, those who ordered these things be taken from you? But that's exactly what Tsutsumida found troubling—that the line of questions led inevitably to answers that would favor one particular type of remedy.

As much as we argued that point, I prevailed in having the survey end with the forthright question about reparations. I told the committee that the intent of the survey was not to construct a survey that was completely scientifically and statistically sound but one that would measure personal views so we could know the minds of our community members. Over Tsutsumida's objections and concerns, we printed up the survey, which we then distributed to every Japanese American group in the Northern California area, going through organizations such as community associations and social clubs, churches (both Christian and Buddhist), martial arts dojos—any source we could find to reach out to our people, whether they were JACLers or not. In the end, we distributed over 10,000 surveys and received approximately 4,200 responses. Of those who responded, approximately 90 percent indicated that some sort of action should be undertaken, and 87 percent supported some form of monetary compensation.

If there was a perceived split in the community on the issue of redress, our survey—flawed though it might have been—demonstrated clearly that in the privacy of their own homes and behind the shield of a questionnaire anonymously answered, Japanese Americans strongly supported our efforts to pursue this impossible dream.

Around the same time that I was working with the committee to develop the survey, Edison Uno introduced me to Dr. Clifford Uyeda, a fellow community activist who would become one of my most trusted and loyal friends as we pushed the campaign onto the national stage. When Edison first introduced Clifford to me, however, I didn't quite know what to make of him because we had strong differences of opinion about certain topics, including poverty and how it related to welfare and education in the black community. As we became better acquainted, Clifford and I grew very close, but I also deliberately avoided getting into debates with him about some of the core issues of the civil rights struggle. Clifford's views were not unlike those of Japanese Americans who touted the value of self-reliance above all else, as exemplified in our recovery from the economic devastation we had experienced during the war. I recognized the fact of this resilience, but I also thought this bootstrap mentality ignored the staggering differences in the histories of the various communities. Fortunately, our shared commitment to the fight for justice for Japanese Americans saw us through these differences, and of course it also helped that Edison, whom I trusted and respected, had introduced Cliff as a good friend; I doubt Cliff and I would have become friends otherwise, let alone such close ones. As we worked together on various issues over the years, I came to see what a remarkable man Clifford was.

At the time I was introduced to Clifford, he was leading a grassroots effort to seek a presidential exoneration from Gerald Ford for Iva Toguri D'Aquino, the Japanese American woman known as "Tokyo Rose" who had been convicted of treason in 1949, having been accused of sharing information about U.S. troops on a Radio Tokyo broadcast. The case was scandalous for a number of reasons, not least of which was the fact that she was found innocent after a year-long U.S. Army military tribunal hearing in Tokyo but was falsely accused and tried again in federal court in San Francisco and subsequently found guilty and sentenced to ten years in federal prison. D'Aquino became only the seventh person to be convicted of treason, and the trial, at the Federal District Court in San Francisco, was at the time the longest and costliest trial in American history. After reading Clifford's files on the D'Aquino case, I decided to join his campaign, which ended with President Ford pardoning Iva in 1977 as he left office.

Around the same time, I also joined Clifford in his efforts against the Sierra Club's planned boycott of San Francisco's Japantown stores, which was in retaliation for Japan's refusal to stop killing whales on the open seas, in defiance of a worldwide moratorium to end the massacre of whales for commercial purposes. Only two countries had refused to join the moratorium: Japan and Norway. The Sierra Club publicly announced that it would boycott all Japantown stores and restaurants as a signal to the Japanese government. Clifford was determined to prevent the boycott because it was, he argued, racist and founded in a kind of ignorant bigotry about Japanese Americans, who, we had to keep reminding the public, had nothing to do with the policies of the government of Japan.

My views of the Sierra Club completely changed when, one day, I joined Clifford on a telephone conversation about the boycott with a representative of the Sierra Club. I mostly listened as Clifford explained to her that the Sierra Club didn't seem to realize that it was boycotting stores whose owners had nothing to do with Japan and its polices. She said, in response, that many of those stores in Japantown stocked products from Japan, which justified the boycott. Then what about white-owned Toyota and Honda dealerships, I asked? Or white-owned electronics stores that sold Japanese Sony and Panasonic products? Or department stores like Emporium and Liberty House, which also sold many products from Japan? Even when pressed by Clifford to explain how the Sierra Club's boycott policy wasn't racist, the representative couldn't explain and just said that if it came to a decision between the lives of whales and the lives of Japanese Americans, the Sierra Club's commitment was to save the whales. To make a difficult situation even more complicated, we were equally outraged at Japan and Norway for their refusal to abide the whaling moratorium (not to mention we were strong supporters of the Sierra Club in all of its other efforts), but that didn't change the fact that the boycott was offensive and racist. Fortunately, the boycott was short lived, in part because large numbers of Japanese Americans protested its racist foundation, a message our community members were more than happy to discuss with the media.

Interestingly, in both the D'Aquino campaign and the Sierra Club fight, Clifford chose to run them independently of the JACL. He didn't quite trust the organization, even when they were on the same side. (The NCWN district voted to support the D'Aquino campaign under Clifford's leadership.) Thankfully he trusted and liked me, and I joined his efforts as an individual, not as a JACL member and committee chairman. I served as a link to the JACL for Clifford, but that was really about as far as he would go with the organization, a decision he hadn't made lightly, knowing that his personal disapproval might be construed as a public criticism of the JACL, which was not his intention.

Uno and Uyeda had extremely different styles of social activism: Edison was a very public figure, while Clifford was, for lack of a better word, bookish. Edison was deeply committed to issues of social justice not just for Japanese and Asian Americans but for all those who were disadvantaged and victimized by unfair policies. Clifford focused on, in addition to Japanese American topics, his intense interest in environmental issues and his concern for Native tribes, in particular the government's continued displacement of the Navajo and Hopi peoples.

There were other well-known Asian American activists in those days, but Edison and Clifford seemed to be at the center of it all. Edison was an activist in the true sense of that word, always working coalitions and cajoling politicians and decision makers to consider alternative ways of looking at policy issues. Clifford, with more of an academic style, loved to research, and loved even more to write about that research; because of his gentle but tenacious ways, people gravitated toward him and invariably joined in his causes. Both men were unique and exceptional.

THE MESSAGE

Without directives from the national committee, I took it upon myself to craft what I thought our message should be, based on the organization's literature and the discussions at district council meetings. If the redress program evolved into interactions with the public, we needed to be prepared with a message and the arguments to back it. However, we still had many unresolved issues, chief among them lack of unity on the matter of compensation for our community's treatment during the war. At this stage, it seemed the only way to draft a statement without a stated campaign objective was to focus on the issue that lay at the heart of everything: the Constitution and the loss of our rights.

To question the conduct of the government in a time of national crisis would, I was sure, cause blowback, and I knew it wouldn't help to push that message through exposing the wartime experiences of a small minority of citizens. From the beginnings of the media campaign I had embarked upon in the Bay Area, I knew that this effort could not be only about Japanese Americans and our suffering and losses. Yes, our experience was the starting point of the discussion, but we also needed to address it as part of the legal legacy of this nation and, more importantly, how that legacy has threatened, and may continue to threaten, the foundations of American democracy as embodied in the Bill of Rights. Ours was a fight to give true meaning to the nation's belief in the Constitution, and by teaching these lessons about the failure of government, we hoped to ensure that what had happened to us would never again happen to any group of Americans. This was about American democracy at its core, and all it stood for as a beacon of hope to the world.

It was a surprisingly red-white-and-blue patriotic message, especially from someone who had lived abroad and become so cynical about the U.S. government and the bigotry of mainstream America, but I knew it was the right message. I knew that we faced certain defeat if our efforts focused on our personal suffering and losses, or on the racist policies of the government. I was convinced that those issues wouldn't work for our campaign because white America just didn't give a damn about us, and if we were going to achieve any degree of success (however we defined "success" at that point), we would have to fight this battle not on our terms but in terms that the rest of the country understood.

For the Nisei, the patriotic nature of the message had real meaning because they felt it deeply. It was what they felt as they were led into America's concentration camps and as they donned the uniform of this country and fought on the battlefields of Europe and the Pacific, and as they died for the ideals of their nation. But it was also about much more than the sacrifices they were willing to make. Culturally, it was about honor and integrity and *giri* (duty), and even though these values sprung from their Japanese heritage, they reflected the Niseis' deep sense of patriotism as Americans. Finally, it was also about demanding our equality as American citizens and forcing the nation to understand the consequences of our experiences during World War II.

Beneath the many forms my public message took was always the larger question "What is justice?" How do you set something right when the violation of a people or an individual is so deeply felt? How do you bring about true justice when the damage has already been done and is irreversible? How is it justice to sentence a murderer to death when it does nothing to bring the victim back or to restore the shattered lives of his loved ones? Is there any comfort in sending a rapist to prison for the rest of his life, to be brutalized by his fellow inmates, when the consequences of his actions can never be erased in the mind of his victim? How do you, generations later, compensate the enslavement of an entire group of innocent people? And if a nation terrorizes and all but destroys a culture, as the United States did with its indigenous populations, what could the country possibly do to make things right? At best, bringing forth justice is a tricky proposition because, as much as you might try, there's never a satisfactory one-to-one equation for redemption, a right that erases a wrong.

Redressing a wrong is, conceptually, a noble and honorable notion, but can it truly heal the victims of wrongdoing, especially when the damage remains, lurking in the dark? Perhaps. This is why we so willingly embarked on such an idealistic venture: to confront that wrongdoing, and to keep it from emerging again. We did not start this movement for just the moment, to fight our own battle and then disappear. We were in it for the long haul.

———

Edison and I talked about the message, and he agreed that its core should reflect the idealism of America; he knew the Nisei would embrace it as their own, despite any reservations they may have about the idea of asking for compensation. Together with Clifford, we also agreed that monetary reparations had to be a part of what we demanded, and that the amount had to be significant. The figure in my mind was $50,000 per individual. I believed that every single Japanese American who experienced internment should be compensated no less than $1 million, but I also figured there was not enough money in the U.S. Treasury to compensate us adequately for what the country had taken from us as Americans. I wanted an official apology, and I wanted enough in the way of compensation that it would begin to at least partially make up for the lifelong humiliation and shame the Issei and Nisei lived with, not to mention all the practical and emotional hardships they suffered after the war in trying to restore their sense of honor and to give decent lives to their families. I wanted the amount of compensation to be large enough to shock the nation and to serve as a deterrent if our nation's future leaders ever again contemplated such odious policies that weakened the foundations of American democracy. Edison and Clifford and I agreed on all of this, even as we knew that we would be up against certain political realities that would limit what we could ask for and what, if anything, we would receive.

We talked often about strategy, and we even talked about the JACL's involvement in the internment, a true sore point for both Clifford and me, and a particularly sensitive matter for Edison, given who his father-in-law was. I tried to avoid the subject when the three of us were together, but Clifford was never shy in discussing the JACL's cooperation with the U.S. government, or the rumor that some JACLers had been informants in the camps. He didn't do it to challenge or offend, and luckily Edison understood this. Cliff was always very honest, forth-right, and fearless when it came to dealing with difficult issues, and while Edison had no satisfactory answers for him, I maintained that it was never Edison's responsibility to defend the actions of Sab Kido and the JACL of the war years.

1976 AND THE
SACRAMENTO CONVENTION

As we approached the 1976 convention, the question of compensation loomed. In my mind, it was important to ask the government for a formal apology—and I was convinced we could get it relatively easily with the right political connections—but I also thought redress would be meaningless without monetary compensation because words could only heal so much. No matter how heartfelt, words are cheap, and we deserved more. Besides, financial restitution was the American way: the civil courts are filled daily with lawsuits seeking monetary compensation for all manner of wrongs. Why shouldn't we be a part of that?

The JACL national convention, held that year in Sacramento in early summer, when the temperatures soared above 100 degrees, was the new Marin County chapter's first convention. We had studied the issues, taken positions on every agenda item, and were ready to do battle where battles emerged. As expected, redress was the central issue of this convention, with monetary compensation hovering in the background, already imbued with memories of the heated debates of the Portland convention two years earlier. Delegates and districts were jockeying to position themselves on the topic and lobbying delegates from other districts for support. This was my first experience at a JACL convention, and I found it fascinating to see how much backroom politicking went on. One group was clearly intent on forcing the compensation issue onto the floor of the National Council plenary session. A smaller group made up of some of the most influential members of the organization—the old guard—seemed poised to hold compensation in abeyance and hopefully push that debate to the next convention, two years later.

I arrived at the convention hotel midweek, on the day the redress discussion was scheduled on the agenda. I could sense the tension in the air as groups everywhere huddled to discuss and plot. Before I could even check into my room, one of my colleagues led me to our district caucus room, where our chapter delegates debated and strategized, and at the appointed hour, we all made our way to the main ballroom for the National Council session, where Ed Yamamoto, chairman of the national reparations committee, would give his report and the much-anticipated debate would ensue.

The discussion that followed at times turned heated and bitter, reminding me of my vague memories of late-night camp meetings when men sometimes became enraged with each other. But unlike those meetings, these were not about survival; they were about honor and our own integrity as a people, as citizens. The focus was redress but inevitably turned to compensation, and thus the long debate began (or continued, depending on your perspective). Delegates were divided into three groups: those who argued against demanding monetary compensation, those who *did* want to demand money and thought it should come as individual payments, and those who demanded money and felt a single trust fund would be adequate.

It didn't help matters that money was a taboo subject in our community. How could we even hope to discuss it rationally? Some of the lawyers in the group (and there were an extraordinary number among the delegates) tried to present the issue as a legal, abstract concept, to depersonalize the notion, but to no avail; others (again, a lot of lawyers) countered by insisting that there was no reasonable way to assess the loss of freedom. How could we possibly determine how much three years of our imprisonment was worth? What was *liberty* worth? Men died in wars to preserve the idea of democracy and freedom, and to give that a monetary figure served only to cheapen it. We could not do that to our fallen comrades who were killed on the battlefields of Europe and in the jungles of the Pacific. We are a people of honor, a people of *giri*, of duty, and we do not debase ourselves by making such demands.

Those who stood on the other side of that argument expressed a point of view that reflected how assimilated we had become as Americans. We had been wrongly accused of disloyalty to the country of our birth, we had been imprisoned without any evidence against us, for no reason other than our ancestry, and to do nothing, even after all these years, would be to allow the government to maintain its claim that we were guilty of *something* and deserved what we got. And *that*, this side argued, would be our dishonoring. In the American system of jurisprudence, financial restitution is a common practice and is, according to some, the most meaningful form of acknowledging a wrong committed against an individual. If we did nothing and let this sleeping dog lie, we were doing a disservice to our children and to future generations of Japanese Americans, who would continue to carry the stigma of shame and guilt imposed upon us by the government, and the public would continue to believe the lies about us and our community's behavior during the war. To lift the veil of shame and be vindicated, we *had* to fight this fight and demand monetary compensation lest we fail future generations. To do less would be to render our wartime sacrifices meaningless.

From both sides of the debate, there was talk about honor, sacrifices, future generations—everything that was important to us as a community. It was a cultural battle we were fighting, not with the government and the mainstream public but within ourselves. This issue hit at the heart of who we were as Japanese Americans, both culturally as people of Japanese ancestry and as citizens of this country. One side of the argument wasn't overwhelmingly stronger than the other because we could all understand how relevant both sides were to our own lives. These topics had been debated not just at chapter board meetings and district council meetings—and not to mention at the JACL convention two years earlier—but in community spaces and in family kitchens. As far as I was concerned, the subject was no longer hovering in the background but was here to stay until we acted on it one way or another. The JACL, if it wanted to move forward as a relevant organization, would have to directly address the idea of demanding compensation. This discussion and debate was necessary, and although, at the Sacramento convention, we seemed a long way from resolving this issue, I knew that until we did, we would remain at the proverbial square one, where we had been for six years now.

And then something interesting happened.

MIKE MASAOKA

Mike Masaoka, at that time still considered the sacred cow of the JACL, was given the floor and began his old-school oratory. Everyone (and I mean *everyone*) in the room listened. I had never met Mike, but I of course knew him by reputation—which was largely unfavorable in the non-JACL circles I tended to choose among Japanese Americans. His name came up at community meetings whenever the discussion turned to the internment, the JACL, or any of the big issues we were engaged in at the time. His name was synonymous with the JACL, and often in a pejorative sense. Mike had a lot of history behind him, but that history was so closely tied to the JACL that it was difficult, if not impossible, to separate one from the other.

Just as Saburo Kido, as the JACL's president in 1942, was accused of selling out the community when the organization advised Japanese Americans not to resist the government's orders to "evacuate," Mike Masaoka was as much a part of that moment and, for many, was considered the real culprit who swayed the opinions of the JACL delegates in that critical emergency meeting at which the organization had made the decision to advise cooperation. At the time, Mike was still a newcomer to the organization, and perhaps it was a testament to his skill as a leader that he could so quickly go from being essentially an outsider to holding so much prominence in the organization. Perhaps they could tell there was nothing fly-by-night about Mike. In the years since that fateful meeting, his lifetime dedication to the JACL and the community raised his stature, and regardless of how one viewed Mike and his policies, he was undoubtedly a true leader.

Born in Fresno, California, in 1915, he moved with his family to Utah and grew up around the Salt Lake City area. He was a champion debater in high school and continued to lead his debate team at the University of Utah, where he majored in political science, with the dream of someday being elected to the United States Congress. A professor

at the university who had befriended Mike advised him to set different goals because, he told Mike, he would never be elected to public
office because of his Japanese ancestry. Mike told me later, when we had
become friends, that that was a hard reality to face, especially in a place
like Utah, where Japanese Americans had never been treated as badly
as they were in California, Oregon, and Washington. In Utah, both geo-
graphically and perceptually, we were not viewed as a threat the way
we were in the wartime designated military zone. He told me he always
felt equal to whites as he was growing up in Utah, and that it had never
occurred to him that he would face racial prejudice if he ran for public
office. That said a lot about Mike and about the lives of Japanese Americans outside of California, where members of ethnic minorities often
lived in enclaves separated from their white neighbors.

Even though Mike said that he was very much a part of the Japanese community in Salt Lake City, he never struck me as someone who
had lived much among Japanese Americans. I had no reason to doubt
what he said, but whatever his experience was in the community, it
seemed not to shape him in the same ways and to the same degree that
it had other Nisei. He was completely at ease in any setting and with
any group, a circumstance that was reflected in his life in Washington,
D.C., where he mixed easily with politicians and political society. He
was a glad-hander and, it seemed, considered himself as good as, or
even better than, anyone else, regardless of color or background. There
was a kind of self-confidence to Mike that turned some people off (many
Japanese Americans saw it as arrogance), but after I had gotten to know
him well, I saw that there was a real vulnerability to him. Despite his
success, he was plagued and even hurt by his reputation within the
Japanese American community, and he seemed always to yearn to
belong more fully to the Nisei generation, to share in their experience
and to be part of who they had become through their hardships and
achievements. Mike was Nisei, there was no doubt about that, but I
always felt that his having grown up in Utah made him a different breed
of Nisei, just as it seems true of any Japanese Americans raised outside
the enclaves that shaped the rest of us so deeply.

Mike fought hard during the early years of the war to convince
Assistant Secretary of War John J. McCloy and Secretary of War Henry

Stimson to create an all–Japanese American combat unit that would give Japanese Americans an opportunity to prove their loyalty to this country. And while that unit, the 442nd Regimental Combat Team, became the most highly decorated unit in the history of the United States Army, despite having served in combat in Europe for only one year, Mike was accused of having created the unworkable situation in which the Nisei faced the decision of either joining the army or resisting and refusing the draft. He was also accused of finagling for himself a soft, noncombat duty throughout the 442nd's assignment in Europe, an allegation that bothered Mike. He told me once that he didn't get his Bronze Star for being a good typist!

After the war, Mike lobbied for passage of a bill that sought to give Japanese Americans an opportunity to file claims for lost properties, but the opponents of the bill in Congress created so many arcane amendments that the final bill became a virtual joke. In the end, Mike was criticized for allowing passage of the Japanese American Evacuation Claims Act as a bill that made a mockery of the hardships and losses endured by Japanese Americans during the war and that also, more than anything, showed Mike to be a yet untutored lobbyist who had been outwitted by cagey opponents of the bill.

Mike's real achievements went pretty much unnoticed or unmentioned in the Japanese American community. (Among the most significant are his personal effort to overturn a presidential veto of the Immigration and Nationality Act of 1952, which gave the Issei naturalization rights after over fifty years of being denied such rights; being one of four major civil rights advocates in Washington who created the all-powerful Leadership Conference on Civil Rights; and being the only Asian American lobbyist who was part of the core team that led the fight for passage of the famous Civil Rights Act of 1964, the result of the work of Dr. Martin Luther King, Jr.) Unfortunately, Mike felt compelled always to justify his actions before and during World War II, but he could never overcome his past with the JACL, nor could he convince his critics to believe his account of what had happened and how much he had fought for the rights of Japanese Americans. Mike knew that his reputation always harkened back to that crucial meeting of 1942. No matter what he achieved later in his life, that decision cast a dark shadow until his death in 1991. And it didn't stop there either. George Takei's 2012 musical *Allegiance,* about the actor's personal experience of wartime incarceration, presents a mocking portrayal of Masaoka. But those who knew Mike and knew what he had accomplished in his life-time remained faithful to him, and although he was the JACL's most controversial figure, within the organization he held a special place of honor and was no less than an icon.

One thing no one could have denied about Mike is that when he spoke, people listened. And on that day in Sacramento, when he took the microphone and began talking about the war years and about camp and about the JACL and about redress, everyone stopped what they were doing and listened.

I had gone to the back of the room to get some refreshments and saw Edison Uno standing back there, so I joined him. Edison had a great deal of respect for Mike, but he could also be one of his harshest public critics (although, to his credit, Edison had a real knack for being diplomatic when he criticized someone publicly). He and Mike shared an inter-esting relationship—mutual respect mixed with an understanding that there were strong disagreements between them. I never heard Edison say anything negative about Mike the man, whether in public or private (and vice versa); Edison liked Mike, he just didn't agree with him about a great many policy matters. Mike represented the past, and Edison was the bridge to the future of the JACL.

As Edison and I stood listening to Mike talk about the war, and about our efforts as a community to reconcile what had happened to us, and what it meant to us as citizens of this country, he brought up Edison's resolution from the 1970 Chicago convention. He talked about the debate that had raged on and on over the issue of compensation, summarizing the arguments both for and against.

And then he did something that I only later realized was remark-able: he stated that, earlier in the year, he had let it be known through the JACL's *Pacific Citizen* newspaper that he not only supported compen-sation but advanced the position for individual payment. He was set-ting the course of the JACL's campaign. He was proscribing for the old guard—all of his colleagues and loyalists—the limits of their objections to the idea of individual compensation. He admitted that as he pondered the difficult question of monetary reparations, he had reversed his initial position. *It was now time for the JACL to ask for compensation; it was the right thing to do.* And with one stroke of his verbal pen, he had opened the door for what was to follow.

I don't remember much of what he said after that or how others were taking it all in, but I do remember turning to Edison and saying, "I think we just got ourselves a campaign."

THE TURNING POINT

That was a turning point for the JACL's redress program. Mike had changed the balance of the argument, and as a consequence, compensation now had a solid base of support among the delegates and the issue was given new life.

The other significant event at that convention was the election of Jim Murakami as national president. Murakami, an engineer who had been imprisoned at Amache (officially the Granada War Relocation Center, in southeastern Colorado), was a member of the JACL's Sonoma chapter and active in the NCWN district. He knew and respected Edison and admired his activism, something not always appreciated by the Nisei. While the convention delegates knew that Jim's election virtually guaranteed Edison's appointment to the chairmanship of the national redress committee, Jim played the political waiting game until he could privately lobby fellow National Board members to confirm his choice. Two months after the Sacramento convention, the executive committee (that is, the elected board officers) confirmed Jim's choice and undercut any controversy in Edison's appointment. To assuage the concerns of the old guard and others from the conservative segment of the organization, Murakami appointed JACL National Director David Ushio to the position of cochair, with Edison. It was a shrewd move for two reasons. First, Ushio, who hailed from Utah and was born after the war, had little knowledge about the internment camps. Second, his father, Shake, who was part of the old guard opposed to redress, was also a close friend of Mike Masaoka, who had just silenced his loyalists at the convention. In a crafty maneuver, Murakami, in tapping David Ushio and Edison Uno for the redress campaign, had handcuffed the opposition and given Edison a free hand to develop the program.

While still in Sacramento, Edison and I met to talk about campaign strategies, which was one of his biggest concerns as the presumptive redress chair. Some of the other districts were already starting to move on the issue—conducting surveys, holding meetings, and the like—but Edison saw what the movement was lacking: a cohesive national strategy. Even as the JACL itself seemed to have more or less coalesced around reparations, the larger community remained divided on the issue, with certain groups and individuals objecting to our making a public spectacle by talking about camp so openly.

It was fine and well—and, I would argue, necessary—that we pushed our own agenda within the JACL, but without wider community support, we could not possibly move forward. My strategy was both simple and risky: since the NCWN district was both one of the largest and the most active in the organization, I figured we could either create the model for the campaign or set a standard as a challenge to the other districts. If we could successfully establish a public dialogue about the internment and force the issue into the open, we could create a starting point for a public campaign. But to do this, I knew it was critical that we educate and convince the public that the constitutional violations committed against us as American citizens were relevant to *every* American.

I knew it wouldn't be an easy road, but I also knew that the challenges we would face—exposing ourselves to attacks, facing the uphill climb of debunking the myths about, and rationales for, our wartime imprisonment, combating the misinformed and bigoted views of the public—were an inevitable part of the journey. If nothing else, I figured that forcing our community to engage in this dialogue would bring us together in an act of self-preservation. It may have been a risky strategy, forcing the community to confront its most painful memories of the camp experience, but we would have to slug this out at some point if we were going to move forward with a campaign. The San Francisco Bay Area being what it was—a progressive region with a significant Japanese American population—I figured it was as good a place as any to begin engaging in the unavoidable verbal fisticuffs.

Edison knew that I was impatient with the JACL's slow progress, and I assumed that with him now at the helm of the committee, things would soon begin to happen at a faster pace. He had his own impatience, and I knew our friendship would keep me closely connected with whatever plans were being made at the national level of the program. His leadership, I was sure, would make a difference.

Edison was the most respected Japanese American civil rights activist in the Bay Area and had a national reputation as a mover and shaker; in many ways, the two of us were a study in contrasts. I was new to the JACL and had just recently returned from more than ten years away from the community, counting my days in the army, college, and Europe. I had been separated from the Japanese American community and everything it stood for in those days, so I was still catching up on how much things had changed in the wake of the civil rights movement, including how the JACL operated and who its players were. Having lived abroad, where America was not the center of the universe, I found my political perspectives much more cosmopolitan than those held by most of my colleagues at work and my new friends in the JACL. I still longed for the *Guardian* and the London *Times* and BBC News.

Perhaps because of this broader life experience, I viewed our community's role in the United States differently than Edison and many other Japanese Americans. He was fearless in his determination to establish an equity balance in American society, and from his perspective, redress was for Japanese Americans what the color-line battle was for the black community: a fight for our place in America. He believed in confrontation, and in this he was more courageous than I. He would sometimes chide me that for someone who was so bound to the European experience, I was still so bound by Japanese culture and its inclination to avoid conflict. "It's the only thing people understand sometimes," he would say, and who was I to argue with that when he had played such a successful role in challenging many mainstream institutions to abolish their discriminatory policies.

Edison and I talked more strategy in the weeks following the Sacramento convention. We agreed that we were shaping a national strategy that would lead to Washington, but all the time, I wondered how straight that road would be. I had already come face-to-face with the public through my work with local media, and I knew there was still a general ignorance about Japanese American history and experience, even in the Bay Area. We figured that, if anywhere, this traditionally liberal pocket of the country would generate the most sympathetic responses to our wartime treatment, and so we were surprised to find that this was not the case. And if we encountered this much resistance in the Bay Area, we knew it would only be worse as we moved farther east with the campaign.

Toward the end of 1976, we decided we would need to sit down and map out a two-year plan. It was getting into the busy holiday weeks, however, so we postponed for a bit our meeting to discuss strategies and the vision for the campaign. Sometime after the Christmas holidays, Edison told me. Sometime in January.

What I didn't know—what hardly anyone knew—was that Edison was scheduled to have major heart surgery at the end of the year. He told me only that he was going to be hospitalized for something routine and would be up and about by January, before the academic year resumed. I looked forward to working with him to develop the details of a national campaign.

But it was not to be. Edison died on Christmas Eve of a heart attack, brought on by a congenital heart condition. I had some vague knowledge that he had had some kind of heart condition, but I had no idea it was that serious. He seemed at times perhaps a little fragile physically but otherwise healthy enough. I was stunned by the news, which felt all the more unexpected because I had been thinking so much about all the things Edison and I needed to discuss. He was only forty-seven years old.

As I thought about him that Christmas Eve, I remembered how he had made light of the surgery, calling it "nothing serious" and "just routine stuff." In retrospect, maybe I sensed his lightness was burdened with underlying seriousness, but it was not my place to ask for specifics, and he never said more about it. In hindsight, it wasn't surprising Edison would have acted that way. It was how he was; it was a part of his modesty and restraint, his *enryo*, his reluctance to draw attention to himself. Some people saw him as a person who liked being in the limelight and would argue that point with me. The real truth about him may have been in between. The man I had gotten to know so well was, if anything, complex and sometimes perplexing. There was a calmness to him, but he was also a tough, even uncompromising fighter; he was a critic of the JACL but was also one of its most effective advocates. He never sought personal recognition and often praised others for things he had accomplished. And when someone took credit for something he had been involved with, he had no need to correct the record. He wasn't a spiteful man or someone who needed people to know of his achievements. That was part of what made him so exceptional.

As an indication of Edison's importance within the Bay Area—and beyond just its Japanese American community—close to eight hundred people attended his memorial in San Francisco, including most of the city's political leadership, its top judges, many state politicians, and a wide cross section of San Francisco's diverse community. I sat among the large audience thinking about how embarrassed Edison would be to have such a grand and distinguished crowd there to pay tribute to him.

I felt at the time, and still do, that Edison's passing was an incalculable loss to the community and to the redress effort. No one ever stepped in to fill his shoes; no one was ever such a complete advocate for so much in the community. I saw his faults and weaknesses, but I also saw his ability to overcome them for the good of the cause, for what it was we all believed in. Some of his friends who knew him more intimately than I felt it was his dedication to the causes of the community that killed him ultimately, that his tireless dedication, his relentless battles against injustice, and his willingness to be on the front lines, all of it wore him down. It's a point that's hard to argue. But I doubt he could have been anything but a fighter on behalf of his people. He was too much a part of the community and cared too much to have turned away. People with greatness in them, however small, never do that, and he certainly could not. Without exception, Edison Uno represented the best our community has ever offered, and losing him left a huge void.

2

LAUNCHING
THE
CAMPAIGN

(1977-1978)

CLIFFORD UYEDA

Jim Murakami, the JACL's national president as of 1976, asked me who I thought would be a good choice to replace the late Edison Uno. Jim had already announced his temporary appointment of former Northern California district redress committee chair Mike Honda to cochair the national redress committee with JACL National Director David Ushio. I knew that Mike, who had become a close friend and would some years later be elected to the United States Congress, was pressed by his work demands and therefore not likely to be cochair for very long. I suggested to Jim that if he wanted a committee that did more than sit on its ass for another two years, he should consider someone like Clifford Uyeda. I was shooting a bit long in suggesting so controversial a figure (Clifford was an outsider whose distrust and public criticism of the JACL was well known), but I also knew Jim wasn't afraid to take risks, as he had thrown caution to the wind in appointing Edison. Jim and Clifford already knew each other within the context of their work in the Japanese American community, and although that might have been an advantage, I was also well aware that Cliff's position on some civil rights issues gave Jim pause. He probably wondered how Edison and I had reconciled our differences with Clifford, but honestly, that was never a problem between any of us.

It was ultimately Jim's decision to make, but the fact that he was asking me for my opinion on who should chair the redress committee told me that he wanted an activist chair. In Clifford, he would certainly have that. I didn't feel any urge to push my preference on him, but when he asked, I shared my thoughts. I'm sure Jim asked others for their recommendations as well, and I have no idea what sort of feedback he got, but several months later he asked Clifford to take over as the national chair—and alone, pushing out both Mike Honda and David Ushio. I assumed he took quite a bit of flak with this appointment, just as he had with Edison the year before.

Cliff told me he was reluctant to accept the chairmanship primarily because of his personal reservations about the JACL. He may have been a harsh critic of the organization, but much to his credit, he was also a member. He always felt that a person had no real credibility and could not gain authority as a leader or a critic of an organization without at least being invested as a member. But his greatest concern about considering the chairmanship, he told me, was that he could not speak firsthand about the camp experience. During the war, his family was sent from Tacoma, Washington, to the so-called Topaz War Relocation Center, in Utah, but he had spent the war years in New Orleans earning his medical degree at Tulane University, having received government permission to leave the camp. I didn't think this circumstance would affect his ability to lead the effort; he may not have lived in camp himself, but he understood the experience through his family and had been part of the Japanese American community his entire life.

So Clifford Uyeda, a retired medical doctor with years of community activism already under his belt, became the chair of the JACL's redress committee almost a year after Edison Uno's untimely death. I always felt his accepting the responsibility was in part to honor Edison, although Clifford would never tell you this. He was a sensitive man, but not particularly fond of expressing that sensitivity. He was an intellectual man of action who grew restless when issues became bogged down in long-winded discussions, he was often tenacious to the point of being single-minded and unmovable, and he was, for better or worse, often oblivious to what others thought of him. He was not an unreasonable man, however, and would always listen to opposing views and could sometimes be convinced that he was wrong. It was his humility, courage, and integrity that made him so unusual and notable within the activist community.

Cliff and I had different ways of approaching the redress campaign. I was much more like Edison in my thinking, focusing on what lurked in the surrounding alleyways, while Clifford's mind stuck to the super-highways. That is to say, Edison and I thought in terms of strategies and the politics of particular situations while Clifford simply saw the larger goals ahead, the destination. I thought of our effort in terms of a campaign, while Clifford thought in terms of a program. He would have preferred to argue the issue in the intellectual setting of, say, an academic symposium, while I was aching for the rough-and-tumble interaction of a debate in the public arena, followed by a fight in the political center of America. One thing we agreed on, however, was how onerous a task it seemed just to educate Japanese Americans on the topic. He would often comment to me how surprising it was that Japanese Americans were still so uninformed about the community's experiences during the war.

———

As the national chairman of the redress campaign, Clifford set about to select members of a committee whose job would be to produce a primer on the internment. His first choice was Raymond Okamura—coauthor, with Uno, of the resolution presented at the 1970 convention that paved the way for our campaign—an obvious selection because of his depth of knowledge about the internment. He also asked Peggy Nagae, an attorney from Oregon, and Ken Hayashi, from Los Angeles, whom Clifford sought for his keen writing ability.

In the late spring of 1977, the committee produced the publication *The Japanese American Incarceration: A Case for Redress*, a succinct history of the internment that described how the government's unjust exclusion and detention policies were guided by racism and greed. Though dismissed by Asian American academicians as something of a quaint publication, *A Case for Redress* laid out a clear rationale for our efforts to seek a formal apology from the U.S. government. The booklet contained facts that most Japanese Americans did not know; it became the bible of the campaign and was widely distributed to JACL chapters throughout the country. It was through this publication that the committee changed the terminology from "reparations" to "redress" to better describe the JACL's intent. The concept of redress went far beyond the idea of monetary compensation and encompassed the altruistic intent to correct the broader injustices of the wartime policies. *A Case for Redress* described the arguments for that greater purpose.

At that time, only a handful of books on the internment had been published, the best among them including *America's Concentration Camps* by Allan R. Bosworth (Norton, 1967); *Prejudice, War and the Constitution: Causes and Consequences of the Evacuation of the Japanese Americans in World War II* by Jacobus tenBroek, Edward N. Barnhart, and Floyd W. Matson (University of California Press, 1970); and *Concentration Camps USA: Japanese Americans and World War II* by Roger Daniels (Holt, Rinehart and Winston, 1971). Unfortunately, none reached large audiences. Daniels's book was the definitive scholarly publication on the topic, but Michi Weglyn's *Years of Infamy* (Morrow, 1976) was the most popular nonfiction book on the internment read by Japanese Americans. Jeanne Wakatsuki Houston's *Farewell to Manzanar* (Houghton Mifflin, 1973), a fictional account of the author's camp experience, was made into a television movie in 1976, and it no doubt reached the largest national audience.

While *A Case for Redress*, a booklet of about fifteen pages, provided in brief form much of the same information these other sources did, the committee's publication was perfect for our efforts because it served the needs of our audience: I had found that many Japanese Americans, while generally high achievers academically, preferred succinct histories over longwinded ones. Thus, the booklet turned out to be a great tool for teaching those who didn't want to read the few available publications at the time. To this day, it remains a wonderful primer on the internment— even though it doesn't cover the information that has surfaced since its publication—and it was truly one of the treasures of the campaign.

It was also at this time that the committee officially changed its name from the JACL National Reparations Committee to the JACL National Committee for Redress, with the new name reflecting the broader goals of the campaign. Whereas the word "reparations" covered the monetary aspect of the effort, "redress" addressed the higher, more altruistic goals of the JACL's program. Ultimately, it was this philosophical change that helped in eventually convincing most of the historically reluctant JACL members to reconsider their position. I'm convinced that if we had continued to focus only on reparations, we would have had a much more difficult time uniting the Japanese American community on the issue.

With the dissemination of the committee's booklet to our chapters and the subsequent revelation of some heretofore unknown facts about the internment, we realized even more profoundly how little most

Japanese Americans knew about the internment beyond what they had personally experienced. As Clifford pointed out to me once, many did not even know the significance of FDR's EO 9066, the order that had led to their incarceration. After the war Japanese Americans were pre-occupied with rebuilding their lives and reestablishing communities, so there was little time to dig into files and understand why all of it had happened. And of course it didn't help that there was a cultural tendency to ignore the troubled past and keep those memories buried in some deep psychological corner, even if it meant never learning the truth about our wartime experiences. It was better to forget than to face the shame of our ignominious imprisonment. While the Freedom of Information Act, signed into law on Independence Day of 1966, opened up new avenues for inquiry, only a few Japanese American researchers examined the internment, a lapse that reflected the community's need to keep the episode in the past. It was still an unpopular subject, and non–Japanese American academicians like Roger Daniels were left to expose the government's manipulations and to begin telling us about our own experiences. Viewed from today's perspective, the degree of ignorance in the Japanese American community was staggering, but that was how it was. We tried to forget, and we did a good job of it.

Clifford, however, had been reading anything and everything he could get his hands on about our wartime treatment, and by the mid-1970s, he was one of the better-informed Japanese Americans on the issue. As the JACL's redress committee chair, he began writing a weekly column for the *Pacific Citizen*, providing historical information about the internment and revealing some of the information that had previously been unknown and unavailable to the public. He saw his role as an educator and was well suited to it. It was the first time Japanese Americans began to understand just how much manipulation and bigotry were behind the wartime policies that had led to their imprisonment.

Clifford and I continued to talk often when we encountered each other at the JACL headquarters in San Francisco, where he did research through the JACL's archival collections. He filled in my gaps of history, and I helped guide his thinking about certain issues he needed to consider as the national committee chair. He kept digging into our past, while I wanted to forge ahead into the future.

THE CANDIDATE

In early January 1978, the power brokers in my district decided they wanted to run Clifford for the national presidency of the JACL, and they invited me to join them, knowing Cliff and I had become close friends and had built an alliance of sorts over the subject of redress. I was surprised that this group in particular—all of whom had toiled long within the ranks of the JACL and had made their way up the ladder to their positions of influence in the district—would champion Clifford for president. If anything, he was a known public critic of the JACL, and yet they had not only reconciled themselves to that fact but they also somehow convinced Cliff to stand for the presidency of the organization.

I didn't know this push for Clifford's election was on the agenda when I was invited to join the group for a meeting. The issue is redress, I was told. I was the last to arrive at Clifford's condo, where the meeting was being held, and I remember the bone-chilling cold of a San Francisco winter night as I walked from my car to his building, expecting the meeting to be about ensuring the progress of the redress program now that there actually *was* progress under Clifford's chairmanship. The biennial convention that year would take place in July in Salt Lake City and would culminate with the election of a new president, and we were meeting to discuss strategies to ensure the continued advancement of the program regardless of who became the next president. Or so I thought.

The idea of running Clifford for the presidency seemed, if not absurd, a huge stretch to me. I couldn't help but see all the negatives of the candidacy of a man who was a JACL member but had been either uninvolved with or even opposed to some of the organization's key efforts. He had rejected the JACL's offer of support while he was leading the effort to get Iva Toguri D'Aquino exonerated of her treason conviction in the infamous Tokyo Rose case; he had never been on the board of a JACL chapter or district; and, in fact, he had never held any position of responsibility within the organization other than that of redress committee chairman, which he had assumed less than a year earlier. I could think of a lot of reasons *not* to run Clifford, and even beyond these and other negatives, there was also the matter of who he would be running against. Looming beyond the horizon was the man who would be his opponent: Mikio Uchiyama, a distinguished and accomplished judge who would be a hard candidate to beat, particularly because he was so highly regarded throughout the organization.

After a lengthy and painful discussion—painful for Clifford because this was all about him and his vulnerabilities as a potential candidate— we all agreed that we would undertake this extraordinary challenge, and I was asked to lead the effort. By the time we walked out into the cold night air, we had developed an entire strategy toward making Clifford Uyeda the next JACL national president. We were excited and convinced that we could make this happen. And there was more than just the next presidency of the JACL at stake here.

Clifford's presidency would guarantee a renewed commitment to set the course for redress, the most important political campaign ever undertaken by the JACL on behalf of the Japanese American community. We were about to embark on a journey that was unprecedented in this country, and whether we succeeded or not, we were about to make history.

⸺

Clifford's candidacy for the JACL presidency was important, certainly, but we needed to think of this effort in terms of larger campaign strategies, beyond the JACL and the Japanese American community, and to project the story of our wartime treatment and our fight for justice onto a mainstream platform. The problem for us, I felt, was that we had no focus, no clear direction. It's one thing to talk about a past injustice and the need to rectify it, but how? And with what? Every debate and discussion about redress that had taken place at each of the JACL conventions since 1970 had reflected the progress in the thinking of the chapters and districts, but redress was a complex issue that ripped at the gut of every delegate; it was so personal that consensus was difficult and progress was painfully slow.

Conventions served as a platform for the various district councils to raise issues, but very few new initiatives were ever presented to help drive the redress effort. The JACL's progress merely reflected the work, whatever it might be, of any current redress committee. It seemed to me that delegates went to conventions without any guidance on what they should have been considering over the past biennium since the previous convention. The regional discussions and debates were good because they were necessary, but we needed something that would help frame those discussions.

My concern was that at the next convention, in 1978, we would once again debate the various components of the redress program and then walk away without accomplishing anything concrete. Two proposals had been placed under consideration, but neither had gone anywhere. The so-called Seattle Bootstrap Plan would provide an individual tax credit as redress payment through the IRS tax return form. There would be a checkbox on the form, and that, in theory, would serve as an educational component for those curious enough to figure out what that checkbox was for. This plan also allowed for those Japanese Americans opposed to redress to exercise their option to *not* receive the tax credit by simply ignoring the checkbox. The second proposal (developed by the national reparations committee under the chairmanship of Edward Yamamoto of Spokane during the 1974–76 biennium), which sought $3,000 plus $10 per day of imprisonment, also went nowhere. Both proposals had already fizzled and would no doubt arrive DOA at the upcoming Salt Lake City convention. What we needed, I thought, was something bold that reflected the collective angst of Japanese Americans and their growing determination to do something, *anything*, to address the injustices of the internment.

Thinking this through with Clifford served a dual purpose: it was obviously relevant to his chairmanship of the organization's national redress committee, but it also influenced his candidacy for JACL president. The two efforts were now tied together because any moves Clifford made as the redress chair would be seen as fundamental to his fitness for the position of JACL president. My job was to make this work at both levels despite the enormous odds against, first, his ever winning the JACL presidency and, second, our redress effort ending in anything but utter defeat. But what we had in Clifford was a man who cared little about the odds; resolute and determined, he was committed to unearthing the truths about our unjust treatment during the war. Through our work together, Clifford and I had built between us an alliance of trust, a bond (due in no small part to our both having joined the JACL with personal reservations), and I felt I owed it to Clifford to get him to the presidency on this journey we had begun together.

The reality for me was that redress had begun to consume much of my life. I was completely focused on my teaching while I was in class, but even as much as I enjoyed my work, I was preoccupied with the redress effort as soon as I left campus. I kept thinking that there had to be some mechanism that would unify the JACL membership behind redress, but I struggled to find the key. And then late one night, after I had finished correcting student papers and turned my thoughts to redress, it occurred to me that what we lacked was a framework to give us direction to our efforts. We had never defined what our goal was other than to rectify the injustice visited upon us as a way to prevent it from happening to other groups in the future, and it seemed to me that until we had a specific goal, a target, our efforts would continue to lack coherence.

I was convinced that that was the key, but it seemed almost too simple and obvious; on the other hand, the idea of a specified goal seemed not to have occurred to anyone. We didn't have a specific objective with a path and guideposts. We hadn't defined the endgame and weren't clear on where we were going.

Later that day, I met with Clifford to tell him what I had been thinking about and showed him a one-page document on which I had scribbled two items, what I described as goals for redress: a $50,000 individual payment *and* a national educational trust fund to assuage the concerns of those who opposed the idea of individual payments. What was important, I told Clifford, was for him to present this plan as a guideline and not a proposal, the difference being that a guideline would state our goal without defining how we would reach that goal, whereas a proposed directive would specify how we would accomplish our desired outcome. A guideline would have the flexibility to define and inform the JACL's next steps as needed.

Clifford liked the idea of presenting guidelines, but, not surprisingly, he wondered if it would be too presumptuous of him to present them unilaterally. He also wondered if it would be better to have me submit the guidelines to a vote by the NCWN district and then present them to the convention as the district's proposal, an idea I rejected outright. The guidelines had to come from the national chair of the redress committee; this had to be *his* idea. Sensing his discomfort with the prospect of presenting the guidelines as a document he had developed, I suggested that he reconstitute his committee with representatives from each of the JACL's districts and then have the committee create a set of guidelines similar to my draft copy. That idea appealed to him because he felt more comfortable having the proposal evolve through a collaborative process, which would help establish its credibility. This was the first time I can recall Clifford thinking strategically: he was going to control the means to reach an end goal that had already been determined.

THE GUIDELINES

As Clifford and I sat in the boardroom at the JACL headquarters talking about guidelines and forming a committee to create them, I was now thinking about strategy on two levels. First, I hoped the guidelines would jumpstart some real action from the JACL on the matter of redress. It was coming on eight years since the Uno and Okamura resolution had brought the issue to light, and I thought that presenting specific talking points could not just further the debate but prompt action by defining what exactly we sought in our demands for redress. And secondly, I hoped the guidelines, if adopted, would commit the future redress committee chair, whoever he or she might be, to follow the course defined by the guidelines. Strategically, I also realized that having guidelines would work to further Clifford's candidacy because, while it had good publicity value for him among delegates, it would also demonstrate that he had organizational leadership qualities, something sorely lacking among his already sparse credentials.

We had been talking and talking about the issue for years, and except for the Seattle group, which was a coalition of JACL chapters in the Seattle area and non-JACL community leaders and interested individuals, no one in the JACL or in the community was willing to take the next step. I hoped that presenting guidelines would at last give a framework and guided momentum to the issue, and if it would also strengthen Clifford's candidacy, so much the better.

As Clifford and I talked about his forming a working committee to develop the guidelines, it quickly became apparent that we personally knew very few individuals in the JACL outside of our district. Rather than consult with anyone in the JACL headquarters where we usually met, like Karl Nobuyuki, the JACL national director, which would have been the wise thing to do, we were more comfortable making selections based on what we knew of them from, or on the recommendation of, our personal contacts.

We began with the obvious names, starting with William Marutani, a Pennsylvania State Court judge from Philadelphia, who was an easy choice simply because he was part of the old guard and had a national reputation within the JACL. I had observed Marutani at the Sacramento convention and, given his demeanor and no-nonsense temperament, I thought he was one judge I would not want to appear before as a defendant if I had committed even the smallest of crimes! The next choice was also easy: Minoru Yasui of Denver, a longtime JACL activist and a civil rights attorney who had defied the government's curfew orders and taken his case to the United States Supreme Court in *Yasui v. United States*. In personality, Min and Bill were polar opposites: Marutani reserved and judicious, Yasui fiery and outspoken.

Next, Clifford selected Ron Mamiya, a young, up-and-coming member from the Seattle group, and from Los Angeles he chose Phil Shigekuni, who was one of the earliest redress advocates in L.A. The others were individuals selected by their district governors in consultation with Clifford: Ted Matsushima from the Salt Lake City area, Bill Doi from the Midwest district, and Tom Shimasaki from Fresno, representing Central California, the only JACL district opposed to redress. Clifford asked me to represent my district, and when I suggested he ask Ray Okamura instead, he equivocated and then eventually decided he would invite the members of his three-person committee as observers: Ray Okamura, Peggy Nagae, and Ken Hayashi.

Over the next day or two, Clifford and I went over the list of committee members to see if he wanted any changes, and we talked about the guidelines and the various iterations we could attempt to develop. We were giving shape and purpose to this effort and dictating the terms of the demands. The guidelines signaled our commitment to take this fight to Congress and to the American public. We would no longer remain silent.

Clifford and I met most days to talk and plan, just as I had done with Edison. In some ways, it's amusing to think about. Here were two people who had been publicly critical of the JACL, now working together to take it down a road that would impact its future and forever change the Japanese American community. It seemed at times surreal, but there we were, the two of us having reached a point where we not only believed in the organization but believed strongly in what it could do on this issue.

———————

Several days before the meeting was to take place, Clifford and I met to discuss the purpose and strategy for the meeting and the importance of developing concrete guidelines for redress. Clifford's concern was how, over a weekend meeting, we would reconcile the still strong disagreements on the compensation issue, which were, first, whether we should even ask for monetary compensation, and then, if so, whether it should be in the form of a trust fund or as individual payments. He felt a need to be inclusive and to process the concept together as a committee, but I thought he should simply lead and direct. I suggested that he ignore the question and begin with the assumption that reparations would be made in the form of individual payments; I wanted him to preempt the discussion that surrounded compensation and inevitably slowed things down. Make the committee members accept that this is a legitimate starting point and that you've already thought this through, I told him, so the issue is not open to debate. We agreed that the committee could work through the concept of a trust fund once there was committee agreement on the amount of the individual payment. If Cliff was comfortable with this plan, it would be an easy way to start the meeting and get past the most difficult question of the entire JACL redress program.

Someone later accused me of manipulating Clifford, but that wasn't true at all. No one controlled or manipulated him, and I certainly didn't have that kind of influence or ability with him. I only knew that if I could give him a suggestion that appealed to him or that had factual legitimacy he couldn't deny, he would give it his own energy and commitment. As we talked, I knew my guidelines idea would pass that test.

———————

In April 1978, Clifford convened his newly constituted redress committee, whose purpose was to spend the weekend hammering out guidelines to present to the delegates at the Salt Lake City convention. We met early on Saturday, with Clifford stating that the discussion would center on how much the JACL should ask for in individual compensation and, in so doing, preempted those who would argue against individual payments in favor of establishing a trust fund. This issue was not open to debate, he declared, and he went so far as to say that, if nothing else, he wanted the goal of the meeting to be deciding on what that figure should be.

By starting the discussion in this way, Clifford got the committee to agree on a monetary amount and he also established a tone for how the program would be run. He was not very subtle in pushing the committee to take such a strong position on a topic that had yet to be decided by the National Council, but no one objected, all of them having come with an understanding that solidifying a plan for individual compensation was the purpose of the meeting. Min Yasui did note, however, that the question of individual compensation versus trust fund was still undecided, and he was hardly fooled by what Clifford was doing. Bill Marutani issued a stern warning that it was problematic that this committee was essentially establishing policy for the larger organization, but some of us argued that, to the contrary, we were only providing *recommendations*, since these were "guidelines" and not mandated positions. Min found it amusing in a cynical sort of way and agreed to go along with whatever Clifford wanted; Bill remained silent on this parliamentary matter for the rest of the weekend.

This initial issue, that of individual payments, was the most difficult of anything we talked about over the two days. All sorts of figures were thrown out: $10,000 from Seattle's Bootstrap Plan, $1 million, $15,000, and several other figures were added to the mix. Just about everyone agreed that $10,000 or $15,000 was not enough, and that $1 million was totally unrealistic. As Min Yasui put it, $10,000 was a "goddamn insult to every Japanese American who was imprisoned"—intentionally (I think) throwing in a dig at the member and observers from Seattle who were at the meeting. When Bill Marutani suggested $50,000, there was silence. That number caused everyone to pause; it was the first suggestion to stick. Ultimately, however, as a group they felt that the total amount, even calculated conservatively, would be so high that we would never be able to get a bill through Congress. With that in mind, someone threw in the number $25,000, which again caused everyone to pause and think seriously if that could work. I favored $50,000, even though, even as a symbolic figure, it was hardly adequate to make up for the abrogation of our constitutional rights, for having to live with the brand of being traitors to this country, for three years' imprisonment and the loss of freedom. Marutani joined in that view. Ultimately, we agreed on $25,000.

Whatever amount we chose would by its very nature be a compromise, I knew that, but I still regretted that I hadn't pushed harder for $50,000. It was the original figure I had presented to Clifford when I had handed him my scribbled outline of the guideline idea, and it was, I felt, an honest amount that would help reconcile our lost honor. I felt that $25,000 was an insult and a sham, and now I wondered if I had stepped back too easily from a figure I truly believed would be a meaningful recognition of what Japanese Americans had been willing to give up, the sacrifice made to prove our loyalty. In my mind, $50,000 was an amount that would begin to give the Nisei a sense of vindication for their belief in a country that had abandoned and turned against them. But I hadn't fought hard enough for that and, in some ways, I felt I had failed.

We were about to break for lunch when someone asked about the disposition of individual payments for those who had already died. What happens to their payments? Should that money go to their heirs? I knew this wasn't an easy issue to resolve; it was fraught with all kinds of problems and would open that huge proverbial can of worms for every group treated unjustly at the hands of a governmental authority. Our case also presented specific questions: How would we define heirs? What if, for example, someone had been in camp and had no wife or children? Would his amount go to his siblings or to their heirs? And what if, say, a Japanese American woman from the camps married a non–Japanese American and had step-children, but she passed away before payments were made; would her step-children, who were not Japanese American and had no relationship at all to the camp experience, be eligible to receive her share? It was mainly Marutani and Yasui, the attorneys, who kept raising legal concerns related to this complex issue, and it quickly became very clear that we would find no satisfactory resolutions to these question over the course of our weekend meeting. In the end, we all agreed that we would ask for an heirs provision without defining the legal terms, and, as an option, we would ask that amounts for those who were deceased be placed in a trust fund, which would also be part of our demands.

When we came back to the meeting, Min Yasui pointed out that we would have to justify the amount we were asking, that we couldn't just pull the number out of thin air and think we would get it. Being an attorney, he pointed out that in a court of law the demand for monetary compensation has to have some basis in actual costs. We had decided earlier that we would not seek punitive damages because (a) this was not a lawsuit and (b) the calculation of punitive damages was impossible. The problem was, of course, that we *had* pulled the number out of thin air because there simply was no reasonable way to determine what the loss of freedom was worth. The amount was at best symbolic, and large enough to catch the public's attention. For the moment, that was justification enough for me. Bill, in his finest jurist pose, looked at Min squarely and said that there was no precedent in the law that would apply to our situation, and any figure we gave would be a number we just pulled out of the air. There simply was no way to justify the amount in concrete, practical terms.

We decided to put that matter aside for the time being and continued the meeting to talk about the other components: the trust fund and the apology. We agreed that the trust fund would be established to provide grants for anyone who wanted to do research on the internment, the idea being that it would prompt historians to publish articles and books on the subject and on the constitutional issues related to the incident. The use of this fund, we said, should not be limited to Japanese American scholars and researchers but to anyone who could present a credible case for receiving a grant to study and provide publications on the internment. The fund would reflect our desire to share the benefits of redress with the general public and not limit the benefits only to Japanese Americans. It would truly be an American fund meant for anyone who had a valid proposal to study this important moment in history.

What amount we would demand for the fund was another difficult matter to resolve. Two influential voices on the committee—Yasui and Marutani—strongly favored the creation of a trust fund over the idea of individual payments. It wasn't that they opposed the concept of individual payments, but they felt a trust fund was a wiser and more honorable (in Japanese American cultural terms) course to follow. If the convention delegates favored the trust fund concept without individual payments, we had to determine how much we should ask for in creating the trust. Without being able to come to agreement on a figure, we settled on a simple formula: the total amount of the trust should be based on what the total amount would be if each camp incarceree received an individual payment. In other words, $25,000 per individual affected by Executive Order 9066. We also stipulated that individuals eligible to receive redress payments but who chose not to apply for that compensation would have their amounts set aside into the fund. At this early stage in our efforts, we had not calculated, nor were we concerned about, the total cost to the government should our efforts to secure compensation succeed.

The easiest matter to resolve was the question about our demand for a formal apology from the United States government; we agreed upon it unanimously. We wanted the apology to come from the President of the United States on behalf of Congress and the American people. Short and to the point. Phil Shigekuni suggested that maybe we should leave the apology out of our guidelines document because it might give lawmakers an easy fallback position, meaning they might agree to an apology but reject the compensation issue altogether. No committee member felt an apology by itself would be enough; that was something we could get easily enough, we felt, and it was the money that gave teeth to our demands. After some consideration, the committee agreed to remove the apology and leave it to Clifford to decide how to present the guidelines.

And so those are where the battle lines would be drawn in our legislative fight. It was all done except for the nagging need to justify the amount of our demand for $25,000.

On Sunday morning, Chuck Kato from Seattle, who was in attendance as an observer, asked to speak to the issue of the justification. Chuck was a numbers guy. He told the committee he thought he had a solution for us and then proceeded to work out a formula. Starting with the figure of $400 million—the estimated value of property lost by Japanese Americans during the internment, as reported by the Federal

Reserve Bank of San Francisco—he took a marking pen and charted out an elaborate formula that actually backed into $25,000 on the bottom line. I suppose some in the room may have questioned the manner in which the calculation was done, but no one objected. It worked.

I would learn several years later that Mike Masaoka was actually the originator of the $400 million figure. When asked at a hearing of the Japanese American Evacuation Claims Act about the value of property lost by Japanese Americans during the war, Mike literally made up the figure on the spot because, as he told me, there were no official estimates and "$400 million seemed as good as any other number." He never expected it would become the "official" figure!

How we derived the $25,000 figure didn't really matter. What *did* matter was that we had come out of the meeting with a figure that was acceptable to everyone, and we also had a set of reasonable demands for redress. It gave us direction, finally. The redress campaign now had a much-needed focus, and our task at hand was now to persuade the delegates at the 1978 Salt Lake City convention to accept our guidelines. The committee had done its job, and Clifford had been the leader I knew he could be. A lot of what transpired was built on everyone's trust and respect for Clifford, and there's no doubt in my mind that he emerged from that weekend with great guidelines because of who he was. And now, for the first time, the JACL had a concrete framework to use in seeking redress.

THE TWO-PART PLAN

About a month before the convention, Clifford asked me if I would consider accepting the chairmanship of the national redress committee if he won the election for JACL president. I was completely surprised by this and in fact had been thinking about candidates for him to consider. I knew he had others in mind and that I wasn't his first choice, but he said he had observed what I had been doing in the Northern California district and noted how much I had accomplished, including creating the survey that had brought the redress issue out in the open and helped unite the district. Above all else, he was grateful that I had initiated the guidelines process with him. He was offering me the chairmanship, he said, because he wanted to ensure a future for the redress program under his presidency. I was flattered, but I was unsure if it was what I wanted.

I told Cliff that I would consider the position only if he exhausted his list of other candidates. I told him I had to be his last resort for the chairmanship and felt I could be more useful to him as a behind-the-scenes adviser to his presidency. What I didn't have to say to him was that a lot of the old guard was not going to be happy if he appointed me. I knew he knew this, but he didn't care; the personal politics of the organization really didn't matter to him at all.

Clifford seemed to feel that I had a clear idea of where we had to go with the redress program if we were going to turn it into a national campaign and grind out successful results. I've often said in retrospect that I was young enough and arrogant enough to think that I knew what the keys were and that, yes, I had a clear idea of where we had to take the campaign and how we would accomplish it. That was when he first asked me what goals I would set for the redress campaign over the next two years.

What I described was a two-part plan that in fact was a long-range single strategy. The first part was a widespread educational campaign. We had already done much work to educate the Japanese American community about the internment, but now we needed the mainstream American public to understand that the government's policies against us, and the arguments backing them up, had been based solely on racist misinformation. Their equation was simple and absurdly simple-minded: we looked like the enemy, so we therefore *were* the enemy. I knew that a key to our effort would be convincing the public that any argument that said our imprisonment was justified was flat-out wrong.

It was the educational campaign that would then shape our legislative strategy, the fight for a bill to seek redress. Until members of Congress realized there was growing support for our position among their constituents, we were not prepared to enter a congressional campaign for redress. We knew there were some congressional members who would be sympathetic to our cause, but I believed, from my own experience, that there were far more who still accepted the wartime government's explanations for imprisoning us. These were the members we would have to convince, and the most effective way of doing that was getting constituents in their districts to support our efforts. And that came down to education.

My timeline for the next two years would have us engage in a national debate with the American public, working our way across the country, strategically targeting geographic areas where our JACL chapters were, and also focusing on major cities, the centers of social influence. In the meantime, we would draft a bill that would reflect the JACL's guidelines (assuming they were accepted by the convention delegates), including the $25,000 monetary demand, and we would present it to the three Japanese American members of Congress to get their reactions. We were counting on the three—Senators Daniel Inouye and Spark Matsunaga, both from Hawaii, and Representative Norman Mineta from San Jose, California—to carry whatever final proposal we came up with, which was completely presumptuous since we did not even have an official proposal for redress yet. We had no idea where Inouye and Matsunaga stood, but Mineta, on the other hand, was an active JACL member and an early supporter of reparations, having appeared at JACL conventions and spoken on this issue publicly.

I laid all of this out for Clifford as what I believed our strategy ought to be, based on what I had experienced running the redress program in our district. Expanding that to a national scale—educating the American public from coast to coast—sounded nothing less than grandiose and maybe even fanciful, but it was the only way we could even begin to talk about legislation.

I believed that the guidelines, if adopted at the Salt Lake City convention, were critical for giving shape and direction to the campaign and would declare that the endgame for redress was restitution. But, I told Clifford, it was important that we never lose sight of why the JACL got into this fight, what it was that Edison envisioned with his and Okamura's 1970 resolution. Edison's words and all the debates in the JACL had led to this point, but we should remember that the bigger goal had always been to engage in the broader discourse about equality in America. Our intent was to raise awareness about the internment in order to question whether the Bill of Rights, as a critical part of the Constitution, had meaning for all citizens at all times or only for some of the people some of the time. Only then, when there was public awareness of the facts, and when it was understood that an injustice had taken place, could we use our experience as a lesson in preventing similar circumstances from happening again in the future. That ultimately was what this campaign was all about.

"Convince the public," I told Clifford, "and you convince the Congress." It would become my mantra over the next two years.

Japanese Americans, while the most political group among Asian Americans at that time, were still reticent when it came to politics. I knew this was the wild card that could cause the entire enterprise to fizzle— whether the JACL had the ability to establish the politics of a coherent grassroots operation in which the national apparatus worked as a unified body, down through to the chapters, which would push the issue further and further into the public arena. We would have to lead the issue out from the hidden corners into which we had placed it thirty years earlier. This effort, if we were going to turn it into a campaign, would have to shatter the comfort zones we had built for ourselves.

Recalling the Iva Toguri D'Aquino campaign and our abysmal failure to get JACLers involved through a modest fundraising campaign, I realized how strongly our community disliked discussing the painful past. As much as our members sympathized with her situation, the campaign to support her reminded them of a terrible time for our community; and for many Japanese Americans, rehashing the unfounded accusations of her case only served to evoke all the negative emotions they had kept so well hidden. I also saw that many Japanese Americans reacted by trying to disassociate themselves from Iva and what she symbolized in the minds of mainstream Americans. The Iva campaign taught me that there was a psychological balancing act we had to be mindful about with the redress campaign. However noble the redress campaign's purpose was, ultimately this effort would fail if Japanese Americans didn't understand that redress wasn't about us as individuals but as a community. It was our place in America, and either the acceptance or rejection of us by our fellow Americans.

Ideas are fine, but what mattered in idealistic battles like redress was understanding the stakes involved. In order to secure their involvement and support for this effort, we needed Japanese Americans to feel an intrinsic personal investment in what we were attempting. They needed to understand that this was a fight to restore our place in America, as well as to preserve the foundations of democracy. What I found remarkable about the passion of the debates about redress was the farsighted and deeply felt belief that this was a constitutional issue that went beyond Japanese Americans, and if it could happen to us, it could happen again to any other group of citizens. It was racial hatred that led to our betrayal and incarceration, and so we would fight this battle on the basis of our collective constitutional rights. We were fighting for what we all, as Americans, valued most about this country: our right to freedom and justice. It wasn't just rhetoric; this was what the campaign was fundamentally about, and that would be our strongest argument.

I also thought back to my experience with the free speech movement at UC Berkeley and the way in which the passion for the principle of free speech had brought thousands of students out of their classrooms and onto the plaza in defiance of the administration. Many of us may have started out as curious onlookers, but we soon understood how important the fight was. The free speech movement was my education in politics, and one of the fundamental lessons I learned was how powerful a belief in principle can be. FSM shut down a world-class university, forced the administration to reconsider an important policy, and became part of the social movement that changed the politics of America. And all that from the power of a groundswell centered on a strong and unwavering belief in a principle.

Remembering the lessons of FSM, I knew that if we could articulate the unifying principle, it didn't matter how small our numbers were because we believed strongly in our cause and would convince others to join us. Whether it was me or someone else leading the effort, what we had to do was build a grassroots campaign in which everyone could participate and contribute. To demand redress from the government for a past injustice may have been unprecedented, but I was convinced that we could do this. Believe in the issue, build it from the ground up. That's where the power was.

And yet, it wasn't quite that simple.

There were a lot of psychological complexities involved, and I approached them from my perspective as a Sansei who was part of the Japanese American community and yet partially assimilated into mainstream culture. I felt I could stand outside the walls of my culture and look in, and in the same way I tried to help my students explore and analyze social issues by thinking beyond themselves and the things that encumbered them, I found myself trying to understand how Japanese Americans, as a subculture of U.S. society, had found a way to live in what for us was a dichotomous world. I was a part of U.S. society, and yet I tried to remember if there ever was a day in my life when I wasn't consciously aware of being Japanese, and I could not. America didn't allow me that luxury, and if I, with one foot in my Americanness and the other in my sense of community, felt so strongly about my dichotomous existence, I could understand how much more strongly the Nisei were affected by the culture of origin that gave them strength. The challenge we faced, therefore, was to find a way for us to break free of the constraints of culture and the very things that guided our behavior as well as gave us strength. The challenge for the redress effort would be to determine how to use those values as the foundation upon which to build a campaign.

The bottom line for me was simple: If Clifford became president and I took over the redress committee, I was going to make it work. I was confident that I knew the keys to the campaign, and whether I was the chair or an adviser to Clifford, I was going to give him a campaign he could be proud of. I felt I owed him that much, both because of our friendship and out of my respect for him. If he won the election for president, I would deliver him a campaign for which he would be remembered. To hell with the odds. He wasn't supposed to win the presidency anyway.

THE JACL'S REDRESS PRESIDENT

Since the JACL conventions of this era were seven-day affairs, there was a lot of time to get things done. Everyone arrived on Sunday and left on the following Sunday. There were parties, some fun events, excursions, plenty of time for business sessions, and adequate time for district caucuses. And a lot of time for campaigning.

We had reserved a room for our campaign operations and beckoned all the power brokers who had offered to work with us to get Cliff elected. My job was to quarterback the campaign, but it was more a formality than anything else because by the time we arrived at the convention hotel we were confident that we had the election locked in. Between the chapters of NCWN (our district) and the Southern California district, we had more than 50 percent of the chapters on our side, and combining the votes of two other districts—the Midwest and the Pacific Northwest—who were strongly supportive of redress, we were assured of a victory.

On Wednesday, July 5, redress was on the agenda of the plenary session for the day, with the scheduled redress workshop immediately following, to provide additional time if needed. Clifford's victory in the election was locked in when he stood before the National Council as the chair of the committee for redress and reported on the progress made during his tenure as chairman, and then presented the magic bullet: the redress guidelines. Copies of the guidelines had been sent to all chapters as part of the pre-convention package, and the *Pacific Citizen* had run an article about the April meeting at which the guidelines had been developed. But the formal presentation and announcement was nevertheless stunningly important. The guidelines suddenly became the highlight of the entire convention and were discussed and debated at length, and the more they were discussed, the more the delegates were convinced that they were viable and an important piece of groundwork for a future campaign.

The $25,000 individual compensation figure and the educational trust feature were adopted by the convention delegates and came to be known as the Salt Lake City Guidelines for redress. There were delegates who raised the question as to why a demand for an apology was not specified in the guidelines and was an underlying assumption of the documents, but we explained that the guidelines committee had deliberated Shigekuni's concerns that Congress might try to take the easy way out by agreeing to provide only the apology, while ignoring the other demands. There were some among the delegates who still insisted the apology should be included, but the proposed guidelines, as written, prevailed.

The acceptance of the guidelines by the convention delegates was a huge coup for Clifford, and it convinced everyone he was a real leader and a strong advocate for the organization's most important program. He walked away from the podium pretty much the winner, both of the redress campaign and of the JACL presidency. The election would take place on Saturday morning, the last day of the convention, and he would be installed at the closing dinner. For the next two years, he would lead the JACL.

When we met that evening as a campaign committee, there was little doubt that the votes we counted on for Clifford were solid. It was rather amazing when I think back on it: here he was, someone who had no formal history with the JACL except for his one-year chairmanship of the redress committee, and now he was going to be president! As a joke, I presented him with an abridged copy of *Robert's Rules of Order* so he would have some idea of how to run a meeting. This was all new to him, and I truly couldn't tell if he was pleased with the results. But he did realize that the delegates believed in him, and he knew he would not lead the organization astray.

As everyone milled about, Clifford took me aside to ask again if I would accept the appointment as the chair of the JACL's National Committee for Redress. When I told him yes, he said that he would stand by me on any decisions I made in that position over the course of the next two years. He knew it wasn't going to be easy and that some of my decisions would be controversial, but he promised me that he would never abandon me, however tough the going got. That meant a lot because it was Clifford telling me this as a friend, rather than just as a president. We were going to be in this together, no matter what.

After Clifford and I talked, I went for a walk. I felt the need to be alone, to take in everything that had happened in the past few hours, to appreciate what had been accomplished. I was certain that when the official election took place three days later, Clifford would become the president of the country's oldest and largest Asian American civil rights organization and would take us in a direction no group had ventured before. The acceptance of our guidelines sent a strong message that the JACL was serious in its commitment to fight for redress.

And with Clifford as president, I was going to lead that fight.

This battle would be waged across America to win the hearts of a public that at this moment didn't care a damn about us. The discussion would be about the ideals that the best versions of us as a nation had strived to uphold for two centuries.

We would talk about the Constitution, the Bill of Rights, the right to be free, and, above all, justice and equality. That would be the cornerstone of this campaign, and before we were through, Americans across the country would know about the injustices of the internment and the ways in which racist policies and the arrogance of power had weakened the foundations of American democracy.

I understood the challenges we faced, that what we were attempting was probably an impossibility. But I believed we could do it in small steps, achieving what we could at each turn and then moving forward to the next step. In my mind, we would do it in two phases, educational and legislative, both campaigns equally important and, while separate, essentially one and the same.

My job would be easier now that I had the majority of convention delegates committed to the issue, but I also knew that once the convention ended and everybody went back home, the majority of responsibility for the campaign would fall on my shoulders. It wasn't that those who had spoken so passionately at the delegates' debate stopped caring about the issue once they left; it was that people get busy with their work, their families, and whatever else is important to them in their daily lives, and they don't always have the time or energy for extra obligations. This was true for me too, but by accepting the chairmanship, I also accepted the commitment to do otherwise. I was willing to put as much of my life as I could on hold and to take a forgotten piece of American history and turn it into a debate in every corner of the country.

I had learned from experience that bringing up our wartime history was laden with risks because any mention of World War II and Japan immediately evoked images of Pearl Harbor. Those images were provocative, as were the never-ending stories of Japan's wartime atrocities against American soldiers taken prisoner. I had constantly faced the challenge of separating what the war in the Pacific had come to mean for Americans from what had happened to us as American citizens on American soil. In those days before our campaign went public, many audiences found it difficult to accept that, despite how I look, I was as much an American as they were. I knew that this would be a battle of reason over emotion, of facts over lies and accusations; it would be finding a way to appeal to the sense of fairness and justice that are the cornerstones of American democracy.

We were also up against a problem of scale. I was only one person, but we needed to spread our message across the country. I thought about the vastness of America and wondered how we could reach as many people as we needed to. Just persevere, I thought. Just persevere. Convince them one at a time, if you have to, and use the media, the same instrument that had turned against us so unmercifully at the war's beginning.

———

I knew that one major part of the battle in educating the public would be to address the issue of race. It was obvious to me that white America had gone along with the internment because they believed Japanese Americans were somehow complicit in Japan's attack on Pearl Harbor, or that we presented a threat to the security of the western coastal region of the country simply because of our ancestry. Japanese Americans had always experienced some degree of racism in this country, and anti-Japanese sentiment raged across the nation not just during and after World War II but, with renewed fervor, into the 1960s and '70s, when an ugly trade war between the United States and Japan grew more heated as America's economy continued to slip. Editorials lamented the fact that we had won the war against Japan and now they were making unreasonable demands on trade policies with the United States. It was a blame game more than anything else, and the truth was that our Made in the USA products simply couldn't stand up to products from Europe and Japan; they might not have wanted to admit it, but Americans *preferred* the superior quality of foreign products.

The tensions of the trade issues enhanced our investment in the ultimate question: Would we be able to convince the American public to objectively examine the principles of this campaign, to see us as equal Americans before the law and not as foreigners to whom the rights granted by the Constitution did not apply? The proposition was simple: if we could prove (as we were confident we could) that our wartime imprisonment was not based on factual evidence of wrongdoing but on racism and greed, we would expose the U.S. government for having violated the Constitution by stripping rights from its citizens based on the color of their skin.

It didn't take a genius to see that our most critical task would be effectively framing the issues of this campaign. Our intent was to have the public and Congress examine whether a policy based on race alone—a policy that therefore violated the Constitution—could and should be ignored and/or rationalized in the context of history, or whether we could agree that the promises of the Constitution and the democratic principles embodied in the Bill of Rights should be sacrosanct and inviolable for all citizens, regardless of race.

As I walked the streets of Salt Lake City, I was proud that we had already gone further than any group had ventured in a redress effort, but with no precedents or models to study as we moved forward, there was no way to know how far we could take this effort or what success would ultimately look like. Would we be successful only if we somehow got a bill through Congress and received reparations payments? Would we be successful if we were at least able to awaken the public to the injustices of the internment, to make our experience part of the American consciousness? Or would it be enough to bring this issue into the public arena and thereby force Japanese Americans to face their painful past and then feel some measure of catharsis for the psychological damage that had been inflicted upon them? Or would it be enough to simply set the record straight, so that mainstream Americans understood that Japanese Americans were not complicit in Japan's war against the United States? Or would it be successful if our efforts eventually helped to prevent the recurrence of a similar injustice in the future, even if the Japanese American community never directly benefited from this work?

On Saturday, the last day of the convention, it was announced that Clifford Uyeda, the dark-horse candidate, had officially won the election and was the JACL's national president for the coming biennium. In his acceptance speech, Clifford repeated the sentiment that had been his campaign theme: he had sought the presidency to lead the JACL in its efforts to seek redress and to restore the honor of Japanese Americans. He also announced in his speech that he had appointed me to chair the JACL's National Committee for Redress, to the shock and dismay of many in the room. The response that reverberated through the halls was "Who the hell is John Tateishi?"

Just as I had predicted, it was a very controversial appointment. Other than the role I had played in overseeing Clifford's presidential campaign, I was essentially unknown beyond my district. I held no leadership position in the national organization and had not made a name for myself. According to the old guard, I was too young (I was thirty-eight at the time) to hold such an important position as the chair of the JACL's most significant committee, and many delegates decided to just sit back and wait to see how badly I would screw up. They were offended that someone so obscure in the organization would be given the plum appointment, but Clifford wasn't bothered at all. He was confident he had picked the right person, and that meant a lot to me.

It's worth noting that the only person who congratulated me among the old guard was Hank Tanaka, who hailed from Cleveland and had been the JACL's national president from 1972 to 1974. Hank spoke words of encouragement and offered any assistance he could give me, telling me to call on him anytime. Hank made this same gesture twenty years later when I agreed to accept the JACL national directorship. Throughout the most tumultuous times of the redress campaign and during my years as national director, Hank was consistently one of my strongest supporters and remained a true friend until his death in 2006.

The delegates from my district, plus those who knew the work I had done there, generally approved of my appointment, but most of the others were filled with doubt. As far as I was concerned, the only thing that mattered was that I *knew* what had to be done to make the campaign work. I was determined that by the time Clifford's term as president was over, we would make real progress on the issue of redress, giving him something to be proud of. That was my pledge to him, and I intended to make it happen.

It was probably arrogant of me to think that I could accomplish anything significant and lasting in the two years that lay ahead in Clifford's term. For at least ten years prior, the Japanese American community had talked and talked about reparations, and by 1978, the JACL had spent eight years debating the issue at the chapter, district, and national levels, digesting the complexities at each turn. There had recently been some movement within the ranks of the JACL, but nothing of note had been *accomplished*, per se. Now it was in my hands.

THE OPENING SALVO
FROM SALT LAKE CITY

Saturday, the final day of the convention, always begins with the election of officers to the National Board and ends that evening with the Sayonara Banquet, the traditional ceremonial dinner at which the newly elected board is installed and special awards are presented. A highlight of the dinner is the guest speaker, always someone of some note, often a politician. That year in Salt Lake City, to the utter dismay of virtually everyone in the ballroom, the evening's keynote speaker was Senator S. I. Hayakawa. To this day, I have no idea how he managed to get invited to the JACL convention, especially with redress center stage on our agenda. Since being elected to the U.S. Senate in 1973, Hayakawa seemed to have made it his mission to undermine Japanese Americans' demand for redress whenever he could, and he seemed particularly hostile to the JACL. He was our strongest critic, focusing his wrath on the JACL's insistence to push forward with the issue. He spoke against redress at the dinner to a chorus of boos and jeers, and, at the heart of his speech, he referred to the demands for $25,000 reparations payments as "absurd and ridiculous."

As upset as I was by Hayakawa's presence, let alone his comments, I knew as I listened to him that I could use his tirade to launch the campaign straight out of the Little America Hotel in Salt Lake City, where we were meeting. Reporters from the city's two major newspapers, the *Deseret News* and the *Salt Lake Tribune*, asked both Clifford and me for comments after the dinner, and we expected their stories would appear in the Sunday-morning papers and would go on the wire services, our words now confirming for the entire country that the JACL and Hayakawa were locked in this battle. To counter Hayakawa's statement, I sent a press release immediately after our interviews to both papers to ensure that, as they filed their stories, they understood the issue from our perspective and did not depend on Hayakawa's comments to define the issue. I made sure, as I did with every subsequent press release sent out in the early stages of the campaign, to state that the JACL was demanding $25,000 for each person victimized by the government's wartime policies. It was a detail that I knew would grab the media's attention.

And with that press release, I launched the JACL's public redress campaign. It didn't occur to me until later that it might have been inappropriate for me to have taken such action without first consulting with Clifford. But the way I saw it, Hayakawa's speech was either the sign of a disaster about to happen or, if we knew how to spin it, an opportunity we could exploit, and I had decided this was a moment we had to exploit to our advantage. It never occurred to me that I perhaps didn't have the authority to launch the issue into the public arena just yet, despite all our discussions about initiating a formal campaign. We knew we wanted to take the issue to the public, but there had only been vague suggestions about how to go about it. Now, none of that mattered because I had seen the Hayakawa statement as an opportune moment to launch the campaign, ready or not.

Three weeks after the JACL convention, the *Wall Street Journal* published an editorial titled "Guilt Mongering," a commentary that held up Japanese Americans as an exemplary segment of society (with the implied "model minority" comparison with other groups) while at the same time undercutting our demands for redress as unseemly and "unflattering," as if to say that we had joined the hordes already guilt mongering white America for past sins. Not coincidentally, there was also a book review titled "Tales of Espionage during World War II" running on the same page, next to the editorial. Clifford and I sent letters to the *Wall Street Journal*, which were published.

It didn't surprise us at all that a paper like the *Journal*, one of the nation's most conservative newspapers in those days, would present such a condescending editorial. What did matter to me, however, was that the very fact of its being printed had elevated the internment issue to a new level, which played in our favor. It was ironic that S. I. Hayakawa and the *Wall Street Journal*, both bastions of American conservatism, had played such a significant role in helping to launch our campaign to heights heretofore unattainable. I hardly expected to reach a national audience so quickly, and yet here we were. As far as I was concerned, the battle had begun. The *Journal* editorial was seen and taken seriously by newspapers across the country, and my follow-up press release was sent to all major news outlets. With that, we stepped into the fray.

I was willing to debate anyone on this issue, whether it was Hayakawa, our archenemy Lillian Baker, or others, whether private citizens calling in to talk shows or elected members of the United States Congress, it didn't matter to me. Baker, a conservative spokesperson who had worked as a regional campaign manager for Hayakawa's successful Senate campaign, was our most persistent foe, often finding her way into congressional hearings on any bill related to Japanese Americans. She continually insisted that we had not been "prisoners" in the camps but guests who could leave once our loyalty had been determined. A World War II widow, she was dedicated to thwarting our efforts to reveal the truths about the wartime experiences of Japanese Americans. Both Baker and Hayakawa consistently ignored the facts of history, and neither was persuaded that the rights guaranteed by the Constitution applied to Japanese Americans. Hayakawa disdained our efforts as misguided and was dismissive of our campaign as being led by "young radicals looking for handouts."

The majority of the earliest editorials, news stories, and letters to editors excoriated us for our greed and for our inability to grasp how desperate the country was feeling after the attack at Pearl Harbor. Responses to our counternarrative varied: some were thoughtful, most were knee-jerk. There were some readers who had the courage to speak out against our wartime treatment and supported our demands to rectify the injustice, but many more of the rare sympathetic letters tended to say that, well, it was a terrible thing to have done to Japanese Americans, but demanding money now makes it all so unseemly. With few exceptions, letters to the editors were strongly negative, even angry, and the majority of them sided with the editorials that, at best, found fault with our demands and, at worst, condemned us as being part of Japan's vicious war machine and now partner to the invaders of America's consumer market. All of the responses, whether supportive or critical, made clear the fact that Americans knew hardly anything about our wartime history.

It was clear that race was getting in the way of our message. Most people were unable to understand that we were talking about an *unconstitutional* policy enacted against *American citizens*—that the issue was not about us but about the Constitution. Many simply didn't understand that people who looked like us were full citizens of the nation, just like them. I was often asked (and still am occasionally), "What is your nationality?" and when I answer that I'm American, the follow-up question is usually, "No, I mean, where do you really come from?" I was being categorized as a foreigner based on looks alone, because I didn't fit the image of what, for that person, an American looks like. In those days, no one seemed to have a problem with understanding the concept of Americans who were ethnically Italian or German or Irish or Swedish and so on, but put an Asian face on a person, and many Americans thought (and still do think) they are not looking at a "real" American. For some, they'd even say we were un-American. We were the Japan that had attacked Pearl Harbor and was winning the trade war with the United States, which was *their* country and somehow not ours.

As our campaign message at last reached its national audience, the initial reporting about the internment was generally fair, but limited. As objective as most reporters tried to be in reporting the news, they had their own biases, especially when it came to historical events, and there were also only so many news sources that reached the general public. In the 1970s, CBS, NBC, and ABC were the principal sources of television news. Cable news did not yet exist, although I met my share of reporters and program hosts who put their own spin on things, and even some who created "facts," but in those days, the extreme and bizarre reporters tended to stay on the margins.

As we churned up the issue in mainstream circles, reporters and program producers around the country sought local JACL members to interview, and we suddenly felt new urgency to further educate our members about the internment, and specifically against the myths promulgated by the government. You cannot fight a grassroots battle without a well-informed constituency, and we knew we needed our supporters to be armed with more than just anecdotal personal information.

One technique that worked well to keep the issue in the media was sending press releases that outlined our demands, accompanied by descriptions with provocative (but accurate) terminology, like "America's concentration camps." The reaction, especially at first, was often outrage and anger, and the responses were filled with all sorts of misinformation. And that was where the dialogue would begin. Over time, this strategy proved effective, and we started to see more and more reasonable commentaries fill the pages of newspapers. The racist accusations and the anger continued (and still do to this day) at some level, but we had seen enough success already to understand that if we persevered, we would eventually win the day.

THE COMMITTEE

JACL protocol demands that all national committees be represented by delegates from each regional district, and the selections to the official redress committee, being such a high-profile and controversial committee, came under some scrutiny on that point. Everyone was curious to know who would get appointments, and as chair, it was my responsibility to make the selections. To the surprise of some, I had no intention of adhering to protocol, in part because there were some districts that either opposed redress or at best only had tepid support among their constituents, and I was not about to waste time going backward to discuss whether we should or should not pursue redress. We were going forward with it, period.

The convention delegates had approved the redress guidelines, and I took that as a mandate, and thus decided to choose five individuals who I felt would best serve the needs of the program. I wanted proven redress activists and landed on the following: Phil Shigekuni from Los Angeles, who had been on Clifford's committee for the guidelines discussion; Raymond Okamura, the Berkeley chemist and virtual walking encyclopedia on redress; Henry Miyatake from Seattle, a dedicated redress advocate and coauthor of the Seattle Bootstrap Plan; Ron Mamiya, a young attorney from Seattle who was also active in the Seattle redress movement and was the person I assigned to draft the proposed legislation that we would send to the Japanese American congressmen; and civil rights attorney Min Yasui of Denver, who had also served on Clifford's guidelines committee. Miyatake and Yasui famously disliked each other, but as an indication of their commitment to the redress effort, both put aside their personal feelings and served on the committee.

When I announced the makeup of the committee, reactions were mixed. Some were angry because I had ignored individuals whom they considered important or at least deserving of a place on the committee.

Others objected to the fact that the committee didn't include a representative from each JACL district. Still others warned me about practically every person I selected: they said Shigekuni was an L.A. "radical" (he was an activist, but hardly a radical); Okamura was anti-JACL and an outsider (both true, if that's what being a critic of the JACL meant); Miyatake was a hothead and unreasonable (i.e., an aggressive and dedicated redress advocate); Mamiya was too young to understand the internment (I still can't make sense of those who think young people can't also be intelligent); and Yasui was an egomaniac and uncontrollable (there was some truth to both, but he was also a brilliant attorney and had a long-standing record of fighting the government on our behalf).

I was also criticized for having appointed two people from Seattle, which I had done in large part because Seattle's redress advocates felt that their Bootstrap Plan hadn't received a fair shake at the convention and that the Seattle group was too often overlooked. In fact, when the convention election results were announced and I was revealed to be the new chair of the redress committee, Cherry Kinoshita of Seattle wanted me to assure her that someone from Seattle would be on the committee, and she had recommended Mamiya. I will admit that part of my decision to include two representatives from Seattle was to ensure they would be an unquestionable part of the process and not feel cheated or excluded.

Overall, though, I didn't feel I had to justify how or why I had constituted the committee as I had. I selected the committee members I wanted for what I wanted to achieve, and I was more interested in finding the right people for the job than following a bunch of rules. It was a unique combination of individuals, I knew, but this was the group I would depend on to help drive the issue over the next two years.

My first look at how the committee would function together came at a meeting I called in September 1978 to develop some media strategies. I was curious to find out what kind of camaraderie there would be, if there was any at all. I knew that Yasui and Miyatake would be at each other's throats at times, but I would handle them. Shigekuni could get along with anyone, and Okamura was mostly unimpressed with others and couldn't care less what anyone thought of him. I knew from previous experience that he wasn't generally comfortable with the JACL crowd, and it puzzled me why he even maintained his membership, but I also knew he was invaluable for what I wanted to do with the campaign. I didn't know Mamiya at all but hoped he would help contain some of Miyatake's fiery personality.

While I preferred we enjoy some camaraderie among committee members, my main concern was to know whether these dissimilar individuals could function cohesively. It was important that the dynamics of the personalities worked because I knew that, if I drove the campaign as I planned, we would, as a committee, need to have a strong foundation if we hoped to achieve success in the face of controversy, both external and internal.

I had invited playwright Frank Chin to attend this first meeting, since he had some media savvy and might be able to give us advice. Frank was a harsh and unrelenting critic of the JACL, and especially of its wartime leaders' decision to cooperate with the government. He was also part of the contingent that asserted that JACL leaders had colluded with the army during the internment. While I did inform the committee members about Chin's positions, I tried to keep those details under wraps from the wider JACL community lest a minor revolt erupt. Min vehemently objected to Chin's presence and referred to him in colorful terms, even as he knew I wouldn't change my mind. Before the meeting happened, word got out about Chin and, as expected, I had to endure endless telephone tirades and the occasional red-faced anger of JACL members who weren't happy with me.

In September we met at the JACL headquarters, located in San Francisco's Japantown, to discuss media strategies. Chin was cordial and tried to be helpful, making various suggestions, but he ultimately offered little that we didn't already know when it came to dealing with the media. After hearing from Frank, I closed the meeting to members only and we turned our attention to discussing how we would undertake the redress effort: through the courts or through legislation. We agreed that if the opportunity presented itself, we would challenge the infamous decisions in the Supreme Court cases of *Hirabayashi*, *Korematsu*, and *Yasui*, in which the Court gave legal authority to the government's policies of exclusion and detention on the basis of race alone. But for now, our limited resources allowed for only one focus, and that was

Congress. We concluded that we preferred a legislative fight. Since Congress and the media were primarily responsible for creating the climate of hate that plagued our community and had put pressure on Washington to force our expulsion, they were our targets. We wanted to spread the message that race-based hatred spewed from the mouths of politicians should never be accepted as anything but the rantings of bigots, and they should certainly not become the basis of governmental policies.

The next question was what type of legislation we would seek.

It was during this conversation that Ray Okamura pointed out that perhaps we were being presumptuous in assuming the Japanese American members of Congress would readily support redress; we would do well to find that out before we made further plans. We knew that Norman Mineta, a representative from California who had been incarcerated in camp, supported redress, but we had no idea whether Senators Daniel Inouye and Spark Matsunaga did, since the Japanese American population they represented in Hawaii had not been imprisoned *en masse* as they were on the mainland. There were camps on Hawaii's islands, but Japanese Americans were only incarcerated there selectively. It was ironic but significant that the military and civilian leadership of the islands opposed the removal and detention of its own Japanese population, arguing not only that they could be trusted but that their removal would bring the economy of the islands to a grinding halt because they constituted a major part of the work force there. In terms of the security of the islands, the local national guard was made up mostly of Japanese Americans—the famous 100th Battalion, who was charged with the security of the islands.

Because the situation on the islands was so different from that of the mainland, we had no idea whether Inouye and Matsunaga would put their political reputations at risk to back what could only be a controversial and unpopular bill. We all knew that without Inouye's support, redress had no chance. Additionally, Ray and Phil expressed concern about what appeared would be the successful election of Bob Matsui, a representative from Sacramento, who had voiced his criticisms about redress.

Ray was right, of course, that we didn't know the degree to which each of the Japanese Americans in Congress would support our efforts.

We didn't know, for example, what their thoughts were about the $25,000 figure put forth in the Salt Lake City Guidelines. Was that figure acceptable, or might we possibly push for more? And did they foresee any problems with demanding individual payments versus a trust fund? There was only one way to find out.

As a volunteer committee chair, I had no authority to instruct the JACL staff to do anything. That power lay with the organization's executive director, Karl Nobuyuki, who by virtue of his position was an *ex officio* member of the JACL's major committees. With Okamura's suggestion and at my request, Nobuyuki instructed Ron Ikejiri, the JACL's Washington representative, to arrange a meeting with the Japanese American congressmen, who would, as it turned out, include Bob Matsui. My concern was scheduling the meeting for the earliest possible date so I could firm up what strategy we were going to pursue if, in fact, we had a realistic shot at a legislative campaign. I was anxious to meet with these men—whom we called the Big Four—because I felt our hands were tied until we knew where they stood.

3
THE STRATEGY

(1978-1979)

ERNEST WEINER

Ideally, the JACL would have been able to rely on the support of like-minded civil rights and environmental groups, but unfortunately those affiliations weren't always available to us. Our early overtures to the ACLU (American Civil Liberties Union) met with silence, and organizations like and including the NAACP (National Association for the Advancement of Colored People), while interested in what we were attempting, were equally unresponsive. We were also cut off from environmental groups because of prior negative interactions with the Sierra Club (i.e., their boycott of Japantown businesses and our accusations of racism had left a bitter taste in both our mouths). But to me the most surprising response was from the leader of a local Chinese American civil rights organization, who told me his constituency would turn on him if he endorsed our efforts. What I hadn't considered was that while I expected immigrant communities to band together against the majority, they often harbored the memories of their ancestral homes, and with those memories all their old-world animosities. And now, here in 1978, Japan's long history in Asia was being carried over as a burden for us. Once again, Japan's actions and history were a plague on our Japanese American house. It seemed like everywhere we turned, the groups we thought would support us instead looked the other way. In those early days, just about every civil rights organization rejected our campaign.

And then one day, while busy with my redress work at the JACL headquarters, I received a telephone call from a man with a deep, resonant voice.

"My name is Ernest Weiner," he said, "and I'm the director of the Bay Area chapter of the AJC." Long pause. What the hell was the AJC?

He continued, "Obviously, you don't have any idea who the AJC is, do you?" He went on to explain that the American Jewish Committee was one of the oldest Jewish organizations in the country and among the four oldest civil rights organizations in the United States. This was my first encounter with the AJC, and through the next thirty-plus years, Weiner would continue to be my contact with the organization and would become my close and, along with Clifford, most trusted and loyal friend.

Weiner and I talked for a time about the AJC and the JACL and the redress campaign. He asked a lot of questions, and occasionally challenged my thinking, but never without offering alternative considerations. He also offered advice in the form of questions ("Have you ever thought about...?") rather than just telling me what to do. I knew from the first words we exchanged that this was not a man to be toyed with, nor someone to be taken lightly. If Ernie Weiner was representative of the AJC, then this was an impressive organization indeed. He was brilliant and sophisticated, but you could see in him the remnants of the scrappy boxer he had been in his youth, a New Jersey lightweight Golden Glove champion, still verbally pugnacious and fearless, a man who could just as easily and without embarrassment shed a tear as he could captivate with his sense of humor. He seemed at ease with people of all kinds, and I imagined he would be as comfortable dealing with kings and queens as with any person walking by on the street. I would learn later in our friendship (from another source) that he had been wounded in hand-to-hand combat in France and was touched in other personal ways by the horrific tragedies endured by the Jewish people in Europe.

It was in one of our early conversations over lunch that he asked if I had considered the idea of a federal commission whose job it would be to investigate the rationale for the exclusion and detention policies and to determine whether a legal wrong, a constitutional injustice, had been committed. I told him no and rejected the idea as both unnecessary and a waste of our time because we were anxious to get compensation legislation introduced above all else. Fair enough, he replied, and suggested ways the AJC might be able to assist our efforts.

Ernie and I met often over lunch, sometimes not to discuss anything in particular but just to get together, to touch base. If we couldn't meet for a while, he would try to make a quick call between meetings to ask how I was doing. "They treating you all right?" he would always ask. On those rare warm San Francisco summer days, he would call and say,

"Tateishi, the sun is out, it's a beautiful day, so get your ass down here and let's go for a walk!" And of course, if I had the time to do so, I would drop what I was doing and we would go for a stroll along the Embarcadero, where his office was located. Regardless of when, where, or why we would see each other, he always wanted to know that I was okay, and he would always ask about the redress campaign.

At that first lunch meeting, I was surprised to see how extraordinarily deep Weiner's knowledge was of the JACL's redress effort, going all the way back to Edison Uno's Chicago presentation in 1970. Because of his proximity to the JACL headquarters, one of his responsibilities with the AJC was to monitor the JACL's redress campaign, and he probably knew more about what we were doing than many of our JACL members. In the parlance of his organization and community, he referred to this as "gathering intelligence" on us, a term that over the next thirty years of my working relationship with Ernie I would hear often, including, in some instances, in rather hostile and critical negative contexts when he was talking about other organizations or situations around the world. When, early in our relationship, he revealed to me that the AJC had extensive intelligence on just about everything the JACL had done with the redress program, he made sure I knew he wasn't just poking around, and he wasn't just telling me about it as a courtesy. He had a purpose.

At one of our lunches, he invited me to meet with him and the AJC's national domestic affairs vice president, Seymour Samet, who was scheduled to visit his office in San Francisco. This was a significant opportunity, and we agreed that Clifford should join us as well. Before the four of us had even looked at our menus, Ernie explained that the purpose of the meeting was to discuss the JACL's redress campaign, and, typical of his style, he then waxed eloquently about the nobility of our effort and the profound implications of what we were attempting. And then he asked if we wanted the AJC's endorsement of the campaign, which, he noted, was not being offered lightly. I knew that this endorsement would bring the full weight of the AJC behind our campaign, and I accepted it, even before I knew just how heavy that weight was, something I wouldn't fully understand until I was introduced to the world of Washington politics.

At this point, the strongest connection the JACL had in Washington was Mike Masaoka, who was by then retired from the organization but still very active as a lobbyist in D.C. In addition to the Big Four Japanese American members of Congress, we had three other influential Japanese American contacts in Washington, but we could turn to them for help only occasionally, so our ranks were thin. Consequently, an endorsement from the AJC—the first national organization to endorse our campaign—would be invaluable because it gave our effort some political credibility. So influential was the AJC that over one-third of the non-Jewish members of the House of Representatives held memberships with the AJC. When I told Weiner and Samet that, yes, we would absolutely appreciate the AJC's support, they started to discuss how they would work the politics within the AJC to arrange for an official endorsement of our campaign.

Weiner asked me (mostly for Samet's benefit, since he himself already knew) what sorts of legislative initiatives I had been considering, and I could see him choreographing where this conversation would go. I described the Salt Lake City Guidelines and stated that we were, for the time being, interested only in pursuing an appropriations bill for the payment of reparations. In response, Weiner explained to Samet that he had earlier suggested to me that we consider the idea of asking for the formation of a federal commission. The internment was still such a little-known episode to most Americans, and a commission would make more credible our claim that an injustice had occurred. I listened, but in my mind I rejected the notion of a federal commission, just as I had done in my earlier conversation with Ernie. We were interested only in a direct compensation bill, I reminded him. If we lost, we would at least know that we had fought the good fight, the one we wanted to fight. Weiner and Samet politely indulged us, something Ernie hardly ever did in the nearly four decades of our friendship. In retrospect, he obviously knew something I didn't when he made this suggestion, but I had no interest in it—at least at that time.

We finished lunch, and then, within an hour, Ernie called me at the JACL office.

"Listen, you schmuck!" he began. (It was a term of endearment in the way he used it.) "We offer you our endorsement and then you tell us to take our suggestion of a commission and shove it up our asses?" And then we talked candidly. He understood well enough why we, why *I*, preferred a compensation bill—we had had this conversation at least a couple of times before, although never in the presence of one of his bosses—and he had always warned me about the realities of Washington and how difficult it would be to get a money bill introduced, let alone seriously considered. One of the obstacles was the ongoing trade war between the United States and Japan. Ernie had spent long hours talking with the consul general of Japan about trade policies, and he knew that as the economic balance tipped in Japan's favor, the American public and their congresspeople would not be in the mood to readily grant monetary reparations to the Japanese American community, even though it had nothing to do with Japan's trade policies. He predicted things would get ugly and was concerned that if the demand for reparations came from the JACL, there was no way it would succeed. If we followed his advice and asked for a federal commission, however, that would put the onus on the government, and any finding of wrongdoing and any demand for redress would come from the government itself. Ernie didn't want our demands for compensation, as reasonable and justified as they were, to become confused with unrelated trade issues. Japan was becoming the enemy once more, and he didn't want us to fall prey to that bigotry again.

Ernie understood our redress campaign in ways that few did, and even better than many Japanese Americans, especially those who grew up outside the community. I didn't fully appreciate at first just how significant the AJC endorsement was and why he had pushed so hard to provide us with his organization's support, but I will forever be grateful for it. It meant that not only would every AJC member learn more about the internment but that all members of Congress who were AJC members would be urged to support our legislation. It also meant that the AJC's Washington office, with its clout and influence, would further help with our legislation. In time I learned that Hyman Bookbinder, the AJC's legendary Washington lobbyist, worked as a stealth lobbyist for our redress bills even after, and maybe especially after, his formal retirement in 1986.

I cannot overstate how important Ernie was to the redress campaign, or to me as a friend. We continued our close relationship through the new millennium until his passing, in early 2014. I once told him that I was going to make him an honorary Japanese American, but, ever attuned to interethnic cultural sensitivities, he told me he couldn't accept because he preferred dim sum to sushi. "I don't do raw," he told me.

THE BIG FOUR

I had made our strategy clear to Ernest Weiner, but the idea of a federal commission did not go away entirely. This time it was suggested during our meeting in Washington with the Big Four Japanese American members of Congress (which excluded antagonistic Senator S. I. Hayakawa, by mutual agreement of all). We met at the end of January 1979 in Senator Inouye's office in the Capitol Building, that location being in itself a sign of Inouye's stature, since only those members who are in top leadership positions have offices in the Capitol when their party is in power, in addition to their regular offices in one of the Senate buildings. As chair of the Senate Appropriations Subcommittee on Defense, Inouye was indeed one of a handful of senators who wielded enormous influence and authority in the Senate. Our JACL delegation included President Clifford Uyeda, National Director Karl Nobuyuki, Washington representative Ron Ikejiri, Ron Mamiya from the redress committee, and me. Much to the displeasure of Nobuyuki and Ikejiri, I had included Mamiya so that he could present the Seattle Bootstrap Plan (the IRS checkbox proposal) as one of two proposals for consideration. The Seattle group had put a lot of time and work into developing that plan and deserved to have their proposal presented by one of their own. Clifford thought it was a reasonable idea and agreed Mamiya's presence at the meeting was appropriate. I had also explained to Cliff in private that if the Seattle plan was rejected in this meeting, which I expected would happen, we would finally have a reason to drop it once and for all. On the other hand, if I was completely mistaken and Inouye, Matsunaga, and Mineta, plus newly elected Bob Matsui, liked the proposal, then we ought to reconsider it, regardless of how much we were convinced it was too problematic, since, we assumed, it required authorizing legislation to change IRS forms to serve the purpose. Inexperienced in legislative work though we might have been, we all knew that trying to change anything in the tax code was setting ourselves up for certain failure.

As we waited outside Inouye's office for his arrival, I mentioned to Ikejiri that the idea of a federal commission had been presented to me by the AJC but that I really didn't like it and hoped no one mentioned anything like that in this meeting. I hoped the Big Four were aware that we, as the ones who had asked for the meeting, were here specifically to present our proposal for direct compensation through an appropriations bill, and we were not interested in discussing alternatives. I suggested that we should preempt any talk of a federal commission, but Ikejiri advised against my trying to dictate terms, even though he thought the Big Four would most likely take our lead on this issue.

Shortly after we were seated, Congressmen Mineta and Matsui arrived, and Inouye suggested we get started. We began by explaining our position on redress as articulated in the Salt Lake City Guidelines and indicated that we had two proposals for redress legislation for their consideration: one that included both individual compensation and a trust fund, and the other the Seattle Bootstrap Plan. Mamiya described the Seattle plan but seemed discomfited by Mineta's impatience. Matsunaga, who arrived during the presentation, seemed uninterested in this proposal, and by the time Mamiya sat down, he had a look of defeat. He was followed by Nobuyuki, who presented the JACL's proposal for an appropriations bill that included compensation in the amount of $25,000 per individual, plus an as-yet-unspecified amount for a trust fund, to be calculated based on the total number of Japanese Americans affected by the World War II policy, including those who were now deceased, plus any amounts unclaimed by those opposed to redress. We believed the number of deceased would be large, considering that most of the Issei were already gone and the oldest among the Nisei were also passing.

Straight off, Mineta and Matsunaga rejected the Seattle plan as too cumbersome and difficult. Mineta criticized just about every aspect of the proposal and said that anything involving the IRS would guarantee dragging the issue into an administrative quagmire from which we would never escape. Such a bill would have to go through the Ways and Means Committee, which he referred to as the "Ways To Be Mean Committee." He wanted nothing to do with such a proposal, an opinion echoed even more harshly by Matsunaga. To my relief, the Seattle Bootstrap Plan was now completely off the table.

Both Mineta and Matsunaga favored the appropriations bill and dove into discussion—exploration, really—about what needed to be done to make it work. The discussion went on for some time, and I was very aware that Inouye had said nothing the entire time. I was curious as to why, especially given that he was the most senior among those present, and certainly the most powerful and influential among them. About twenty minutes into the meeting, Inouye finally spoke when Matsunaga and Mineta had finished sharing their thoughts on an appropriations bill.

"Have you fellows thought about a commission?" he asked, and my heart sank. Mineta was the only one of the Big Four to immediately reject the notion.

"Aw, hell, Danny, we don't need a commission to tell us what we already know," he objected vehemently. I was surprised by his response, and also that he would refer to Inouye in such familiar terms with the rest of us sitting there.

Our group kept our mouths shut and waited to see what would happen. True, we had somewhat anticipated the suggestion of a federal commission, and given how much we needed Inouye on this issue, we weren't prepared to reject his idea outright. Fortunately, Mineta's objections expressed pretty much what the rest of us thought about the idea, and what Clifford and I had discussed in our meeting with Ernie Weiner and Seymour Samet: it was unnecessary; it would add another step to a process that would ultimately lead to a fight for an appropriations bill anyway; it would take longer, as we meanwhile lost more and more Issei; and it didn't accomplish anything we couldn't do ourselves. We had heard that, typically, commission studies ended up on shelves collecting dust and taking up space, and we simply didn't have the time or the patience. We had already waited more than thirty years.

Inouye sat patiently and said, "If you go with an appropriations bill at the beginning, my good friend here," turning to Matsui, "won't be in the House for a second term." Matsui blanched and was visibly shaken by that comment, which was Inouye's way of saying not only would a direct compensation bill get killed but Bob would not last beyond this first term in office and would be part of the collateral damage of an ill-considered bill. But the main point was that we would fail miserably if we attempted a compensation bill without first laying down some much-needed groundwork.

Both Mineta and Matsunaga stayed silent as Inouye continued. The problem, he explained, looking at me, was precisely the same problem I had identified as the reason we needed to wage our battle in the public arena rather than on paper behind closed doors: we needed the support of the American people.

Inouye said, "We know that the internment was wrong, but our colleagues in the Senate and House think the World War II policies were appropriate and just, and the American public has no idea that this ever occurred. Until we can convince them about the injustice, we will not be able to get the needed votes in Congress."

A federal commission, Inouye said, would serve a number of purposes to achieve that goal. He said the Big Four would ensure that a blue-ribbon panel of distinguished Americans would be selected to serve on the commission, and the commission would have a research staff capable of conducting a thorough study of all the available documents and facts, which would help them reach a conclusion independent of us as representatives of the JACL and the Japanese American community. The commission report would be an official government record of the events surrounding the internment decision, a more permanent and impermeable chronicle of all that had happened to our people.

"If you work the angles just right," he said, going with a federal commission would also get us more publicity than we could ever dream of—certainly more than the JACL could afford. Inouye pointed out that we could mandate that the commission hold public hearings around the country to give Japanese Americans the opportunity to testify and tell their side of the story, and this, he thought, would be the most powerful part of the hearing process.

"Just imagine," he said, "hundreds of Nisei telling the story of their travails in a way that would touch the hearts of Americans across the country." He added that a press conference to present the commission's findings and conclusion would make national news, as would the presentation of the commission's recommendations. We could stage it so that the recommendations would not be presented for at least two or three months following the issuance of the report, meaning we could double the amount of national publicity.

I still didn't like the idea, but I said nothing to counter Inouye's comments. Some redress histories state that Mineta went along with Inouye's suggestion, but I can say, as someone who was in that meeting, that this was not the case at all. Mineta continued to reject the idea and insisted that an appropriations bill was the better way to go; fight the battle up front, he said. Matsunaga, whose initial response mirrored Mineta's, tempered his own comments in deference to Inouye's position. We were still in the middle of the discussion an hour later, but the meeting was brought to a close because, as Inouye put it, they had "business of state" to tend to. As we said our goodbyes, Inouye told us that we should talk amongst ourselves about which direction we wanted to go and then let them know. It was our show, he said, our decision. They would follow our orders.

As we filed out and the others were in conversation, I told Clifford that it almost felt like we *had* to follow Inouye's recommendation. With someone so powerful giving us his political advice (and he had obviously thought the matter through), I didn't see how we could do otherwise. In this moment, it looked like it was federal commission or nothing if we were serious about succeeding in the legislative phase of our campaign. Granted, I was sure Inouye would have helped with an appropriations bill if that's what we had decided on, but I wasn't sure how successful we would be, given how strongly he believed in the wisdom of, and the need for, a federal commission. Besides, he wasn't dismissing or side-stepping our desire for compensation; he was simply making real the incredibly poor odds we would face in trying to push a compensation bill through the United States Congress.

Before I walked out of the room, Inouye took me aside and said he'd like an opportunity to meet with me privately in his office in the Senate office building to discuss everything. I was leaving D.C. later that day, so he told me he would have his personal secretary, Sally Watanabe, squeeze me in for a meeting before I left.

In the cab back to the JACL's D.C. office downtown, we went over the options before us. Given that Inouye felt so strongly about a commission but Mineta insisted on appropriations, we weren't sure what to do. Ikejiri was close to Mineta, and I got the sense that Nobuyuki was also, which meant they would probably go along with Norm. Clifford and I said we were noncommittal, but I knew that, based on the strength of Inouye's argument and his position in Washington, we had both accepted that the commission was probably our best, and maybe our only, choice.

I called Sally and arranged for a quick meeting with Inouye later that day, and with most of the afternoon left for us all to relax or to go sightseeing, we scattered and agreed to meet back at the JACL office later that afternoon. I told Clifford that Inouye had asked me to meet with him, but I thought Cliff should be there as well. He was the JACL's national president, after all. I felt awkward not including him, but Clifford said he'd be fine to spend the day walking around the capital and taking in the sights. If there was anyone who wouldn't be bothered by this sort of thing, it was Cliff.

I went to see Inouye, but I didn't tell the others about it. It was a very short meeting, and he got straight to the point. He said he was counting on me to persuade the others to seriously consider the commission strategy because he honestly didn't think we could get a compensation bill passed without doing some groundwork first. He assured me that at least half the members of the Senate knew nothing about the internment and that most of them would not vote in favor of a reparations bill. And despite comments Mineta had made to the contrary, it was even worse in the House. Inouye told me to see if I could get Jim Wright (D-Texas), the House majority leader, or Neal Smith (D-Iowa), chair of the House Appropriations Committee, to commit to a money bill. Inouye said he would arrange meetings for me with either or both of them. He insisted that they were both critical to a victory in the House, and without them and others of their stature to support the bill, we would not succeed. He advised me that we would have only one chance at getting a bill through the House and Senate, and that if a compensation bill failed the first time, it was unlikely to ever pass, no matter how many times we kept reintroducing it in different forms. He said he was counting on me to convince the JACL National Board to make the right decision.

As I prepared to leave, he told me again that, whatever I decided, he would follow the lead of the JACL. "It's your decision," he said, "so tell me what you want me to do, and Sparky and I will do whatever you decide." I didn't doubt his sincerity about that, and I knew he and Matsunaga would never abandon the Nisei buddies with whom they had served in the 442nd during the war, but I also understood what he was saying: we had one shot at this and one only, and whatever we decided would then determine the fate of the Japanese American community. Everything, he was telling me, rested on my ability to make the right the decision. At that moment, I fully understood the gravity and finality of our next move.

Like just about every Japanese American in the country, I admired Inouye for all he had accomplished throughout his remarkable career and was in awe of the power he commanded. He had served on the Senate Watergate Committee, cochaired the Iran–Contra hearings during the Reagan presidency, become one of the most powerful members of the United States Senate, and had been awarded a Distinguished Service Cross in 1947, later upgraded to a Congressional Medal of Honor in 2000. Before I left the Hill, I walked through the halls of the Russell Senate Office Building, where Inouye's office was, and looked at the names on the doors. I saw the names of politicians who were in the news every day, whose decisions affected our lives and events throughout the world. It was sobering to think of what went on in these buildings and chambers. These were the individuals who, in one way or another, would play a role in changing the lives of Japanese Americans. And in the midst of it all was Dan Inouye.

When I met up with Clifford again, I told him about the meeting. We were walking on the National Mall, emptied of people on a winter's afternoon. I remember how cold it was as we talked for over an hour while we strolled. I told Clifford that if we made the wrong choice here, it was all over. We still both strongly favored an appropriations bill, but there was no way I could ignore the challenges that would lay ahead by choosing the option whose odds were so overwhelmingly against us. I knew that ultimately the money itself wasn't important—because, for many Japanese Americans, seeking monetary compensation, especially for something as priceless as the loss of our freedom, was a denigration of our cultural values—but I was fully convinced of the importance of fighting this fight in order to make a statement about the injustice that had been inflicted upon us as American citizens. This was what would help memorialize the lessons of our experience and, hopefully, prevent similar atrocities from happening again.

As Clifford and I talked, we also acknowledged that, if we went with the commission idea, we'd have hell to pay in the Japanese American community for that because it would be seen as a "soft" approach, a coward's choice to avoid the tough fight. I knew I, personally, would probably be skewered, but I also knew that Clifford would stand by me, no matter what. After reflecting on the benefits of pursuing a commission as described by Inouye—public hearings, enormous publicity, the opportunity for Japanese Americans to tell their side of the story, an objective and thorough examination of the circumstances of the wartime policies, and a report with recommendations—I found myself most taken with the idea of the official report, which would be based on facts and the personal testimonies of the Nisei. It would set the record straight that we were the targets of a racist policy, and it would objectify the extent of the government's culpability. I saw then how good for our cause it would be to have an official conclusion of wrongdoing, as the facts themselves aren't always enough to convince even intelligent and reasonable people when they want to cling to beliefs that contradict the truth. The more I thought about it, the more the idea of a commission seemed the wise course to take. I had made up my mind, and now I just needed to bring the JACL along with me. The good news was that I was certain that whatever choice we decided on, we would have the support of the Big Four.

What we needed now was publicity. How could we get front-page coverage in every paper across America and major stories on every television evening news program?

––––––––––––

Karl Nobuyuki and I had several long conversations about the meeting with the Big Four, and we found we both favored direct compensation but agreed that our best chance for success would be to go with Inouye's suggestion. Karl had been talking to Ron Ikejiri, who also believed the commission strategy would advance our cause; Karl saw the wisdom in Inouye's plan and all the benefits it offered, including giving us a much greater advantage in later pushing a redress bill through Congress. We were all concerned that the commission process would lose us valuable time, especially as the Issei generation was disappearing, but although we all felt a sense of urgency to push forward as quickly as we could, we knew we needed to balance that with our desire for the campaign to succeed. Nobuyuki called Ikejiri, and the three of us talked. And talked. Finally, Ikejiri suggested we wait to see what Mineta would decide because he was just as key to our efforts in the House as Inouye was in the Senate. Mineta had enough power and influence among his colleagues that no one, including Republicans, would be foolish enough to introduce any bill having to do with Asian Americans without the courtesy of running it by him first. Though still relatively new to the House (he was first elected in 1975), Norm Mineta was already viewed as a rising star and was rumored by many, even at this early stage in his congressional career, as a potential candidate for Speaker of the House of Representatives. Later, President Bill Clinton would appoint him U.S. secretary of commerce, and then President George W. Bush would appoint him secretary of transportation. But even back then, he was highly respected, had a likable personality that made him popular among his colleagues, and possessed an ability and willingness to work both sides of the aisle that made him particularly effective. We knew we couldn't move any kind of legislation in the House without Mineta's blessing and support, but we also knew with absolute certainty that Mineta supported redress and had been one of the early advocates both as a JACL member and as a public figure.

As preoccupied as we were about the decision before us, I took a moment to appreciate that our first task in going to Washington—to find out if the Big Four supported even the basic idea of redress—had come out in our favor. Any misgivings we had about Inouye and Matsunaga's support because they were from Hawaii were wiped away. They would help us because what ultimately mattered was that they were Japanese Americans. They had both served in the war with the mainland Nisei and understood what the community had endured, and they were fully committed to the cause. In the earliest days of the campaign, Matsui, who had just been elected to Congress, was not yet a factor in influencing votes in the House. At that point, we were unsure how he would position himself on redress legislation because it was public knowledge that he had had some strong misgivings about the issue, which left many in the community skeptical about him. But Bob could read the direction of political winds, and as the mood of the Japanese American community turned more in favor of redress, there was little doubt among our inner circle that he would bend in the direction the political winds blew. The Big Four meeting had revealed that Mineta, Inouye, and Matsunaga all supported redress, and Matsui would surely recognize that among Japanese Americans, this was an issue too important to ignore or resist. It was easy to see that Matsui could become an important factor in our fight for redress.

About a week after our meeting in D.C., Nobuyuki called to tell me that Norm Mineta had changed his mind and was now supporting the creation of a federal commission. Privately, I still had misgivings about this strategy and had hoped Mineta would force the idea of a compensation bill back on the table, but now that he agreed with Inouye's suggestion of a commission, the direction of our campaign was determined.

THE MOST CRITICAL DECISION

As chairman of the National Committee for Redress, I could easily have made a unilateral decision and informed my committee and the board that we would be pursuing the creation of a federal commission to investigate the internment. But process is an important part of an organizational function, and because the decision to pursue a commission strategy would have ramifications throughout the JACL and the Japanese American community, the decision about the strategy we would pursue would have to be processed through my committee.

And yet I had already committed to Inouye's commission plan. I needed to convince my committee, but I had no idea how I was going to do it. I shared with Clifford that the committee, as constituted, would most likely reject the strategy by a three-to-two vote. If that happened, I would have had to take the committee's recommendation to the National Board, which would have the final say. I felt I could count on Yasui and Shigekuni to vote for the commission, but I knew that both Miyatake and Mamiya would vote for the appropriations bill strategy, as would Ray Okamura, a real hard-liner when it came to redress and legislative matters. As the chairman, I wasn't allowed a vote except to break a tie.

I had three options. The first was to circumvent the committee and make a unilateral decision, but that was even more problematic, especially for a decision this monumental. It would have been the easiest option, but it was also the worst, and the political ramifications would reverberate through the JACL and the Japanese American community. Ironically, Clifford was the one who suggested this option to me, maybe remembering my having suggested the same move when he was chair of this committee and we were talking about pushing what would become the Salt Lake City Guidelines onto the national stage.

My second option was to wholly reconstitute the committee to ensure the vote would go my way, but considering that I had formed the committee less than six months ago, the move would look suspicious.

And finally, my third and probably best option would be to bring one new person onto the committee, to even the vote and allow me to be the tiebreaker. It would have to be either someone conservative and predictable or someone who understood and respected Inouye and Mineta and was politically astute enough to know which way to cast his or her vote. I would need someone who could ensure the vote went the way I needed it to go. At the same time, though, I would need someone who had unquestionable integrity and could not be swayed by others. Clifford agreed that this was my best option but wondered how I was going to add another member to the committee without it being obvious why I was doing so.

I resolved the dilemma by adding Bill Marutani, the judge from Philadelphia who had served as the East Coast representative on the committee Clifford had established to develop the redress guidelines. If questioned about why I had added a committee member and why it was Marutani in particular, I would explain that we lacked an East Coast perspective and thought it was important to fill that gap. I would deal with whatever challenges this move created, but the important thing was that Marutani would vote for the federal commission strategy. I was sure of that, as in those meetings with Clifford's committee, he had voted against including monetary compensation in our list of demands.

Shortly after Bill had accepted my invitation to join the committee, I sent a memo to the other members to inform them that he would be joining their ranks. If anyone accused me of stacking the vote, I would remind them that Marutani was fiercely independent and prided himself on being so. At the same time, however, I knew he was a political animal who understood Washington politics and what was at stake with the committee's decision. And it didn't hurt that he was friends with Inouye and Mineta and was part of the old guard along with Masaoka.

I scheduled our first six-person redress committee meeting for March 1979, with only one purpose: to decide what legislative approach we would use to seek redress for Japanese Americans—direct-money bill or federal commission? In the days approaching the meeting, I talked to Yasui and Shigekuni to make sure I had their votes, and I called Ray Okamura on pretense of clarifying some factual information but managing to slip in a few words about Inouye's (and now Mineta's) political perspective on the whole redress matter. Because I knew he would find it objectionable for me to try to influence his thinking, I focused on what the Big Four had said, without suggesting why their approach was the better choice. To try to lobby Ray on this matter was foolish, so I simply provided him with facts, answered his questions, and assured him that I would lay out both approaches at the meeting.

I also called Marutani, under the pretense of catching him up on what had taken place at the D.C. meeting with the Big Four. As I was explaining how Mineta had changed his mind, he made sure I knew he would not tolerate being lobbied by me on any committee deliberations, and I of course agreed. It mattered not at all because I was certain he had already consulted with Masaoka to discuss what Mike thought was our best course of action. We were all three of us doing a kind of dance, each thinking he was leading, but my advantage was that I knew they were two-stepping. As far as they were concerned, I was just some naïve guy from the coast who hadn't a clue, that they were the ones moving me. At this point in my efforts to establish a viable and legitimate campaign, I wasn't bothered by the shenanigans others engaged in because I was clear on what I needed to accomplish. And what mattered to me at this moment was that I could count on Marutani to be mindful of what our friends in Congress wanted—something he would have learned from Mike. It also helped that Bill fancied himself as among the more politically savvy members of the JACL—which was true—and I knew by the end of our telephone conversation that he would vote for the commission, resulting in a split vote for which I would be the tiebreaker.

I called Inouye and told him I could guarantee the committee's vote and that I would get to work on the key board members to ensure that the National Board accepted the committee's decision and recommendation.

———

We met the first weekend of March 1979. The weather was beautiful—one of those incredible San Francisco spring days when the air is crisp and sharp, and the view of the city's skyline is stunning as you drive down the grade approaching the Golden Gate Bridge. It's the kind of day

I love being outside, but I knew I was going to spend the weekend locked in tough discussions with my committee members. Looking back, there were many critical moments to the campaign, but none compared to this one. Whatever we did this weekend would forever change the course of Japanese Americans in this country. The meeting was that important.

I opened the session late on the Friday afternoon of March 2, to tend to administrative matters and bring everyone up to date. I allowed only two visitors to observe the weekend's proceedings: Kaz Oshiki, administrative assistant for Representative Robert Kastenmeier (D-Wisconsin), and Pat Okura, former JACL national president. Both were longtime JACLers. Very noticeably absent was Mike Masaoka, who had graciously declined my invitation, citing a possible conflict of interest because of his extraordinarily close relationships with Inouye, Matsunaga, and especially Mineta. I was disappointed not to have him there, but his absence told me that I could count on him to work the redress campaign from behind the scenes; he would be the wizard behind the curtain, pulling the strings, playing the players. I sometimes wondered what was behind his commitment to the issue: Did he simply like the game of politics, or was it, I wondered, his way of redeeming himself for his controversial involvement on behalf of the JACL during the war?

Also present at the meeting were Clifford, as the JACL's president, and both Karl Nobuyuki and Ron Ikejiri, as national director and the JACL's Washington representative, respectively. Debra Nakatomi, who was an ex officio adviser to me on media as well as internal JACL political matters was there in her role as executive assistant to Karl Nobuyuki, who had requested she take notes.

As I opened the Friday session, I laid down the ground rules by stating that, once the meeting was officially called to order and until we adjourned on Sunday, only committee members would be allowed to participate in the discussions unless I formally recognized others present in the room. I was determined that only committee members should exchange their views because it would be incumbent on them to take full responsibility for the final decision.

I don't know what anyone thought about my restrictions on who was allowed to participate openly in this meeting, but, frankly, I didn't care. I wanted the committee members to decide without distractions because they were the individuals I had chosen to make this decision. These were the people who best knew what Japanese Americans in their regions felt about the issue, I thought, and I wanted them to be free in their thinking as they struggled with the decision. It would not be an easy decision by any means, and if I could have, I would have vacuum-sealed the room to keep it free of outside influence.

That meeting was the tightest I've ever run. Once I started the deliberations, I rarely allowed digressions or any comments that were out of order. I knew Clifford well enough to sense when he wanted to say something—even when he didn't overtly signal to me—and I let him participate in the discussions. Occasionally I called on Kaz when I could see him getting fidgety, but only if I thought his contributions at that point might further the discussion.

I began with presenting both of our legislative options and included the Seattle Bootstrap Plan, even though the congressmen had already rejected it. We spent all of Saturday talking about the various options before us. One phrase that kept coming up was "political reality." It was important when discussing our ideals that we remained mindful about what was actually politically possible. We had to dismiss any macho (or, really, naïve) ideas about charging the Hill and fighting the good fight to the death. We had a huge responsibility to the Japanese American community, a duty, *giri*, to do what was right and to do it the right way. For the most part, we stayed on task, and the mood was serious. Only now and then would someone make an attempt at humor, but it didn't carry very far because of the intensity of the deliberations. People chose their words carefully, sometimes haltingly. By late Saturday afternoon, I decided that we had started to talk in circles, with little new information or insight coming to the discussion, so I recessed the committee for a short break and informed the members that when we reconvened it would be time to vote.

It was already late enough that I could have adjourned for the evening and reconvened in the morning for the vote, but I didn't want anyone to have a chance to lobby any other attendee. Up to that point, I was still sure we would have a tie vote, and I wanted to make sure no one was persuaded to switch their vote to the money bill. I needed the vote to take place as soon as possible.

When we reconvened after the break, I told the committee members that this was a historic decision that would determine the future of the Japanese American community, and that because of the magnitude of what we were about to do, I was going to allow each member to make a statement for the record before casting his vote. At Karl's suggestion the day earlier, I attempted to arrange the seating so that votes for the commission would be cast first, but as committee members arrived, they chose their own seats. Based on that, I knew there would be one voter who could swing either way: Ray Okamura. I had expected him to vote for direct compensation legislation, but Clifford and I agreed that Ray could be swayed by persuasive reasoning, even at the last minute, and so his vote was up in the air.

We had expected Mamiya and Miyatake to remain committed to direct compensation, and they were. Before they cast their votes, both Ron and Henry expressed their objection to the weekend's proceedings, stating that the JACL's National Council had given us a clear directive to seek a compensation bill. Marutani echoed this concern that we follow the directives of the organization, but he also revealed his political savvy in recognizing the "political reality" of Washington and our dependence on the support of our friends in Congress, no matter what our personal desires or views might be. He then cast his vote for the commission strategy.

By the time it came to Okamura, it was clear that his vote would determine the committee's decision.

I admired Ray. I admired his gutsiness in speaking out on unpopular but important issues; I admired his integrity and the way he was always guided by reason and not by what was easy or by what others necessarily wanted. He deserved to be the voice to express what so many of us felt so deeply. As he began his statement, he talked about how much he distrusted the idea of the federal commission and how uneasy he felt about putting the fate of our lives in the hands of a bunch of political appointees. We didn't need to have a study to explain that what happened to us was unjust and racist. That was already clear, based not just on expert research by scholars and historians but on personal memories and evidence, including files he himself kept on the internment experience. Despite all the benefits Inouye had put forth as possible outcomes of a commission—the publicity, the report, the support of the nation—Ray said he was not persuaded that any of this was guaranteed; the history of commissions was that the studies were completed and the reports ended up on bookshelves, never read, collecting dust. He then said, however, that despite all his serious misgivings about the commission approach, and his innate distrust of politicians on this issue (even Mineta and Inouye), and as much as he preferred a money bill and an honest fight for redress through legislation that laid out our claims and presented our demand for compensation, win or lose, he had been persuaded by the weekend's lengthy discussions about the political reality of Washington, and so, with reservations, he voted for the commission.

Shigekuni and Yasui voiced similar misgivings but also let the realities of Washington direct their votes for the commission.

Yasui was the last to speak, and I was glad to have him close out this procedure because he would do it with the passion it deserved. He was vim and vigor, piss and vinegar. He was a fiery speaker, the likes of which we rarely see in the Japanese American community. He had a silver tongue. Min talked about the wrongs committed against Japanese Americans and the damage to the Constitution and the very concept of democracy and individual rights, which should be sacred rights. He talked about how he preferred an honest fight, which a money bill would give us, but he said that our responsibility was to succeed in seeking justice for the internment and he was therefore voting for the commission.

Relieved that Min hadn't followed his heart on this matter and instead showed his political astuteness by voting for the commission, I felt some disappointment that, with the vote now at four to two, I wouldn't get a chance to vote at all.

As I adjourned the meeting, I told the committee that our decision would most likely be an unpopular one. All the reservations we had expressed about the commission would come back to us as criticisms once we made our decision public. I said I wanted the committee to take responsibility for the decision and for everyone to stick together and respond to what I envisioned would be an onslaught from the community. This would be the fight before the fight.

After the voting, we recessed for the evening and reconvened the next morning, when I began the process of describing the next steps for the committee: namely, to draft language for legislation to establish a federal commission. I wanted us to draft the language for the bill rather than leave that to one of the offices of the Big Four. At his request, I assigned Mamiya to write the draft, setting a hard deadline for two weeks from then.

After the meeting adjourned, there was very little conversation. The mood was subdued. Ron and Henry were the first to leave. Min and Bill were having a quiet conversation in the corner; Phil quietly gathered his stuff and then talked briefly with me before he left to catch his flight back to Los Angeles, shaking hands with Ray before he went. And Ray, the one who had saved the day, stood alone sorting out his papers and materials.

Bill left with Min and the D.C. contingent of Kaz Oshiki and Pat Okura, without acknowledging anyone else on the committee. He and I had hardly talked since my call inviting him to serve on my committee, something Clifford noted and commented on more than once. I knew that Clifford had tremendous respect for Marutani, although he seemed not particularly fond of him. It wasn't so much animus as it was that Bill was aloof and distant. As far as I was concerned, however, Bill was inconsequential to me, which was probably a mutual feeling. I didn't do much to disguise, even to Bill himself, that he had been invited onto the committee only for his pro-commission vote. He had served the purpose and I was done with him, and he with me. Or so we thought.

After everyone had left, Clifford and I went up to the office we had commandeered after his election as president and talked for a long time, for what seemed like hours. We critiqued the meeting and discussed various things different people had said. He asked me if I intended to keep this committee together, but I couldn't really see any purpose for doing so. Both of the Seattle members were undoubtedly going to resign, and both Marutani and Okamura had served their purpose, which was to make the tough decision. As soon as the JACL board accepted and approved the committee's recommendation to pursue a commission strategy, I intended to reconstitute the committee to serve a different purpose. As I set my sights on moving the campaign into grassroots lobbying, I envisioned needing a representative from each of the JACL's eight regional districts, and that would require a complete redesign of the committee. I knew both Phil and Min would continue to assist however they could in their respective districts, and they would be the only two possible carryovers into the new committee.

For the moment, however, the most important part of my post-meeting critique with Clifford was our discussion about what to expect from the JACL membership and the community in response to our decision. I told Cliff he needed to get the National Board to accept the committee's recommendation and suggested we might want to consider having the individual chapters reaffirm the board's decision. It was a risky proposition, I knew (what if the majority of the chapters went against us?), but if there were any strong doubts, it would be better to find out through a chapter-level ratification process before we took the campaign to the U.S. government and the American public. We couldn't risk our own members derailing everything. Despite his confidence that the community would understand the logic of our decision, Cliff agreed that it was better to be safe than sorry. Once again, I was glad to know Clifford would stand with me no matter how unpleasant things got.

"LIKE 1942 ALL OVER AGAIN"

I knew our decision would be unpopular and controversial, and that the JACL's critics would take us to task for choosing this direction, but the intensity of the vitriol it evoked, not just from our critics but from legions of JACLers, far exceeded what I had anticipated and was worse than anything I could have imagined. The majority of JACL members criticized us for selling out, and the community focused much of its anger toward me. Our critics said that this was typical of the JACL, that we had betrayed the community just as before, that we had violated the language and spirit of the Salt Lake City Guidelines, and that the JACL had taken the easy way out once again.

I was accused of personally leading and manipulating the committee to a decision that had been forced upon us by Senator Inouye, and in doing so, I had betrayed the Issei, who would not survive long enough to see the creation of a functioning federal commission. Our decision, we were told, was a cowardly act on my part and was tantamount to the cooperation agreement Mike Masaoka and Saburo Kido had made with the Roosevelt administration. This was 1942 all over again, and instead of Masaoka stabbing the community in the back, this time it was me. I had given in to appease Inouye, they said; many called for my removal as the redress chair. No sooner had the announcement been made than the criticism started flooding in, and it quickly turned from harsh to vicious to downright ugly.

In the middle of the firestorm, Ernie Weiner called to see how I was holding up (he had of course been following the subject closely) and asked if I wanted to take a break and meet for lunch. I told him I didn't have time; I was getting my ass beat and was feeling a sense of what it must have been like for him in his last boxing match, the one that had convinced him to quit!

As I responded to all the letters sent to me at the JACL headquarters and as letters to the editors of Japanese American papers, I made sure

132

that neither Inouye nor Mineta was implicated in the committee's decision. It's true, I stated, that Inouye had suggested we consider the idea of a federal commission and that Mineta supported that suggestion, but the decision was ours alone and was based on the available options, which included a money bill. Based on everything we knew, it was our judgment that the compensation bill had a good chance of dying a slow and meaningless death, whereas the creation of a commission would pave the path to a compensation bill that would have stronger legs to stand on.

True to his promise, Clifford stood by me during those many days and weeks of attacks on me and the committee, defending me in articles and interviews when he could. As the criticism continued, I sought occasional refuge in lunches with Ernie, who commiserated and would always share some apt boxing metaphor, like "Take the eight count, but show them in the fifteenth who's the real chump."

As uncomfortable as it was in the weeks following the meeting, the tumult, I knew, was part of a process we had to endure as we attempted to navigate our way through the yet uncharted landscape of a redress campaign. The committee's decision, while it had considerable weight, was only a recommendation to the National Board, which had the final say. The board met quarterly and was not scheduled to hold another meeting for a few months, but the cost of holding an emergency meeting of the sixteen board members was prohibitive. I was understandably anxious to have the board make a decision (we couldn't do anything until it had), and so encumbered by logistical and costs problems, Clifford convened a National Board meeting on the earliest possible date, the first weekend of June. The discussion of the committee's recommendation lasted over three hours, becoming heated and even acrimonious at times. But it was curious that some of the board members who would normally be expected to contest the recommendation didn't do so, which suggested they had been lobbied—by whom, I don't know, but the criticism of the committee's decision was so widespread among the chapters that it was difficult to know which of the district governors at the board meeting had changed their views. Karl Nobuyuki and I had calculated that the vote would be close and had even discussed a ratification process should we need to overturn a board decision.

After more than three hours of debate, there was a call for the question, and the board was nearly unanimous in its approval vote, even as the underlying sense was strong opposition to, or an uneasiness with, the proposal. None of that mattered, however, because it was now the JACL's official position to pursue the creation of a federal commission whose responsibility would be to investigate the circumstances surrounding the government's wartime policies of exclusion and detention, determine whether it was justified, issue an official report to Congress and the president with its findings and conclusions, and provide recommendations as remedies, if warranted. We were on our way, sort of.

Just before the vote was taken, Nobuyuki announced that there would be a ratification process of all JACL chapters to affirm the board's decision, implying that the expectation was that the board would approve. It caught me completely by surprise. It was a risky game of politics, and Karl acknowledged this when we met as soon as the board adjourned. Clifford joined us in the conversation about ratification but disagreed about the usefulness of the process. We had gotten the board's approval, and a ratification process could backfire if chapters voted against the commission idea. Because there was so much dissention among the rank and file of the organization, we argued, a successful ratification would silence our critics from within the JACL once and for all. But that very factor concerned Clifford: there were so many chapters and members that had voiced their dismay at what they thought was a cowardly decision, and we would not be involved in their dialogue as they made their decisions. It was a legitimate point, but we were eventually able to convince him that the prudent course was to seek a vote, no matter how narrow we worried the margin might be.

Karl and I calculated the risk. We went through each of the eight JACL districts, chapter by chapter, noting even individual members who might influence a chapter's vote. We worked late into the night, putting each chapter in one of two columns, and finally concluded that we had enough votes on our side. It would be close, but we were reasonably confident that the chapters would ratify the board's decision. We informed Clifford of the plan.

But what if the chapters didn't vote in favor of the federal commission? Well, I would have to decide on the next course of action, with the complication that we *had* to move forward with the commission idea. By this point, I was absolutely convinced that a direct compensation bill would end in disaster. I had begun doing talk shows around the country and consistently had to deal with ugly, racist views and knee-jerk reactions, and so it didn't take much to imagine the harsh reactions we would encounter in Congress with a money bill. A vote to ratify the commission strategy was critical, and if the vote backfired, I had no idea how we would manage if not by dictatorial decree, and while Karl and I privately discussed the idea of a decision by executive fiat, neither of us wanted to risk crossing that bridge. We would have to do what we could to secure ratification by our chapters.

We sent out a very carefully worded ratification document to all JACL chapters shortly after the June board meeting and assigned a strict deadline of July 9, 1979, giving chapters just over a month to call emergency meetings of their boards and members and to submit their votes to the national headquarters. Each day when I finished my teaching schedule and went to the JACL office, I would be greeted with a stack of phone messages from chapters and members with questions about the commission concept, what the alternatives were, what the consequences would be if a choice was made in one direction or another, and some even sought a parliamentary procedure to stop the ratification process.

While I was committed to the commission strategy, I endeavored to answer questions objectively, even talking about the advantages of a direct compensation approach if we could find a way to make it work, or the downsides of a commission as a means to achieve a goal. I tried as best I could not to try to persuade the thinking of anyone who called. My role in this process was to present information and hope for the best, whatever that might be.

At the close of business on July 9, Karl and Clifford officially announced that the polling was closed. The *Pacific Citizen*, the JACL's newspaper, announced that the vote was five to one in favor of the commission and quoted Clifford as saying he was gratified by the confirmation of the board's decision. Karl was elated that we could now move forward. But the reality was that the vote was much closer than the numbers showed because almost half the chapters would not subject themselves to the ratification process, which they considered illegitimate, being of the opinion that the committee's recommendation and the board's decision were in violation of the Salt Lake City Guidelines mandate. In protest, they did not submit their votes.

The final tally approved the commission strategy, but it was not the enthusiastic endorsement we had hoped for. Because of a large number of abstentions, we could only declare a confirmation of the decision, rather than announce that the JACL membership had unified behind the cause. But the official result was the same nonetheless. Karl sent a memorandum announcing that the JACL chapters had ratified both the redress committee's recommendation and the National Board's acceptance of that recommendation, and the commission strategy was now the official position of the JACL. One hurdle down, countless more to go.

THE MEDIA BREAKTHROUGH

The cacophony that reverberated within the Japanese American community over our decision was so consuming that it seemed odd to me that it was so wholly absent from mainstream media. But of course it wouldn't stay that way forever. For the time being, and from the outside, it came off as nothing more than in-fighting among Japanese Americans that had no relevance to anyone else. Not yet, at least.

While to us this wrenching experience dragged on for months as the JACL—the committee, the board, the chapters—processed the decision and faced the community's reaction, and while the Japanese American vernacular newspapers around the country followed our moves closely, none of it had caught the attention of mainstream papers, nor was it covered on any newscasts, even in places like Los Angeles and San Francisco, where the nation's largest Japanese American populations resided. Big occasions, like the Days of Remembrance events in Seattle and San Francisco, drew their own media attention, but it was only local. We had tasted wide coverage in the wake of S. I. Hayakawa's statement at the Salt Lake City convention, but for the most part our coverage was still limited.

What we really needed was regular exposure about the internment: editorials and investigative reporting in newspapers, human interest stories on local television news programs, interviews with influential members of the community. We needed to find a way to convince the media that this was a sustainable story, one that could be picked apart from a number of angles. I knew that debating the issue on the air would be our most effective way to reach the American public across the country, so that's where I focused my efforts.

What interest the media did show in our campaign came from producers of public television and National Public Radio affiliates. I appeared on several PBS programs that aired around the country, but the story I was able to tell still centered on the Bay Area, where the JACL was headquartered, and PBS was still relatively new at that time, not yet "mainstream" television. The commercial network affiliates were not even a little curious, and our efforts to get the media's attention for news-oriented stories proved only partially successful.

Fortunately, breaks often come when, and from where, you least expect them, and ours came one day when I got a call from Anna Chavez, at that time a new anchor at the local ABC affiliate KGO. Up to that point, the reporters and program hosts I had encountered on Bay Area stations had generally been critical of the redress movement and seemed to see this subject as easy pickings because it was an unknown issue. The hosts had not figured out that it was in their interest to take us seriously, and when they did not, they did so at their own peril because as soon as we got into a conversation, it was easy to overwhelm them. But Chavez was different from the very beginning. She had grown up in the Bay Area but had only recently heard about the internment, she told me during our first telephone conversation. She wanted to know more, wanted to understand how this could have happened and why no one—not she, not her colleagues at the news station, not her professors at Stanford—knew anything about so profound an injustice on American soil. This was a new experience for me, and a hopeful one. As we explored the issue, her inquiries told me she was on a quest for truth, and when her story later appeared on KGO, it aired as a special report.

A few months after the KGO story, Wendy Tokuda, a news coanchor at KPIX-TV, the local CBS affiliate in San Francisco, called to tell me she was interested in producing a segment on the evening news about the internment. I was pleased, of course, but felt she needed to know that she would get hate mail if she did this story because, unlike Chavez, who was Latina, Tokuda was Japanese American. She wasn't concerned (she said she got hate mail when she reported on the trade war with Japan), and she had a personal interest in the internment and redress issues, for obvious reasons. Perhaps because of that investment, Tokuda's reporting took her story to a new level. Chavez's piece was underlined with the questions "Why did this happen?" and "How could it happen in this country?" and raised the fundamental issue of our campaign: "Does the Constitution truly stand for what it says, or do the rights of U.S. citizens apply to some and not others?" The Tokuda piece, while raising similar questions, told a more personal story about the profound impact of the wartime experience on the lives of Japanese Americans, laying bare the story of racism and greed and the political corruption that fueled the injustice. The next night, KPIX ran part two of the program, this one centered on our redress effort, and the unusually extensive coverage was no doubt made possible by Dianne Fukami, Wendy's news director, who was also Japanese American.

A few days later I received a call from anchor Tritia Toyota, who wanted to get the story of the internment on her local news program in Los Angeles, which was the second largest television market in the country. I found out later that, while Tritia and Wendy knew each other, they hadn't talked to each other about running stories about the camps and had done so independently. I flew down to L.A. to interview with Tritia for her program. In the space of two months, major stories about the internment and the JACL's demands for redress aired on three major broadcast affiliates: Chavez (ABC), Tokuda (CBS), and Toyota (NBC).

Not long after Tokuda's story ran in the Bay Area, I received a call from Bernard Goldberg, the West Coast reporter for *CBS Evening News*, who was interested in the internment and redress stories because, as he put it, it was such an "American story." He asked about the camps, the government's wartime policies, and our demands for redress. As we talked, he asked if any of the camps still existed (remnants of some, yes) and if there were any within reach of the Bay Area. I described Manzanar and Tule Lake, both within a day's drive, and he was immediately intrigued with Tule Lake and all it symbolized, especially because it was the camp in which the No-No Boys and other "troublemakers" were held. He asked if I could connect him with someone who might be willing to be interviewed about life at Tule Lake. He said he understood it was a sensitive topic and that sharing memories about camp might be hard, but he hoped someone would be interested in telling their story.

It was early 1979. It was difficult enough to get a Nisei to talk publicly about camp at all, but to find someone willing to talk on national television about life at Tule Lake, and to expose him- or herself to the scorn of a community that preferred to keep such things private, would be nearly impossible.

Among the few people I knew who had been at Tule, Ben Takeshita, my fellow cochair of the district's redress committee who had stunned us with the declaration that he had been a No-No Boy, surprised me once again and agreed to accompany Goldberg to Tule to do an interview on camera.

Goldberg and Ben traveled to Tule Lake, the high-security camp where Ben and his family had spent most of the war years. The interview went well, and I had arranged, in addition to Ben, to have a couple of 442nd vets also do interviews with Goldberg, and I did an interview as well. It was exciting to know we were so close to having the internment story finally reach a national audience. We had gotten some exposure through the television movie of *Farewell to Manzanar* and Michi Weglyn's book *Years of Infamy*, but Goldberg's story was network news. There was no mistaking this as fiction or an exposé told from our point of view. This was part of the factual history of the United States being told for the first time through a major news outlet.

Before the story ran on CBS, Goldberg called and asked to interview me for a story on the trade war between the United States and Japan. Before I could respond, he said the idea for this story had evolved from my interview about the internment story, specifically my statement that we Japanese Americans are frequently blamed for Japan's policies and actions, which was obviously a part of the rationale for our treatment during World War II. I initially declined his request because I didn't want to be identified in any way whatsoever with Japan and the trade issue, and I knew that as soon as viewers saw my Japanese face, they would see me as Japanese. And then to appear in the other story as the person leading the redress campaign, which extolled our rights as Americans—it all seemed potentially too confusing, not to mention risky. That said, I eventually decided to do the trade issue story, despite the risk and even though I was no expert on trade issues. Who better to talk about Japan's arrogance and the horrible impact their policies were having on the lives of all Japanese Americans? For us, it was another case of mistaken identity, similar to what we had suffered after Pearl

Harbor; mainstream Americans never bothered to even try to distinguish us from policies of the Japanese government. In many ways, it was the height of insensitivity and stupidity, and who better to say that than me?

It was a calculated risk, certainly, but the more I considered the plusses and minuses, I realized it was an opportunity. From having worked with Goldberg before, I knew he would not betray the trust we put in him, especially on a story with which we could easily be exploited. Just as I figured, he didn't betray that trust.

The story on the trade war aired on network news the day after we did the interview, but the Tule Lake and redress story was delayed, or perhaps preempted by more pressing news. Goldberg assured me the internment story would get on the viewing schedule because it was too important not to air, and I tried to be patient. As we talked about various aspects of the story, he told me about his experience in the Tule Lake area while he was there conducting interviews. Between shoots, he had decided to go to the neighboring town of Newell with his cameraman, hoping to knock on doors and interview a few residents about the camp. Most people didn't want to be interviewed, and one man even came to the door with a shotgun and threatened both men if they didn't get off his porch. Goldberg pondered this response and noted that the residents of Newell had reacted in much the same way residents of towns near the German death camps did after the war. The older Newell residents didn't want to share their thoughts about the existence of a camp like Tule right in their backyard.

I told him about the time a year earlier, in 1979, that I had gone up to Tule for a dedication ceremony of a monument the JACL had erected at the old camp site. I had driven through the night to get there and was trying to catch a short nap in my car before the ceremony was to begin. As I slept, a man knocked on my window and asked me if this was the monument ceremony for the camp. He told me he had grown up in Newell and, as a nineteen-year-old when the war broke out, had volunteered for the army and ended up in the Army Air Corps in the Pacific. He didn't know about Tule Lake until he returned to Newell after the war. At that time, the camp still held Japanese American incarcerees.

He told me that he had gone to war to fight the axis powers and to protect democracy and the American way of life, and when he came back and learned about the camp right outside his town, he got so angry that he left and ended up in Idaho, where he worked as a crop-dusting pilot. Now, thirty-four years later, he had received a news clipping from a friend about the monument dedication and had come back because, he told me, all he wanted was to be able to tell someone he was sorry for what had happened.

"I went all the way across the Pacific to make sure this kind of thing didn't happen in this country, and then I came home and saw this. I was so goddamn mad that I couldn't stay. But I came back because I wanted to say I'm sorry."

I asked him if he would tell his story during the ceremony, but he said no, that wasn't what he came back for. He said the ceremony was for Japanese Americans and he didn't want to interrupt anything. He just wanted someone to know how sorry he was that we were put into the camps.

And then he left.

When I got word from Goldberg that the internment story would air on *CBS Evening News*, I called Ken Kashiwahara, the West Coast reporter for *ABC World News Tonight* and an acquaintance, to let him know about the CBS story. By the next morning, Ken was interviewing me during a break between my classes at City College, and I was then able to parlay that meeting into convincing a reporter for NBC to do a story on *NBC Nightly News*, anchored by John Chancellor. Within a week's span, the story of the World War II imprisonment of Japanese Americans, as well as our demands for redress, had aired on all three major networks, this time to national audiences.

By the late 1970s, most Americans still got most of their news from newspapers, but television was fast becoming an important outlet, reaching into practically every household in the country. And now our story was airing in front of an incredulous American public that was learning about our wartime experiences for the first time. We had broken through the barrier that had kept this story closed off in some dusty corner of history, and our country was finally learning about the fate of Japanese Americans during World War II.

Clifford had only been the JACL national president for about a year by then, and in that time we had already accomplished so much. I had flooded news editorial desks with information and managed to get our story running in the editorial pages of some of the country's major newspapers; helped establish the internment and our redress effort as a newsworthy issue in various local and regional papers; orchestrated debates between letters to editors of newspapers around the country; pushed a decision—however controversial it was—for our legislative approach to seeking redress from the U.S. government; worked on getting the internment and redress story aired on all three major television network news programs; and been lucky enough to secure the endorsements of two national organizations, the American Jewish Committee and the National Hellenic Society. Looking back on it all, it was gratifying to see how much we were able to get done, especially since each of those achievements was, at the time, nothing short of monumental. We had gone from nothing to national awareness in just a few years. And we would keep going.

CAMPAIGN BACKLASH

One of the consequences we experienced as a result of national media exposure through the network news stories was a sudden increase in the interest of local news outlets around the country. And that meant more exposure, both good and bad. We were still in the early stages of the campaign and exposing the government's machinations against us, and we knew it would be a lot to take in for most people. The network news stories were objective and fair, but viewers for the most part jumped to their own conclusions. Unlike newsprint articles about our wartime experience, television, with its visual imagery, seemed to create a storm of reaction we hadn't seen before.

On the call-in programs I participated in after the three big network stories, the airwaves were flooded with callers dedicated to either justifying the government's actions or denying the camps had ever existed, or certainly not in the way I had described them. Temporary resettlement facilities, yes, perhaps, but not concentration camps with barbed wire and armed military guards.

I was also attacked on the matter of reparations. "Why should you get anything?" some would say. "You were just a kid." My response: "Oh, so it's okay to imprison children, is that your point?" Rarely did anyone speak from authority or factual knowledge; and those who criticized us seemed to do so because they were offended by *my* criticisms of the government's actions during a war that, for most people, had brought out the best of America.

"It was wartime and we had been attacked, so what were we to do?" was a frequent challenge. Or some would insist that there was "no way to tell if any of you were spies." I always threw back the same retort: "So the solution was to imprison the entire population, including women, children, the infirm, even orphans?" I would then ask, "And what about the matter of evidence? When did it become okay to imprison people without any evidence, without even an accusation of wrongdoing?" My questions were usually met with silence.

It became clear that the primary objection to us and our campaign was that the idea of Japanese people seeking justice for something done during World War II was flat-out repugnant. Didn't we understand that *we* were the enemy? Their bigotry was unabashed, and they made no apologies for it. Most of these callers didn't see me as an American who espoused the rights of citizens as guaranteed by our Constitution. What mattered to them was that I was a Japanese person who obviously didn't understand that the government was forced to treat us as it had because we were a threat to the country. They were offended that I would question the facts of history (at least as they knew it, or as they wanted it to be) and that I would denigrate the image of the venerated Franklin Delano Roosevelt. A frequent comment I heard was "Someone like you shouldn't be allowed to smear the good name of a great president."

While working with the media opened more opportunities to reach large audiences, it also brought out what I referred to as "the crazies," and I was often their target. I didn't mind the oddballs or even the sincere racists—their arguments afforded me an opportunity to debate the issue—but dealing with the crazies always gave me pause. "Good Americans like me are here to get rid of people like you," I was once told. These are the people who wanted us gone, and their comments often seemed to have an underlying threat. As the campaign built momentum, threats became more frequent. I'm sure that other Japanese American organizations and individuals in other parts of the country had similar experiences, but because of my position within the JACL, and because I was often the face of the cause in the news stories the public was seeing, I become a convenient focus of the animus against our efforts.

What began with hate mail sent to the JACL headquarters soon morphed into vague threats and then specific threats, some to my life. The hate mail wasn't entirely unexpected—the thoughts people were putting on paper were the same I heard from people calling in to talk shows or speaking out at public events—but the threats were a different matter, and it was hard not to be concerned, even though

I understood this abuse and anxiety came with the territory. Anyone who has been a voice for any unpopular civil rights matter encounters similar situations; it seemed an inevitable consequence. People were lashing out because we were presenting facts that didn't conform to their views, facts that threatened their sense of order. And when I was able to fight back and respond effectively to their bigotry and misinformation, they were unable to handle having been made to feel even a little powerless by someone like me—a nonwhite, a Japanese American. Ironically, I could measure the current success of our media strategy by not just the amount but the *kind* of hate mail we were receiving at the JACL headquarters.

Although we were one of the oldest civil rights organizations in the country, going back to 1929, we were unused to getting hate mail with such frequency, not to mention the level of vitriol it expressed, indicating that we were reaching deep into the hostility of a segment of the public. For the first time in its history, the JACL installed a security system at its headquarters and took precautions to ensure the safety of the staff. This was all new to us, in a time before security systems became commonplace, and even though I was most often the target of the anger, everyone who worked in the building felt vulnerable. Karl Nobuyuki, who had ordered the security system and established the safety protocols, told me the caution measures affected everyone, but it was Yuki Fuchigami, our receptionist and the first line of contact for people calling or entering our offices, who knew how serious the threats were becoming.

What began as occasional calls and hate mail grew as we got more exposure, and there was a point at which I could see the toll it was taking on Yuki. The telephone calls were one thing—a spur-of-the-moment rant by someone needing an outlet—but the hate mail was something else. The letter writers seemed to have a deeper level of commitment, springing from a different mindset, and some seemed driven by a different motive. At Yuki's urging, we reported the threats to the San Francisco Police Department, and because the letters were being sent through the U.S. Postal Service, the SFPD called in the FBI, who advised Yuki on how to physically handle the mail and how to measure the potential for danger. She was stern in advising us to take the hate mail more seriously—that is, as a real threat and not just crank mail. None of this could have been easy for her, and when Karl offered to change her position, both in function and in location, she insisted on staying where she was. Because of her proximity to my office, she also decided to take on the role as my personal secretary and guardian angel. Yuki was a constant for me during those years, and I don't think she ever realized how important she was to me, in part because I never let her know just how much I appreciated her. When she and her husband, Walt, moved to Portland, Oregon, in the early 1980s, I thanked her for all she had done, but I never truly found the words to express how much she meant to me. That was one of my biggest personal regrets during the redress campaign.

At the headquarters, we tried to keep worries contained, and I definitely downplayed the stress of it all the few times I mentioned anything about it to my wife, Carol. I made certain my two kids, Stephen and Sarah, who were in elementary and middle school, were never exposed to this side of the campaign. As much as I tried to shield my family, however, I couldn't deny the seriousness of the situation when the police informed me that they had learned there was a contract out on me, and it was credible enough that they urged Carol and me to take safety precautions. I had tried to protect my family from this aspect of the campaign, but they were now a part of it.

For a time, I paid very close attention to what was going on around me. I didn't change what I was doing—I continued to speak to public audiences and seek any opportunity to be on the air—but I found myself hesitating when I came out of studios or event spaces after particularly heated discussions. I never got used to the threats, but I'm grateful they were never serious enough to stop me from doing what I knew I had to do. The battleground of this campaign was on the airwaves, and I was willing to go there. This was my job, and I took it seriously.

THE REDRESS STAFF

As we got deeper into the campaign, I began to understand why Edison Uno had been so insistent that, if the issue of wartime incarceration ever turned into a campaign, the JACL was the only organization in the Japanese American community capable of carrying such an effort. It wasn't just that the Japanese American members of Congress were JACL members and aligned with our values, and it wasn't just that we had chapters spread across the country, with a large volunteer force of around twenty-eight thousand prepared to do battle on the ground (although this reach proved critical as the campaign evolved). The real benefit the JACL held was the structure of its professional staff in key areas, including Washington, D.C. Because the JACL's members didn't always agree with the decisions that came out of the redress committee, it was the staff at the regional offices—especially those in the major West Coast cities and, perhaps most critical, in Chicago—upon whom we counted to be the steady force in the local communities. It was they who mustered the support needed from our chapters, and they who guided grassroots efforts. Although the dedication of volunteers is the heart and soul of an organization like the JACL, unpaid workers can only do so much while also prioritizing their careers and families, and thus we depended heavily on the paid staff who worked hard every day in regional offices across the country. And as the campaign progressed, I found myself in dire need of extra staff support at the headquarters.

With a limited budget, I set out to hire a part-time assistant and found Carole Hayashino, who met all my criteria: she was knowledgeable about the incarceration and its complexities, she was involved with and understood the Japanese American community, and she was willing to do what was essentially a full-time job on a part-time salary.

Carole was perfect for the job, but some within the ranks of the San Francisco JACL objected to her past dealings with the organization. She had been an activist in the Bay Area for years, in particular as a member of an organization that opposed the JACL's support of redevelopment in the city's Nihonmachi (Japantown) during the 1970s. The government's urban renewal plan sought to rid its inner-city communities of urban blight, but their controversial method involved displacing whole ethnic neighborhoods in favor of constructing new stores, apartments, and condominiums. The Fillmore District, once a thriving community that featured some of America's best jazz clubs, was completely wiped of its soul by redevelopment. The impact on Nihonmachi, which was a solid middle-class and well-maintained neighborhood, was devastating. Hayashino was then part of the community-based Committee Against Nihonmachi Evictions (CANE), which was viewed by the J-town business community and the JACL as a radical left-wing organization. Ironically, the fact that Hayashino had been part of CANE raised her value in my eyes; had I been around in San Francisco in those days, my sympathies undoubtedly would have been with CANE. As it turned out, redevelopment of Nihonmachi ultimately displaced most of the Japanese Americans living in the area, many of them Issei, and the effect on the community was devastating. This style of urban renewal drove a stake into the heart of J-town and forced the closure of many old neighborhood mom-and-pop restaurants and shops. Many in the community compared the J-town evictions to the forced removal of the community's residents during World War II and were again critical of the JACL's support of the government's program.

Carole came on board as my staff despite the objections from grumpy JACLers in the San Francisco area, and her influence was immediate. We were able to stay abreast of requests and develop new materials for the campaign, and Carole's role eventually expanded into a full-time position as our principal researcher. She was an integral part of the campaign until its conclusion.

————

Chicago, at the heart of the heartland, has been home to the largest Japanese American population outside the West Coast since World War II, when Japanese Americans who had secured permission to leave their respective camps found their way to the bustling Midwestern metropolis. After the war, many Japanese Americans who wanted nothing to do with the West Coast—a place suffused with memories of how easily they had lost their homes and businesses, and a place where anti-Japanese feelings still ran especially high—chose to resettle in various parts of the Midwest, notably in Chicago, a cosmopolitan city with, at that time, a small Japanese community. Chicago's Japanese American community grew considerably after the war and was the most populous outside the West Coast. Smaller communities began to spring up in other parts of the region as well, in states such as Minnesota, Michigan, Ohio, and in some Plains areas. As Japanese Americans found new homes, new jobs, and new opportunities in these cities, JACL chapters were established there, adding a strong Midwestern element to our national network.

By the mid- to late 1970s, the effects of the trade war between the United States and Japan were being felt especially hard in places like Detroit and Ohio. A crippled economy, the loss of manufacturing jobs in the auto and steel industries, and the introduction of more and better-made Japanese products in the consumer market gave rise to strong anti-Japanese sentiments in the Midwest, fermenting a kind of racial animosity that felt always simmering just below the surface. The economic depression that befell the region that came to be known as the "Rust Belt" found a useful scapegoat in the Japanese, and many mainstream Americans could not and would not distinguish between Japanese people living in Japan and the Japanese Americans who were their fellow U.S. citizens. In fact, many could not distinguish between any ethnic Asian groups, which made us all vulnerable to various prejudices, as we tragically learned in the highly publicized 1982 murder of twenty-seven-year-old Chinese American Vincent Chin in Detroit. Two unemployed auto workers, Ronald Ebens and Michael Nitz, bludgeoned Chin to death with baseball bats in retaliation for the negative impact of Japanese imports on the American automobile industry. The incident was memorable not only because of its brutality but because of the light sentences the men, who were white, received for their crime. They were both convicted of manslaughter, but neither served a single day in prison. Many unemployed auto workers hailed them as heroes. Given this atmosphere of anti-Japanese fervor, we perhaps shouldn't have been surprised that it was in America's heartland that our redress campaign would encounter the strongest opposition and hostility.

That was the environment into which Bill Yoshino stepped when he took over the challenging job as director of the JACL's Chicago office, with the responsibility of overseeing the civil rights landscape of the Midwest and managing its volatile situations. Although he was born in Seattle, Washington, Yoshino was a product of a Midwestern upbringing and understood better than I the social landmines we would face in the heartland. It was fortuitous that Bill came to my attention among the cadre of JACL regional directors because, at that time, I was still very much West Coast–centric: it was where the internment had hit hardest, it was where the majority of Japanese Americans still lived, and it was where I had the most connections.

Because I had no one with whom I could talk about regional strategies, I asked Nobuyuki to assign Yoshino to the campaign, and once on board, Bill and I talked frequently. He played an invaluable role as we moved into the legislative phase. The Midwest loomed as a vast, hostile area where we would have to fight some of our most volatile battles.

Former JACL president Hank Tanaka, from Cleveland, warned me that ignoring the Midwest would be fatal to the redress campaign. True, the region was a cauldron of mixed reactions on civil rights matters, but, more importantly, the combined congressional power of the Midwest states far outweighed that of the West Coast. Vibrant, metropolitan Chicago, a Democratic stronghold, may have been at the center of the heartland, but it was surrounded by rural, small-town America with its traditionalist mores and conservative politics. Add to that cities like Detroit and Youngstown, whose dying industries of automobile and steel manufacturing introduced other complex issues into the political mix, and we faced a major challenge in bringing the redress campaign to this region of the country.

Chicago would be the base from which we would work the issue in the Midwest. With its relatively large Japanese American population and a JACL office there, we would develop a Midwest strategy for redress, and Bill Yoshino would be the one to oversee and implement it.

THE FLAG AND APPLE PIE

I was never one to wave the flag or join the heartfelt throngs filled with emotion whenever some great display of patriotism was being show-cased. Like many of my generation, I expressed love of country by questioning the powers that be and demanding that things be made right or made better. When called upon to serve in the military, I had done what I was asked to do and more, but at heart, going back to my teenage years, I had always maintained a cynical edge. For me, much of what people said they loved best about the United States—freedom, equality, opportunity, democracy—seemed to be a reflection of what they *wanted* to be true, rather than what actually was. Our country's checkered history on issues of race and social justice kept me from ever being a flag-waver.

Of course, there was also the fact that I never forgot standing at the barbed-wire fence looking out on America and wondering why we had to have armed soldiers in guard towers looking down at us. And I never forgot the hatred and prejudice aimed at us when we returned to the West Coast, and how we were belittled and sometimes treated, and how our parents and other Nisei were humiliated so often by white people who exalted in their Americanism and patriotism. So yes, love of country had some serious caveats for me, a sense that was driven even deeper by my days at UC Berkeley, where questioning assumptions became a preoccupation. Some might say I was not the right person to head up the redress effort, which would have run more smoothly had it been painted red, white, and blue.

In my earliest days as the chair of the national redress committee, I jotted down a list of strategies for the campaign. It was in the middle of the night and I was alone with my thoughts about where we were and where we needed to go. I started with an item that said something like, "Make this America's campaign—the flag and apple pie." I wrote it with a hint of cynicism because I knew how easily the flag and apple pie could be taken away from anyone who didn't fit what mainstream

Americans thought was acceptable, like the color of one's skin. Nevertheless, the campaign had to be about America as it was meant to be. It had to be about democracy, about foundations, about taking lessons from the past to build a stronger America for the future. And, at the bottom line, it had to be about the Constitution.

Outlining the issue in terms of American idealism was not some kind of political gimmick wrestled into service for the campaign but was indeed the very framework within which the JACL had been discussing redress since the topic's introduction at the 1970 convention. It was also extremely important to the Nisei; everything they had done during the war, including putting on uniforms to fight for the country that had stripped them of their fundamental rights and imprisoned them, was evidence enough of their unwavering belief in American idealism.

If our campaign hoped to succeed, the effort had to come from within the Japanese American community, and with a unified voice and purpose. The problem, however, was that we were still not in full agreement about even the very idea of seeking redress. In choosing to pursue the issue, the JACL may have expressed the will of the majority of its members, but in fact we represented only 4 percent of the Japanese American community, which in itself was barely half a percent of the nation's total population. We still had people opposed to bringing up the issue of camp at all, preferring to keep it buried in our past, and then of course there were those who opposed our chosen strategy, and those who only wearily supported it. Passage of the Salt Lake City Guidelines in 1978 had only momentarily united the membership at the convention, and until the JACL could be fully unified in its support of the purpose and goals of the campaign, the divisions within the Japanese American community would only widen.

Clearly, we had to set our own house in order, which meant finding a way to soften the opposition from some of our most influential members, including, among others, psychologist and former national president Pat Okura, in the D.C. area, and Denver journalist Bill Hosokawa, both of whom energized redress opponents. And there were many others like them. Approximately 75 percent of JACL members favored redress, but the number dropped to around 60 or 65 percent if reparations were part of the discussion. But monetary compensation was not going to be ignored or dropped from our demands—both the Northern California survey and the Salt Lake City Guidelines mandated its inclusion—and so we would have to work to change some minds.

As long as we had majority support in the JACL, I would push the issue forward, assuming that the opposition would eventually be forced to accept the will of the majority. It was with this in mind that I attended the Tri-District meeting in 1979 in Fresno, California, which brought together the state's three districts: Northern California/Western Nevada, Central California, and the Pacific Southwest, which together represented 75 percent of the JACL's chapters. Both the Northern California and Southwest districts were on record supporting redress, but the Central Cal group, while much smaller, was still officially opposed, in part because it represented a rural, conservative part of the state. Nisei farmers were a major presence in California's Central Valley, and many of their leaders had gained statewide prominence and influence representing the old guard, who were among the JACLers most adamantly opposed to redress.

I used my time at the podium to articulate what I believed was at the heart of the campaign: honor and vindication and what we could contribute to the nation. Yes, we would be asking for reparations, but only because money has the power to make Americans understand the significance of an issue. This was the same message I had been spreading to Japanese American audiences across the country, but now that the campaign had gotten some wider public traction, it held even more weight with the Tri-District delegates. And the message stuck. We came away from Fresno with the Central Cal district no longer officially opposed to redress. This was a big shift because it was the Central California District Council that had raised the strongest opposition to the campaign within the JACL. We always knew we would need broad support from across the state of California, home to the majority of the country's Japanese American population, and once Central Cal joined us, I knew we could persuade most of the Nisei elsewhere to join also.

I spanned the country to talk to JACL chapters about the state of the campaign and to discuss any aspect they wanted to know more about, to help with any challenges they were having at the local level, and to lend an ear to those who wanted to give voice to anger they had about our campaign. The subject still hadn't garnered enough interest outside the community that non–Japanese Americans would be interested in attending these meetings, which was good, since, for now, members-only meetings were preferable, as they allowed us the space to talk candidly amongst ourselves about the significance of what we were attempting with this campaign. I wanted a forum in which I could speak not only about strategies but also about the cultural imperatives that drove both our demands for justice and our self-imposed demands for silence, because those imperatives were one and the same. I needed an opportunity to talk about the very things that were at the heart of the Japanese American soul, to begin to peel away the protective layers that had kept us strong through the ignominy of the camps and in the years following the war, as we continued to struggle against those who hated our very existence. I was convinced that the Japanese Americans who still resisted our effort based on cultural reasons could be won over if they understood the altruistic motives driving this campaign, which sought to reinforce this nation's commitment to democratic principles.

Despite my own personal cynicism, I truly did believe that this was the purpose and goal of the campaign; otherwise, why even bother? I thought we could make a difference, and if I've ever believed in anything about this country, it's that it's important to fight for the rights of everyone. I had always been a strong believer in social equality, but I also knew that you had to work for what you got. No handouts. Prove yourself and always endeavor to achieve what's right; and if you can't, then we'll fight for and with you. And for the Nisei, it was much more: it was a belief in what America stood for, embodied for them in our cultural sense of honor. And that was what I talked about to the Nisei who opposed our campaign and found our demands offensive. Was I successful? Slowly, even one by one, as they started to understand the goals of the campaign and the ideals it was founded on, they began to change their views. But we would not see the community unified on this issue for another two years.

THE GRASSROOTS MACHINE

While the JACL had an envious legislative record, there was nothing in its recent past that would indicate how effective it still was, or could be, in a major lobbying effort. This was the organization that had successfully fought to eliminate alien land laws in western states and had effectively challenged constitutionally questionable state laws and discriminatory municipal ordinances throughout the West. And this was the organization that responded so effectively when called upon to support the effort to override President Truman's veto of the 1952 McCarran-Walter Act, also known as the Immigration and Nationality Act, which would provide naturalization rights to the Issei. But McCarran-Walter was almost thirty years in the past; we were a generation removed from any large-action efforts of that nature. We didn't know how well the national JACL chapter network would function as a grassroots lobbying machine. We hoped, and even expected, that we would be able to mobilize our network simply by invoking marching orders, but we wouldn't know until we tried.

Yoshino and I decided we needed to put the chapters to a test, thinking it would only be a matter of fine-tuning the machine in preparation for a full-out grassroots campaign. Chapters were asked to seek resolutions of support for the concept of redress from their city councils and then provide us with copies of the resolutions, which we would use once we began lobbying Congress for redress legislation. The resolutions were important as evidence of the broad constituency support we had in 105 chapters across the country. It seemed a good and solid strategy. City councils, being local entities, were very accessible and were good targets for our grassroots operation. If chapters encountered resistance or outright rejection, so much the better: it gave our members the opportunity to hone their lobbying skills on individual city council members, and if they failed to get the city council resolution in their area, it did us no harm overall; rejections would be for our records only, and we would have measurable information about the level and nature of resistance we would encounter from the congressional representative in that district. But the main objective was to provide experience to our chapter members in order to prepare them for the big fight, which would be pushing our bill in Congress.

In some ways, the JACL was ideally structured for the kind of campaign we were embarking on: we had chapters located throughout the country, but approximately 70 percent of them were in California, where the majority of Japanese Americans lived. Los Angeles had, and continues to have, the largest ethnic Japanese population in the nation, and its influence spreads south down through San Diego and all the way to the Mexican border. The San Francisco Bay Area comes second, with thirty-four chapters making up the region from as far south as Monterey and extending far north and inland beyond Sacramento to the surrounding farm towns. And finally, there was a strong Japanese American presence in the Central Valley along the Highway 99 corridor, where Japanese American farmers established some of the most productive and successful farms and created a monopoly in the truck-farming industry by 1940, one of the primary reasons behind the push to remove the Japanese population from the state.

Beyond California, there was a strong JACL chapter in Portland, Oregon, and several in Washington State. Away from the West Coast, JACL chapters were present in many cities with Japanese American communities: in clusters around the Salt Lake City area; around Denver; in some of the Plains states; a swath in the Midwest, from Ohio and Minneapolis through Chicago to St. Louis; and in the East, with chapters in Boston, New York, New Jersey, and Washington, D.C.

Bill and I wrote a draft resolution for our chapters to adapt as needed and submit to their city councils. To our knowledge, no legislative body, at any level, anywhere in the country, had gone on record criticizing the United States government's WWII policies of exclusion and detention. With our resolution, these cities would be the first to adopt an official position condemning the injustice of the policies enacted against Japanese Americans. Keeping in mind that the vast majority of Americans had yet to be convinced that our treatment was unconstitutional, we were careful in crafting the language of the resolution, and we laid out the arguments in as logical and straightforward a manner as possible.

The resolution strategy was a provocative idea that we expected many, if not most, city councils to find offensive. The resolution sought to push city councils into taking a decisive position as to the constitutional rights of all citizens, but it did not include any mention of monetary compensation. If some of the more progressive city councils wanted to include a supporting statement about reparations, then, yes, by all means, our chapters should work with them to include it. We armed our chapters with the draft resolution and informational packets and asked them to provide us with copies of the resolutions that were successfully adopted.

Within a week of our sending the draft resolution to our chapters, we heard from a number of chapter representatives who expressed reservations about calling on their city council members. Their reasons varied, but most were concerned about their lack of experience in the political arena. Some were gun-shy, and some didn't feel confident that their city council members would even bother with a resolution of this nature when neither they nor their constituents knew anything about the internment. Bill and I discussed this reluctance coming out of our local chapters and realized that while, yes, inexperience in politics was a factor, there was also something more specifically rooted in our community that was holding us back.

To an outsider, such reservations might seem like timidity or lack of confidence, but Bill and I recognized it as the cultural inhibition embodied by the Japanese word *enryo* (to show restraint, reserve, deference to others). It's one of the most fundamental and most deeply felt cultural values in Japanese culture and is very much a part of who we are as Japanese Americans. From the time we're children, we're raised to consider others before ourselves: don't impose yourself on others, don't make them feel uncomfortable, be considerate and aware of how others feel, defer your needs or desires to those of others. It's so fundamental in Japanese American culture that I doubt there are any among us who hasn't heard someone say, "Please, don't *enryo*." Others might interpret it as being submissive, but we see it as being polite and considerate of others. Others may see it as weakness; we know it's part of what makes us better.

It's easy to see why this doesn't translate well to lobbying. *Enryo* directly conflicts with what we were asking our chapter representatives to do: impose their demands on others. But if we wanted to press forward with the campaign, and especially if we wanted to have a chance at getting a bill passed in Congress, we would need to find a way to make it work. We needed our chapters to be both ready and, more importantly, willing to look beyond the boundaries of *enryo* and do what needed to be done. There was no campaign otherwise.

The results that came in were mixed: some chapters were enthusiastic and had pushed their city councils to adopt the resolution, while others never got past the first phone call. When chapters reported that their city councils rejected the resolution or refused to take action on it either way, I saw this as an opportunity for our members to engage in a true lobbying effort by learning to argue facts against what were clearly opinions. If nothing else, it would be good practice for the fights ahead.

Next, we pushed our members to go to their county boards of supervisors with similar resolutions, and once again, we got both positive and negative results. In this second round, some chapters that hadn't participated in the first request came back with successes. Our grassroots machine was getting stronger and more solid.

This effort was really quite remarkable. Many of our members were, for the first time, talking to total strangers about their own experiences during the war—what they had personally endured, not just statistics and talking points. They were asking their local politicians to judge the value of their lives and to judge them as Americans. They risked rejection and humiliation all over again. In essence, they were asking these people to share common ground with them as Americans.

Although our success rate for the resolution campaign was moderate at best, the effort was an important and even critical first step in building the JACL into an effective grassroots lobbying operation. When I think back on that exercise today, from a place of knowing how it all turned out and where we are now, I'm amazed at how far our chapters and members have come since this initiation into grassroots lobbying. Less than a year later, these same JACLers were out on the campaign trail, hustling votes from their congressional representatives. We had laid the groundwork and were becoming a force to be reckoned with. We would not be ignored.

4

THE FIRST LEGISLATIVE FIGHT

(1979 - 1980)

THE WAITING GAME

Once we made our decision to pursue a federal commission on redress, I became impatient to begin the legislative fight. I wanted to further defy all prognosticators who had said we would never get even this far in the process. True, this would not be the battle for the appropriations bill, the battle I really wanted to be fighting, but I knew by this time that the commission strategy would help clear the garbage and political morass from our path—if we could execute it successfully.

By summer 1979, we still had no word from Ron Ikejiri, our man in Washington, that a bill had been drafted, only that Representative Norm Mineta's office was working on it. It was agony waiting, partly because we were eager to start the next phase of our campaign, but also because there were still strong voices in the community critical of our decision and we wanted to quiet them with definitive action.

In early June, I was surprised by a phone call from Senator Spark Matsunaga. My only encounter with him ("Call me Sparky," he insisted) had been observing him in the Big Four meeting earlier that year. He had discounted Senator Daniel Inouye's suggestion of a commission strategy in favor of joining forces with Mineta to take a direct-compensation measure straight to their colleagues, Norm in the House and Sparky in the Senate, and I remembered watching his subtle reactions as Inouye reasserted his idea of the commission. Sparky was calling from his office in Hawaii to assure me that his staff was in communication with Mineta's office on drafting the legislation, and he predicted a bill would be introduced sometime following the summer recess.

"Politics is largely a waiting game," he told me, "like a chess game." He sensed my impatience and was reassuring me that he and Inouye would carry this issue to its conclusion in the Senate. "There's a gestation period for any bill or issue to make its way from an idea to legislation to an act signed by the president." Be patient, he told me. "Be like Buddha; see the end." It was advice that would serve me well in that moment and for the rest of my career dealing with Washington.

As much as I still disliked having to delay our eventual fight for an appropriations bill, my experiences facing mainstream audiences had convinced me that taking the extra step to work through a federal commission was critical if we hoped to succeed. It seemed that the more people learned about our demands for redress, the more they ignored the facts and assumed our guilt and culpability in the war in the Pacific. I knew we would continue to see hostile reactions, that some people would never believe what we were telling them, but it remained important for us to talk about our experiences because that was the only way we could make an impact and discuss the lessons of the internment. We had had some success on national platforms already, but the commission would give us the biggest forum in which to tell our stories, and it would offer us validation of our claim that we were not collateral damage of a justified policy but victims of an unconstitutional and racist policy. I was banking on the commission placing our story on the largest stage possible.

I finally got word at the end of July 1979 that a bill had been drafted by Mineta's office and was circulating among the Big Four. The strategy in terms of language for both the House and Senate versions was to have parallel language as a way to facilitate reconciling the House and Senate versions of the bill once approved in each chamber. A conference committee, made up of equal numbers of members from each house, would meet to iron out the differences, and then, once reconciled, a single bill would require a vote of each chamber for final approval. Every additional step in the process created an obstacle that slowed things down, so a bill with duplicate language would avoid one extra procedural step. For the same reason, it would be up to the sponsors of the bill to fight off amendments being added in each house.

The so-called commission bill, as it finally evolved, sought the following: to establish a federal commission to be named the Commission on Wartime Relocation and Internment of Civilians (CWRIC); to examine the facts and circumstances that led to the issuance of Executive Order 9066 and the policies to exclude and detain American citizens and legal residents of Japanese ancestry; and to present to Congress and the White House a report of findings and conclusions, and, if warranted, to provide recommendation of remedies. The bill also sought an appropriation of $3 million to accomplish its task.

We, the JACL, on behalf of all Japanese Americans, were rolling the dice. After what we had experienced at the whim of the government during the war, we were now daring to put our fates in the hands of yet another government entity, with the expectation that it could, and would, be fair and just. Based on the research I had done at the National Archives in D.C., however, I was convinced that an objective examination of wartime documents would lead to only one conclusion: that we were the victims of a racist policy that could not be justified by facts.

For good reason, the Japanese American community was skeptical about the outcome of such a strategy. The entire history of Asians in this country was one of mistreatment and being lied to and lied about, perpetually the victims of institutional racism. Given this history of over one hundred years of mistreatment in this country, the community wondered what made us think this time would be any different. Why, suddenly, would this country even give a damn about us and what we demanded? Everyone was certain that the commission would take an inordinately long time before beginning its work and then get bogged down in delays that would result in a half-hearted body doing a half-assed job to complete its mission. Or better yet, it would delay long enough and then most of us would be dead and gone, and then where would that leave our community?

Against this atmosphere of doubt, we needed to muster as much support as we could among Japanese Americans. The problem, of course, were the divisions that remained in the community, on both this issue and our chosen strategy. Even if we had the entire Japanese American community in support of redress as an issue, our numbers at best would have seemed quixotic for a major political campaign: Japanese Americans comprised fewer than one half of one percent of the entire population of the United States—we numbered 650,000 according to the 1970 census, a number so small that we were, statistically, insignificant as a political cohort. The even greater challenge was that while a substantial part of the Japanese American community still opposed the very idea of redress, of those who supported, many remained critical of the JACL's decision to pursue the federal commission strategy; more than half of the chapters were opposed to it. As an organization with a membership of approximately 28,000, it was disheartening to know that even this small of a group was further divided. Full support of the commission strategy was an even smaller piece of the population pie; we had just a sliver of the community pushing this effort. The hard reality we faced was that we had only a handful of chapters that would form the core of our grassroots efforts. Fortunately for us, the Midwest and East districts were part of that small cadre of chapters that became the heart of our grassroots machine.

As we awaited our plunge into the legislative fight, Clifford and I looked at the available data and concluded that, yes, our numbers were ridiculously small. Regardless, this group of dedicated legislative warriors was going to fight for the bill to establish a federal commission that would conduct a historical investigation of the World War II policies of the U.S. government. I continue to be amazed that such a small group of politically gun-shy amateur activist citizens had the will to take on such a daunting challenge.

With the language of the bill drafted, the next step was designating principal sponsors for both the House and Senate bills. In the Senate, Inouye and Matsunaga were the obvious choice to be coauthors and principal sponsors because they had the political credentials that would serve the intent of the strategy. Both were World War II veterans, both had worked as public servants for years, and both were highly respected and liked by their colleagues.

Ikejiri and I met with the two senators to talk about legislative strategies. They agreed that it would be best to introduce the Senate bill first and let its momentum carry over to the House. Sparky estimated that he and Inouye could get no fewer than fifty and as many as seventy-five members, or three-fourths of, the Senate to support the bill, but they would probably introduce it with only a handful of sponsors to move it strategically toward a vote. The precise numbers didn't really matter, Matsunaga explained, because sometimes congresspeople feel obligated to sign on as cosponsors but then they don't necessarily vote in favor of the bill. Quality, not quantity—at least initially—was what we wanted, he explained. The main thing was to get the commission bill into the hopper and get it passed as early as possible in order to start the gears rolling, and then he and Inouye would find ways to ensure that a follow-up compensation bill would get the necessary votes. He would work his colleagues to try to get a comfortable margin over the required fifty-one-vote majority.

Inouye suggested that he and Sparky could arrange for the Senate bill to be referred to the Committee on Governmental Affairs, which, before it became part of the Department of Homeland Security in 2004, did exactly what its title stated: examine the conduct and actions of the executive and legislative branches of government. The committee was chaired by Senator Henry Martin "Scoop" Jackson (D-Washington), a close ally to both Inouye and Matsunaga. Jackson had already agreed to cosponsor the bill and would work closely with Inouye and Matsunaga to move the bill at an appropriate time, and then Inouye and Matsunaga could get the legislation to a floor vote fairly rapidly. Having momentum from the Senate bill would help the cause of the companion bill in the House, where we would encounter the most resistance. The Senate, Inouye and Matsunaga agreed, was a more manageable body than the House, with only 100 senators to deal with compared to 435 House members—who were often cantankerous, according to Inouye.

As an aside, Inouye noted that we ought to get Senator S. I. Hayakawa onto the bill, a move I personally found objectionable, even as I understood it was a reasonable strategy. Inouye knew that Hayakawa and I had gone at each other on a live-televised program in Los Angeles in 1980 and suggested that I shouldn't be anywhere close to their meeting with him. On that particular program, I had shared my astonishment at how a senator and self-professed Japanese American (he was born in Canada) could be so ignorant of the facts; his response was to scold me for my lack of respect for him as a United States senator. "On the contrary," I responded, "I have tremendous respect for the office… if not for the man." He rose from his chair, glaring at me, and the program moderator went to a commercial break to cool things down on the set. Inouye had contacted me within a few hours after that program to congratulate me on keeping my head, but he warned me against further provoking those whose support we needed.

It was decided that Ikejiri would arrange the meeting, thus sparing either Inouye or Matsunaga the indignity of it seeming as if they were acquiescing to Hayakawa by asking to meet with him. But the bigger surprise was that the meeting took place in Hayakawa's office. I was dumbfounded to see it happen that way because Inouye and Matsunaga both held more rank over Hayakawa. Sparky explained that they would play on Hayakawa's ego to get him to sign on to the Senate bill. I hoped it would work.

Ikejiri and I conferred later with Mineta and Matsui about the timing on the House bill. No doubt Mineta had already talked to both Inouye and Matsunaga and seemed to want to hear from us how the JACL felt about this strategy to have the House bill follow the one in the Senate. That seemed logical to us because whatever problems Inouye and Matsunaga faced in the Senate would be fourfold in the House, with its larger body of representatives. To say that he sought our approval would be stretching it, but like Inouye and Matsunaga, he did us the courtesy of at least letting us feel we were part of the decision-making process. Neither Ron nor I had any illusions about who was in charge here, but this entire enterprise to seek redress was as personal for Mineta as it was for the rest of the community; we all had a lot at stake in making this work.

The Senate bill would go first, and in the meantime, before the introduction of a House version, all four of us would try to get as many cosponsors as possible, with an eye on Mineta rallying as many influential Republicans as he could. While the sheer number of 435 House members presented a challenge for our grassroots campaign, we could simplify our task by supporting Mineta's effort to have the bill referred to the House subcommittee that mirrored the one to which the Senate bill had been referred. Both commission bills had been drafted to focus on constitutional and government action in order to get them referred to their respective Judiciary subcommittees, which would simplify their progress, the theory being that as one bill moves, it gives incentive to move the other. The next important factor was that the Senate Judiciary Committee was chaired by Ted Kennedy (D-Massachusetts), who looked favorably on our effort, and that beneficial atmosphere was mirrored in the House, where Peter Rodino (D-New Jersey), a legendary figure in his own right, chaired the House Judiciary Committee. If the bills got similar subcommittee referrals, our task would be to get hearings on the bills, and then get them out of their respective subcommittees.

After working through all these calculations, Mineta suggested that he and Bob attempt to convince Jim Wright (D-Texas) to author the House bill. Wright was the majority leader in the House and closely aligned with House Speaker Tip O'Neill (D-Massachusetts). Wright would bring a lot of clout to the bill, and his being from the southern part of the country might help soften some of the resistance we anticipated from that region. Mineta indicated that together they could probably get as many as one hundred cosponsors on the bill by the time of its introduction.

Getting Wright to carry the bill was an interesting strategy because as majority leader he was, of course, one of the most powerful members of the House of Representatives, and his endorsement would ensure strong Democratic support. There was also an added symbolism in having his name as a principal on the bill. He represented the Austin, Texas, area, and those who knew their World War II history, as Wright did, knew that the all–Japanese American 442nd Regimental Combat Team had rescued the 1st Battalion of the 36th Division, formerly the Texas National Guard. The 1st Battalion, which came to be known as the Texas Lost Battalion, had been cut off and surrounded by crack German troops in the Vosges Mountains and was close to being annihilated. With the Texas battalion in a desperate fight for survival, and after U.S. forces had made numerous failed attempts to break through the German lines to get to them, the 442nd was called in. After five days of fierce fighting, the 442nd finally rescued the battalion, although at a heavy cost. They suffered over 800 casualties to rescue about 230 men; the ranks of the 442nd were decimated in what has since gone down in U.S. military history as one of the great battles of the war.

Wright, who had fought with the Air Force during the war, knew this history and felt personally indebted to the men of the 442nd for their sacrifices and heroism. He didn't have to be reminded that members of the 442nd had found their way to the European front lines via the internment camps, and I knew from my conversations with him that he felt deeply about the heroic sacrifices of the 442nd.

While Wright and many others who had fought in the war may have been familiar with these facts, the story of the 442nd and the internment of Japanese Americans was still largely unknown, even to members of the United States Congress. Most would have only a vague idea about the experience of Japanese Americans during World War II, and as Ike-jiri and I began lobbying the House, it was apparent that most knew very little, if anything, and what they did know was often based on misinformation. Yet again, we faced people who were adamant that Japanese Americans had either deserved their wartime incarceration or were simply unfortunate victims of a difficult but necessary decision handed down by the president. After all, the Supreme Court had affirmed the government's policies, and that was enough for most people to dispel any arguments about the constitutionality of the order.

Because of such attitudes, we knew we were in trouble in the House even before the bill was introduced. In a carefully considered strategy, Norm talked to Speaker O'Neill about getting the bill referred to the powerful House Judiciary Committee, chaired by Peter Rodino. Norm said that if we got the first bill, the one establishing a federal commission, assigned to the House Judiciary Committee, whatever money bill followed later on would likely be referred there as well. He said we'd have a better chance with Judiciary than, say, Ways and Means, where most bills died. Plus, the Judiciary Committee seemed an appropriate route, since the language of the bill intentionally focused on the question of constitutional authority.

When I checked the long list of almost forty members who sat on the House Judiciary Committee, I was familiar with at least half of them, so I had an idea of what we faced. Norm and Bob obviously would lobby their party colleagues on the committee, but the JACL's responsibility, with its diminished numbers supporting the commission strategy, would be to work the members who needed more persuading. Most of the Republicans were unwavering in their opposition, but some of them supported the bill; likewise, most Democrats were on our side, but there were also some hard nuts to crack, like Texans Jack Brooks and Sam Hall, Mike Synar from Oklahoma, and Lawrence Smith from Florida, all influential members of the Judiciary Committee.

Although working with the Judiciary Committee promised to be less challenging than working against the strong opposition in the House at large, it would still be a major undertaking. To make the process more manageable, we focused on the subcommittee to which the House bill had been referred, the Subcommittee on Administrative Law and Governmental Relations, chaired by Sam Hall. It was, as planned, a referral parallel to that in the Senate, and in many ways it was a perfect example of the differences we would face in the two chambers: in the Senate we had Scoop Jackson, a friend and supporter, and in the House, Sam Hall, who had made it known that he opposed the bill.

———

The focus of our campaign now moved away from educating the public and toward legislation (although I knew that, at least through my lifetime, we would never stop educating the public as long as there were racists and bigots who resented our presence in America and would not accept us as equal). We had made great strides with our grassroots efforts thus far and I could only hope we would continue to do so, although I had my doubts. We still had only a small part of the JACL membership supporting the commission strategy, and I wasn't at all sure that our grassroots lobbying operation was going to work. We had learned a lot about the process when lobbying city council members and county supervisors, but I didn't know if we had enough bodies out there in the JACL rank and file to push two bills from the bottom to the top, from grassroots to Congress.

And yet here we were, already defying the odds, and this was only one year into Clifford's tenure as president and my tenure as the redress chair. In that period, we had established a national platform from which to awaken the nation to the facts about the internment, and now we were going to push a bill through Congress, even though it was seriously handicapped by majority opposition from within the JACL's membership, not to mention within the larger Japanese American community. We truly were only a handful strong inside the JACL, but now that we had reached this point in our quest of an impossible dream, I began to believe we had a real chance of going all the way. I knew that if we succeeded getting this first bill through Congress, we would change the way Americans viewed our wartime experience and begin to shatter the dark myths and stereotypes that continued to shadow our community. For the first time in almost thirty years, the JACL was going to enter the legislative arena and fight for what felt, in some ways, like an existential battle for our place in America.

INTRODUCTION OF THE
COMMISSION BILL

Call me naïve, but at the beginning of this process I thought our bill to form a federal commission was so benign it would easily pass. It sought no more than to create an investigative commission whose purpose would be to examine the circumstances that led to an incident in the nation's past, and what was there to fear about the truth?

A great deal, apparently. It's amazing how viciously those in power will fight to keep the truth in the dark.

On August 2, 1979, exactly 151 days after the JACL National Committee for Redress had made its fateful decision to pursue the commission strategy, the Senate commission bill (S. 1647) was introduced. It was authored by Dan Inouye, with Spark Matsunaga, S. I. Hayakawa, and Ted Stevens (R-Alaska) as principal sponsors. The surprise was Hayakawa; unbeknownst to many, Inouye and Matsunaga had cajoled him into putting his name on the bill as a sponsor, despite his opposition to redress! Getting Ted Stevens to sponsor the bill was a strategic move; as chairman of the Senate Appropriations Subcommittee on Defense when his party was in power (Inouye was chair when the Democrats controlled the Senate), he held great influence among his fellow Republicans. Stevens's inclusion as a principal sponsor would do much to defuse Republican opposition in the Senate.

Although the bill was introduced with only six sponsors, Sparky, true to his word, had hustled and lined up eighty committed votes in favor of the bill. Its passage in the Senate was a done deal so long as it was given a hearing and made it out of committee.

The following month, on September 28, 1979, the House bill (H.R. 5499) was introduced, with Majority Leader Jim Wright of Texas as the author and principal sponsor of the bill. Mineta and Matsui could easily have put their names as coauthors of the bill, but the symbolic value of having the House majority leader as the bill's main proponent was an important signal to fellow House members that this bill had personal significance to him, not to mention the symbolism of having a Texan honor the 442nd in this way. The bill was eventually dropped in the hopper with 114 cosponsors, an incredibly large number for a bill whose intent focused on a past government action that, on the surface, appeared potentially controversial.

The serious grassroots lobbying in the House would now begin.

As we toiled at getting support for the commission bill, Mike Lowry (D-Washington), on behalf of the Seattle Japanese American coalition, introduced a money bill (H.R. 5977) that sought $15,000 in a lump sum plus $15 per day of internment for individual victims. This was a remnant of the old Seattle Bootstrap Plan, which had been rejected three times by the JACL, and it caught those of us in the JACL leadership completely by surprise; we had heard no mention of the bill and had no idea that Lowry's office was working on it. "Blindsided" most accurately describes how we felt about the situation.

Lowry had the right to introduce any bill he wanted, of course, but what puzzled me was that he must have known that his bill was doomed from the outset. Mineta said not to worry about it, but Matsui, as a new congressman, did not hide his displeasure and made it clear that he was not one to be toyed with. He was infuriated with Lowry's bill because it provided the members of Congress a way to side-step our redress bill.

As it turned out, a significant number of those behind the Lowry bill were JACL members, a discovery that was problematic because we were trying to speak on behalf of the community and here they were acting contrary to official JACL policy, which had been dictated by the National Council and further guided by the National Board. I talked at length with Clifford several times and suggested imposing sanctions on the Seattle-based chapters that supported this legislation. A sanction had no enforcement consequence and was essentially nothing more than a public chastisement, but I felt we needed to make clear that the national JACL in no way supported the Seattle proposal, and that those chapters were acting in defiance of the organization's policy decisions. I personally thought their move was naïve and that the pro-redress rationalization they gave—that they wanted a direct-compensation option—

was absolute hogwash. They were jeopardizing the bill that the Japanese American members of Congress had agreed unanimously was the most prudent approach.

Lowry's bill did not go away, but, ultimately, it proved to be little more than a distraction. It may not have seemed that way for those of us, Matsui included, who—unlike Mineta—had little experience on the Hill, but we were generally able to push the matter aside and turn our focus again to getting our own bill through Congress.

THE OPENING ROUNDS

In the year since the JACL's National Committee for Redress had made its decision to pursue a federal commission, the cacophony of protests leveled at us persisted and made me wonder to what end the criticisms and accusations were being made. My committee had chosen the commission strategy, the JACL's National Board had accepted and approved our recommendation, and the JACL chapters had ratified the decision. After that agonizing process, did our critics think we would consider revisiting the decision and changing our minds? No, of course they didn't. Their criticism was simply condemnation. They said that in choosing to have a federal commission go through a pointless exercise to determine the causes for the wartime policies against us, we had taken the easy way out, the coward's way. They accused Senator Inouye of misguiding us to a meaningless route, and they accused Norm Mineta of caving in to Inouye and turning his back on the community when it mattered, lacking any courage at all.

In the six months between our decision to pursue the commission strategy and the introduction of the commission bills in the House and Senate, the vehemence of the criticism never faded, never wavered, and in fact intensified. But now that the bills had been introduced, our opposition became moot, merely background noise. The issue was beyond debate, and there was no going back. Frankly, shifting our focus to D.C. and the legislative battle that lay ahead was a welcome change from the constant barrage of local hostility.

Our attention now turned to the matter of forming a lobbying team. We had a full-time D.C. lobbyist in Ron Ikejiri, and the expectation was that he would work with us on the redress bills. But he also had a full plate of other issues that were priorities on the JACL's action agenda. Immigration was an increasingly important concern facing the Asian community overall, including refugee issues brought on by the end of America's war in Vietnam as well as the further growth of the U.S. Asian population following the passage of the Immigration and Nationality Act of 1965. The trade war with Japan continued to manifest in increased violence against Asian Americans, and there were regular attacks on civil liberties through various legislative initiatives that sought to limit our rights. As the only Asian American civil rights organization with an established record and longevity in D.C. at that time, the JACL, and Ikejiri in particular, was constantly dealing with issues affecting the rights of the nation's ethnic minorities and its noncitizen immigrants, not to mention collaborating with other civil rights organizations to strategize on ways to protect vulnerable cohorts in minority population groups. While redress was one of the major programs on the JACL's agenda, if not *the* priority, these other matters were of equal importance to the JACL's Washington presence, and Ikejiri therefore could not devote himself to our campaign full time.

Back in San Francisco at the JACL's headquarters, Clifford, Karl, and I agreed that we needed a lobbyist dedicated specifically to the redress bill, and for obvious reasons we felt the best person would be a Japanese American. Mike Masaoka was our first candidate, and he would have been a logical choice. He was by then a forty-year veteran of Washington lobbying, was well known and highly respected by many members of both the Senate and the House, had a personal connection with Mineta (they were brothers-in-law), and was close to Inouye and Matsunaga (all veterans of the 442nd Regimental Combat Team). He was familiar to, and highly respected by, the top civil rights advocates in Washington, and no living person in this country could match his knowledge on the political machinations related to the internment. Being the controversial figure he was, however, Mike would have brought some pretty heavy baggage with him into this issue, and while that didn't matter so much in D.C., we agreed that it would negatively influence how the Japanese American community would perceive our campaign. It would come down to the issue of trust, which was already on thin ice given how the commission strategy decision had gone down.

Nobuyuki pointed out, only half-joking, that hiring Mike to be our lobbyist on this bill would just be asking him to do up front what he was going to do behind the scenes anyway. There was no question in any of our minds that Masaoka, whether he was our hired lobbyist or not, would use his considerable skills and influence to insinuate himself in the process to control the redress lobbying effort, but we also knew he would never allow himself to be our "deep throat," our contact on the inside, because it would relegate him to an advisory role, giving him too little leverage. For Karl, Clifford, and me, it came down to where we thought Mike could do his best work. Clifford pointed out that ultimately it didn't matter if we hired Mike because he would help us no matter what. No one in that room doubted for a second that Mike would not only aid but probably control much of what happened in our fight for redress, and we would probably never know about it. One thing we knew for certain: he would be the constant in the campaign, regardless of who thought he or she was the brains behind it, and that included the three of us. We laughed to realize that Mike probably didn't realize we understood this about him; it was one of those amusing "he didn't know that we knew that he knew" situations. It's a good thing we weren't in it for the power and didn't take ourselves too seriously!

The question for the three of us was whether we could afford a professional lobbyist. In the end, with the JACL's limited budget, we decided against such a move. We determined that I would have principal responsibility for lobbying any and all redress matters, in concert with Ikejiri in the Washington office. I had extensive knowledge about the World War II experience; I had faced hostile public audiences, so dealing with elected officials would be no problem; and we assumed my teaching schedule would be flexible enough to allow me to devote time in Washington. In reality it wasn't, but I would find a way to manage it.

I thus became the JACL's principal redress advocate in Washington; Karl informed Ron and the JACL's regional offices throughout the country, Cliff notified the National Board, and I set about to arrange my teaching schedule in such a way that I would be able to spend a considerable amount of time in Washington for part of the year. Though I didn't realize it at the time, it was, for me, a transitional time moving from teaching to lobbying. Both during and after the redress campaign, I would end up spending most of my professional career doing business in Washington, advocating on civil rights issues, working on public-policy matters, and lobbying. It set me on a road I never expected to go down on my life's journey.

On average, there used to be anywhere from five thousand to twenty thousand bills introduced in each session of Congress, and just about every one of those bills represented the welfare of one group or another, whether private industry or public interest. Most bills die through the natural process of attrition, and so most bills that made it through Congress, at least in the 1970s and '80s, usually—but not always—had bipartisan support. It's rare that any bill gets through the gauntlet of sub-committees and committees and the amendment process and the seemingly endless procedural obstacles of both houses of Congress without powerful lobbying interests behind it, either through the representation of high-powered lobbyists or a broad, deep public interest. And then, even if a bill finds its way to the president's desk for signature, there's always the possibility of death via presidential veto, or through simply being ignored. The bills that stay alive through the entire process and eventually earn the president's signature, however, become part of the canon of federal law and are contained in volumes that line the walls of law libraries and law offices across the country. For good reason, Mineta used to say that the two things you don't want to watch being made were sausages and legislation!

This was the world I was entering and learning to understand, but although it was daunting, I was happy to be there. All the work that had come before had brought us to this moment. This was the battle for which we had been preparing.

Norm Mineta would carry the bill for us in the House, and we would coordinate with his office to assist in any way we could. We were confident his influence and the respect he generated among his colleagues would get this bill passed. Bob Matsui, having just been elected, was new to the job and therefore limited in what he could do, but he was ambitious and determined to make his mark. Because they were both Japanese American, Matsui purposely charted his course separate from Mineta and generally away from Japanese American and Asian American issues, which he would leave to Norm. He had his own agenda to carry him up the political ladder; he was not about to play second fiddle to Mineta.

It wasn't the best time for a rivalry to begin, but it did make for some intriguing drama. Matsui, for some reason, made it almost a competition for who could gain the most support on the bill, and everyone noticed. I never talked to Mineta about any of this (we never had that kind of relationship), but Ron told me once that Norm seemed amused by it all. In 1981, his second term in office, Matsui would gain prominence when he managed to get assigned to the Ways and Means Committee, one of the most powerful committees of the House. Little by little, he made his way, and over the next twenty-five years, until his death in 2005, he showed just how effective he could be as a politician.

Normally, the way to lobby a bill is to target key members of the committees and subcommittees to which it gets assigned, plus any non–committee members who have considerable influence among their colleagues on either side of the political aisle. Not to be ignored, ever, are the subcommittee chair, the ranking minority member, and, in most cases, the committee counsel (a staff position). The chair, whether of the subcommittee or full committee, is critical to woo, of course, because if the chair dislikes a bill, he or she can simply not place it on the hearing schedule or ignore it at a markup session, basically refusing to breathe life into the legislation. Meanwhile, it's also important to lobby every member of a committee because a majority vote is required for a bill to get pushed to the next level of inquiry. From subcommittee to full committee to the full chamber, whether House or Senate, and at every step of the process, the dynamics are similar: you need the support of the chair, the ranking minority member, the other key members, and the majority.

When I started to lobby subcommittee members on the commission bill, I was keenly aware of how uninformed and sometimes downright ignorant the public was on the matter of internment. But even as I began my work in Washington, I expected those who worked in the offices of the United States Congress to be more informed, more intelligent, more insightful about the significance of the constitutional implications of our treatment. Even if they were biased either for or against redress, I expected they would at least have the basic facts down.

Not so. Not by a long shot.

The first person who usually sees a bill is a congressperson's administrative assistant (or chief of staff) or the legislative director, the one who oversees and directs the legislative work in the office. When our commission bill was introduced, many of the AAs and LDs had no idea what this bill was even about. And then, after they had seen the bill and read the opening contents of the intent of the proposal, many seemed unable to get beyond the word "Japanese." As often as not, I walked into an office for the first time to find that the staff was confused about which aide should handle this issue. Sometimes the bill was sent to aides assigned to U.S.–Japan trade issues, or aides who dealt with immigration, or Asia-Pacific bilateral issues, or defense or intelligence or criminal justice ("internment" being the operative word in the last case). I was told more than once that this bill belonged in the Senate because it was a foreign-relations issue. One person said the referral should have been to the House Committee on Natural Resources because that was the committee that was handling Japan's defiance of the worldwide moratorium on commercial whaling. In most of these cases, it was a guessing game for the congressional staffers, and most of them guessed the bill was about Japan, not Japanese American citizens. I had to explain, time and again, that this was a proposal dealing with constitutional matters and that the bill was properly referred to the Subcommittee on Governmental Affairs, which fell under the Judiciary. After working through the confusion and getting the bill to the proper aide, the next challenge was often dealing with the incredulity or skepticism of a legislative aide who, whether out of ignorance or bias, seemed unable to comprehend what could possibly have been wrong with our wartime treatment.

As lobbyists, we figured we would have to visit every single office in the House, all 435 members, in order to straighten things out because we could not assume members or their staffs would be familiar enough with the issue to handle it properly. There were plenty of offices where aides were either informed or interested in learning more, and we would sometimes be surprised that the unlikeliest of offices understood the issues behind the legislation. On the other hand, and not unexpectedly, we encountered many offices—and some even of West Coast representatives—who were still being led by their biases rather than by the facts. I still couldn't believe how much resistance we were seeing for a bill that sought nothing more than the formation of a commission to study what, to most people, was an insignificant historical event. Overall, we assumed we would have some degree of push-back, and we were always grateful when we were unexpectedly met with understanding.

While we tried to figure out how best to work the House, Matsunaga and Inouye continued building support for the Senate bill. They said they wanted to try to get the bill approved by spring of 1980, which meant we had a short window of possibly six months for working the House bill if we were to stay abreast of the Senate bill, and we would not have time to visit all 435 offices in our initial lobbying effort. We eliminated over 100 offices as either clear supporters or those dead set against the bill, and in consulting with Glenn Roberts, Mineta's brilliant legislative director, we eliminated another 50 or so members whom Norm would contact directly. That winnowed our number down to approximately 280.

As I focused on key members, I encountered many congressional representatives who were opposed to the idea of a commission simply because they found no fault with the government's treatment of Japanese Americans during the war. Some even took offense because the very idea that the government had done something wrong was seen as an attack on a great president who had saved the nation in a time of crisis. They were the same arguments, based on the same misinformation, that I had encountered in all my public speaking on the internment, and the racist reasoning behind it all was the same as that which had led to the internment in the first place. Just as it had been with the audiences I had educated on air and in meetings and public events, my challenge was to begin the process of chipping away at the "facts" as they understood them and to force a wedge of truth into their misinformed beliefs.

———

Unlike many other bills that move through Congress, ours was not a party-line issue, meaning partisanship usually prevails over doing what is right. While Democrats were more inclined to support the bill, there were Southern Democrats who stood staunchly against it, and likewise, there were Republicans who didn't reject it outright and were even willing to consider its merits. Thus, I focused my lobbying efforts on both Democrats and Republicans who I thought could be persuaded to support the commission bill. Because this bill made no mention of the huge monetary package we hoped to introduce in later bills, I found we had more opportunity to debate not the outcome of the bill so much as the political, social, and philosophical issues behind it. I knew these debates would pay huge dividends when it was finally time to introduce the monetary compensation bill.

It's easy to say in retrospect that the commission bill was hardly the challenge the compensation bill was later, and there's a good deal of truth to that. But in my experience of lobbying both bills, the commission bill faced unexpectedly huge challenges because we were bringing a *new* issue to Congress and had not yet built members' sympathy to our cause. Some members worried that supporting the bill could be misconstrued by their constituents as support for Japan, or as a vote in favor of ignoring the wartime treachery of Japan. Others, of course, thought our wartime imprisonment was perfectly justified. It was also easy to see that some congressional offices just didn't like us and resented what we were doing in stirring this particular pot.

I had some very gratifying success in convincing many members to at least *consider* the possibility that our arguments were valid, pointing out that, if this bill won congressional approval, they would be able to examine the findings produced by the commission and make up their own minds. Although some needed more convincing than others, I liked their willingness to keep an open mind and, more importantly, I appreciated their deep concern that America maintain its integrity as a democracy. I talked to people from both sides of the aisle who felt that partisanship should not get in the way of uncovering truths about our nation's conduct.

There were, of course, both Democrats and Republicans who remained dogmatic and closed minded in their opposition, willing to obfuscate truth and fact in favor of what they needed to believe, which was that the United States was morally infallible. They were as yet unwilling to admit that we as a nation are in fact fallible and have made regrettable mistakes in the past, and that our greatness is measured in part by how we face the truths of our darker moments.

I found it ironic how much time and effort I spent debating the merits of the arguments for or against the internment, despite the fact that the purpose of our bill was to create a commission to investigate the very subject about which we were arguing! It was the horse and cart trying to get ahead of each other, and yet there was no avoiding it because the aides to whom we were talking obviously needed to understand the issue before they could be effective allies. They needed to be able to justify to their bosses—meaning the congresspeople—why they were either recommending or rejecting consideration of the legislation and, for those who remained opposed, on what basis their bosses would explain to Mineta the reason for the negative vote, knowing full well how personal this particular issue was to Norm as a camp survivor.

It was an exhausting process, but we soon began to see the fruits of our labor, both in D.C. and at the grassroots level. It was always gratifying to walk into an opposition office, see an aide with whom I'd become acquainted, and have him or her tell me, sometimes grudgingly, that our JACL members had done a good job in their home district of convincing the boss, who had changed his or her position on our bill. Sometimes a representative would tell me that he had changed his thinking on the issue after reading our material. "You'll have my vote" was always such an exhilarating thing to hear from someone who had started out strongly opposed. It didn't happen often, but it happened enough to keep us encouraged and plugging away at the opposition. Each conversion got us one vote closer to our commission, one more vote that would open doors toward our ultimate goal of redress.

COULD A NATION JUDGE ITSELF?

Despite the odds against our succeeding at each phase of the campaign—from reaching across the country to educate the majority of Americans, to succeeding with our initial bill, to publicizing the findings of a commission (assuming we got that far), to having the president sign a monetary compensation bill (again, assuming we got that far)—I was determined that we would succeed at each turn, even if success didn't mean fully achieving the demands of the Salt Lake City Guidelines. We had already begun to change the way Americans viewed Japanese Americans and our wartime experiences, and as much as I wanted to take our demands all the way to the president, I would consider our campaign a success if, when it was all over, Japanese Americans would be free of the guilt and shame with which they—*we*—had lived for four decades. I would do everything I could to accomplish this.

Although part of my lobbying strategy was to point out the benign nature of a bill that sought simply to open an investigation into the internment, it was no secret that our ultimate goal was monetary restitution. The JACL had made our intent public on that subject, and we were in no way attempting to mask it. The thrust of our lobbying was insistence that our imprisonment was unjust and therefore needed to be addressed; the commission would examine the facts objectively and determine whether we were right. To those who were confident in their opposition and certain that EO 9066 was entirely justified, we asked them what had they to lose? If they were right, the federal commission would prove it. As for the cost, the $3 million authorized for the commission was less than the cost of paving a mile of highway.

One of my greatest challenges as someone new to lobbying was that, as an advocate of a cause, I could not tell a representative or even an aide that he was naïve, stupid, bigoted, or any of the other faults I encountered on the Hill. I knew most of the people I was dealing with had been to law school, and most were even familiar with the landmark

Japanese American cases *Korematsu* and *Hirabayashi*, but I saw, time and again, that knowledge did not necessarily translate into wisdom. And some of them were simply operating from a place of fear: many congresspeople and their aides seemed to feel threatened by what secrets might be revealed by a federal commission investigation.

If anything, their arguments became more nuanced. They worried about setting a bad precedent by allowing a group to criticize the government and the president in this way. They were concerned that bringing such matters to light was not in the nation's best interest. They rejected the idea that this or any other generation should pay for the sins of past generations. In our case, it was a simple case of national security: Japan had bombed Pearl Harbor, and the government had to keep the nation safe, as well as keep Japanese Americans safe from the hysterical mobs on the West Coast. That rationale invariably begged the question, Why is it that we, the innocent victims of a crime, were the ones imprisoned while those who threatened us went free? If I point a gun at you and threaten your life, should you go to prison so you can be safe from me while I remain free? It was a senseless and, to be quite candid, stupid rationale, not unlike most of the arguments directed against us. I loathed the idea that we had been imprisoned for our own good; it was such a condescending insult. Some of the aides seemed to be driven by a need to find an excuse for our wartime treatment. Even if our imprisonment was a mistaken judgment, some would say, yes, it was regrettable but, well, many past misjudgments were too.

Little wonder that every political pundit who commented on our issue said we had no chance in hell of ever getting our bill through the grueling process of Congress.

At the heart of it all, even beyond what the cause meant to the Japanese American community, was that the commission would address an essential issue: Could a nation judge itself? Could it judge fairly and objectively an event that was buried so deeply in emotion and nationalism and anger that, even after almost forty years, it still evoked the collective passion and outrage that it had in the moment the country learned of Pearl Harbor, and in the hours and days, and indeed weeks and years, that followed?

For someone to accept that Japanese Americans were disloyal, or at least felt questionable loyalty, to this country, he or she would have to accept that all of those imprisoned—the elderly and infirm, children and infants—were all somehow also culpable. How else could you justify the imprisonment of those groups under armed guards? If you dared to argue—as some did—that the imprisonment of children was actually a humane act because it kept families together, don't you then have to wonder why the government didn't move families to states in the interior of the country, where they could remain free, rather than to camps, where they lived behind barbed wire and under the surveillance of armed guards? What it came down to was that a prison was a prison, regardless of whatever awkward rationales people might make to call them anything else.

Since there were no defined criteria for our imprisonment other than race—a clear infringement of our constitutional rights as American citizens—how can you accept so flagrant a violation of the very ideals upon which the nation was founded? If your argument is that people of Japanese descent were a threat to the security of the nation, you would have to show definitive and *a priori* evidence of their involvement in *Japan's* effort against the United States, or produce specific evidence proving that each of these Japanese American individuals was guilty of action against the country. And if you think there *was* evidence that could somehow prove the guilt of an entire community, why were Japanese Americans not given the right of a fair trial to prove their innocence? If you argue that the government could not know who among the Japanese American population *might* prove to be disloyal, and therefore the only safe measure was to imprison every person of Japanese ancestry, regardless of the Constitution and the guaranteed protections of American citizens and legal resident aliens, the logical conclusion of that argument is that what the Constitution says does not matter and its promise of certain inalienable rights is meaningless.

In retrospect, it may seem that passing a bill to create a commission would have been easy. After all, there was no demand for huge sums of money. This was a bill simply to create a study commission. But the subject of our incarceration was so new that the fact of our imprisonment alone brought about responses that surprised us. Rather than question how or why it could have happened, in some offices it seemed to harden the reaction against us, as if to assume our guilt. I realized that initiating a discussion on the commission bill with a measured approach was critical lest knee-jerk reactions closed minds on the issue. In a time when intelligent discourse was the means by which opposing sides reached compromises and was the political tool for laboring over challenging legislation that would serve the interest of the nation, it was important that the offices we lobbied remain open to us. But I was keenly aware that, in that Congress, memories of the war in the Pacific still lingered, and the strident dissonance of the trade war was the sound of caution for many. We were also mindful that by 1978 there was a growing movement that called itself the Moral Majority, which signaled the emergence of a new conservatism in the country. For us, the combination of a religious conservatism and the sense of patriotism borne of memories of World War II demanded an awareness in how we broached the subject in our initial endeavors with Congress. We were there to open minds, not close them.

In the aftermath of the civil rights movement, we were a nation in which ideas about race were still evolving and, for many in the majority, were still disrupting their sense of well-being. The movement had opened the door of self-examination and brought about a new acceptance of racial differences, but for some in the majority that revolutionary concept raised the deep-seated fear that those who had suffered injustices at the hands of the majority were now a threat to the security of mainstream Americans. And therein lay the power of the redress movement: we dared now to speak out about our unjust treatment, and we dared now to make demands, even if they threatened the assumptions the majority of Americans held about us.

Within a week of my starting to lobby the commission bill, I was relieved of any doubt I had about the wisdom of following this strategy versus the option to directly pursue an appropriations bill. If we had gone the other way, we would have failed miserably. The Big Four would have obligingly introduced whatever bill the JACL asked of them, but I knew now that trying to get sponsors of a compensation bill would have been nearly impossible, and the handful of sponsors who would have signed on would have done so only out of personal loyalty to the Japanese American members. The bill would never have made it out of committee—no matter Inouye's power and influence, no matter Matsunaga's passion, no matter Mineta's stature among his colleagues in the House, and no matter Matsui's determination. It would have taken years just to get to a hearing, and even that wasn't a sure thing. Once a bill like that is passed over, it only very rarely sees the light of day. I was thankful we had followed Senator Inouye's advice.

AN AMERICAN TESTIMONIAL

When the JACL national council of delegates voted in 1978 to approve the Salt Lake City Guidelines, in typical fashion it didn't have adequate funds to back its support of this, its priority program. Redress was given a $12,500 budget for each of two years, which was a substantial amount for a committee budget of the JACL, but that number did not reflect an expectation that redress would evolve into a national campaign. The publication of *A Case for Redress* under Clifford's chairmanship absorbed practically all of his committee's biennial budget in a matter of months, so I knew the committee for redress didn't have adequate funding to do all I wanted to do—all we *needed* to do.

The unexpected success of the campaign and its expanded budget demands became the problem of Karl Nobuyuki. As national director, he was responsible for authorizing program expenditures and keeping an already tight budget balanced; lucky for us, he was more than willing to scour the JACL's budget to support the program, an almost herculean task given the organization's limited resources. Nobuyuki proposed to Clifford and me that we could generate additional funds by hosting a black-tie tribute dinner to honor all of the Japanese American members of Congress together, something that had never been done before. His idea was to use the balance of funds in my program budget to organize the fundraiser dinner, which he anticipated would generate over $100,000. (For perspective, these were the days when $25,000 could get you a hot Porsche and $100,000 could get you a big house in the hills.)

In addition to Clifford, Karl, and me, the dinner-planning committee included National Board Treasurer George Kodama from Los Angeles, Min Yasui, and Mike Masaoka, who was important in this enterprise because he was probably the one person who could convince all five (including Hayakawa) of the Japanese American members of Congress to participate. Given his long tenure in Washington, D.C., he had a personal relationship with each man and was an old hand at these types of events, not to mention that his participation would generate a large audience of his followers from within the JACL, where he still held tremendous influence.

As much as Mike was revered by many of the old guard in the JACL while at the same time he was reviled by many others in the Japanese American community, his Washington credentials were impressive and, apart from Dan Inouye and Norm Mineta, he probably had more credibility as a political operator than any other Asian American. Mike would be crucial in guiding us through the politics and protocols of attempting something this big.

We were all agreed that the purpose of this dinner would be to honor the Big Four Japanese American members of the United States Congress and that it would be called "An American Testimonial." The hitch came when Masaoka insisted that Hayakawa had to be included. To exclude him would be an insult, he said (which was precisely the point, as far as I was concerned), and as an organization we should at least honor the office he occupied. My objection was that I just didn't like the man's politics and the arrogance he had shown the Japanese American community. His very existence offended me, and I didn't think he was worthy to sit at the same table as the other four men.

Masaoka, however, was insistent and in the end prevailed. So the dinner was planned as a salute to all five Japanese American members of Congress, however much we grumbled among ourselves and predicted there would be a price to pay in the community when people found out Hayakawa was included among the honorees.

The dinner, "An American Testimonial," which was held on March 22, 1980, turned out to be a considerable triumph despite the fact that both Inouye and Matsunaga had to cancel their attendance at the last minute. Tickets cost $100 per person, and we nearly filled the grand ballroom at Los Angeles's Bonaventure Hotel, the only downtown hotel that could accommodate two thousand guests. We raised a grand total of $75,000.

And yet the event itself wasn't without its problems. Even before it began, the Los Angeles Japanese American community, among the most dedicated to social activism in the country, was unhappy that the "elitist" JACL was holding a dinner in L.A. (instead of San Francisco, where we were headquartered) that was so expensive that only the rich could afford tickets. The expensive dinner, they claimed, sucked money out of the L.A. community when those funds could be put to better use locally. They were also not pleased that the list of honorees included the community's archenemy S. I. Hayakawa. The evening's program itself, which included long speeches by Masaoka and Yasui, had its own drama. Hayakawa, not unexpectedly, spoke out against the JACL's demands for redress and monetary compensation, and the audience, almost all Nisei, and including some of our most influential community leaders from all over the country, didn't take his criticism sitting down. There was jeering and shouting—shocking behavior for the Nisei—but perhaps it helped influence those in attendance who also opposed redress, inspiring them to give second thoughts about their position once they saw the passion with which their peers, in tuxedos and evening gowns, were willing to raise their voices against Hayakawa.

The program was structured so the three congressmen spoke in the first half of the evening, followed by a short intermission. As we began the second half of the program, Hayakawa's chair sat empty, eliciting murmurs throughout the audience about his ungracious departure. Some made jokes about the catcalls during his speech having scared him away! The empty chair took on a life of its own, with people saying it symbolized Hayakawa's empty head and vacuous heart, plus other similar insults, and it remained a focal point for the rest of the evening. As Norm Mineta took to the podium, he looked at Hayakawa's empty chair and said, "I'm sorry to see that the Ayatollah's left because I wanted to say a few things to him!" The audience responded with laughter and cheers.

Not surprisingly, the dinner ended with mixed reviews. As a fundraiser, it had been a success, but the strongest criticism was definitely the inclusion of Hayakawa, which many, and perhaps most, in the community found reprehensible and hypocritical. How could the JACL claim to champion redress and then include Hayakawa at an event like this? He had earned such loathing from the community that to honor him for *anything* was seen as unforgivable. The JACL was accused of hypocrisy, and we were again criticized for putting on an expensive, elitist event that sucked money from the local community.

The financial result, however, was salve on the wound for us. Even though we fell short of our goal of $100,000 (and came under harsh criticism for that "failure"), we netted $75,000 for the redress program, which would put that money to good use. But no sooner had the check been deposited into the program's account than the board treasurer for the JACL, George Kodama, asked that we loan half the earnings to assist with shortfalls in the national budget. I was reluctant to consider this proposal, if for no other reason than that Kodama had been a harsh critic of the dinner, and the whole thing stunk to me. Kodama warned that if I refused to even consider this request, he could always take the matter to the National Board, where he had much more authority than I. In the end, I agreed to split the proceeds and "loaned" the national budget half of our $75,000, which I knew I would never see again. But since the redress campaign had already absorbed so much of the national budget by that point, ultimately it seemed fair enough.

MY COLLIDING WORLDS

Although I had thus far been able to balance my roles as a teacher at City College and the head lobbyist for redress in Washington, the balance became problematic once the commission bill was introduced in the House. At that point in my tenure as a faculty member, I had additional campus-related responsibilities to perform, and I found myself torn between the two worlds I tried to straddle.

I hadn't yet admitted it to myself, but I was being drawn deeper into the political world of the campaign and, whether consciously or not, that was the world I was choosing. We were on the threshold of a major milestone in our long-awaited battle for redress, and I never thought about giving up the duties of the campaign, especially not at this point. I wasn't yet prepared to give up my teaching career, but I knew that was in my future. I didn't have any visions of grandeur that I, as an individual, was somehow integral to the success of the redress effort—the campaign was bigger than any one of us, and I would be a fool's fool to think I was anything more than a cog in the machine—but I knew that the redress effort was an integral part of who *I* was. In the continuum of the Japanese American experience that stretched from the days of camp to where we now were, my commitment to the cause started as I stood behind the barbed-wire fence, looking out to the unknown world that had banished us. There were so many in our community who had sacrificed so much, including those who, like Edison and Clifford, had risked their personal reputations to help bring us to this moment, never seeking personal recognition for their contributions. Like them, I had grown up in the milieu of the community's long fight for acceptance, and now that we were on the brink of what we had sought for so long, the choice between continuing with the campaign or going back to full-time teaching was simply not an option for me, and in fact it never occurred to me. I felt a deep responsibility for having gotten us this far, and I would continue to be part of the process, no matter what it might take and wherever the path we were paving took us next.

I knew the process was taking its toll on my wife, Carol, and I wasn't sure how to cope with that, in addition to everything else I was juggling. It would be disingenuous of me to say now that circumstances overtook me and the situation was beyond my control, but, simply and honestly put, I made my own choices, one of which was to focus on the responsibilities I had accepted both as a teacher and as the chair of the JACL's redress campaign, even at some cost to my life as a husband and father. I was somewhat consoled by the success the campaign was having, especially having gotten to the point of finally introducing our bills into Congress, but that doesn't mean I was free of regret.

The success of the lobbying effort gave us all a boost of energy and a renewed sense of purpose, and for me personally, it became easier to ignore the community's bitching and moaning. Our goals were now in sight, and reaching this latest plateau was giving me a stronger resolve to make it all work. It was also a time to focus on what lay ahead, and one of the aspects of the process I was most excited for was that the investigations of the federal commission would become a forum in which Japanese Americans would be able to tell the country who we were and what we have always been as citizens of this nation. The commission would be more than just a research team and then a deliberative body; it would be a stage from which our community's voices would be projected to its largest audience yet.

The commission would hold public hearings in the cities where the largest and most significant Japanese American populations resided, and the entire community would have the chance to be involved. The Nisei would be given an opportunity to testify about the effects of the internment in front of an official body of the United States government. Handled correctly, a federal commission could help heal the community by hearing its voices directly from the people themselves.

The Matsunaga-Inouye strategy to shepherd the bill through the Senate first, as a way of giving it greater momentum to make it through the House, proved effective. The Senate bill was introduced in early August 1979, with the House bill following in late September of that same year. By March 1980, just seven months after its introduction, the Senate bill would be put on track for a hearing.

The hearing would be held by the Senate Committee on Governmental Affairs, chaired by Scoop Jackson, a moderate Democrat from Washington State, which had a large population of Japanese Americans and Japanese immigrants. He was a strong supporter of redress.

This initial bill and everything about it was exciting to me because it marked a step forward, and every bit of progress we made seemed worthy of drumrolls and news flashes. But relative to everything else that goes on in Washington on a daily basis, our bill was virtually a nonevent. The scheduling of the hearing was not newsworthy and would not (as I would have liked) draw network television cameras into the hearing room to record the proceedings for posterity. Weighed against the issues of the day—the gas shortage; the combative relationships within OPEC; tax reform; social issues including housing, welfare, and employment discrimination—a hearing to discuss the necessity of establishing a federal commission to do yet another investigation and to issue yet another report had little meaning for most people. This was a small crumb in a place where feasts of monumental proportions were served up daily.

Still, it meant a lot to me, and to us. This was the first time that the United States government would address the issue of the World War II internment, the first time the United States Congress, the body that had played such an influential role in the events that led to our forced exclusion and imprisonment, would discuss the consequences of the attitudes and actions taken by others who sat where they now sat. We were finally going to have the opportunity to force the truth of our lives upon the highest representatives of this nation and compel them to conduct an honest investigation of political racism on a massive scale. We had waited forty years for this, an examination of the hidden past that had destroyed our place in this country but had not destroyed us and our belief in our rights as Americans.

I called Clifford from Inouye's office to let him know that Senator Jackson's office was searching for an open date on the committee's calendar to schedule a hearing. What I intended to be a short call stretched into a long conversation during which we talked about what this all meant. Phone calls with Clifford usually lasted maybe five minutes at most, and even then, only if I talked to keep him on the phone. He was like many Nisei men, adverse to small talk on the telephone, an instrument meant to convey information only.

But when I called to let him know that we would finally have a hearing date on the Senate bill, I was surprised that we talked—no, I should say *he* talked—at such length about what this meant for us, for the community, for the country. Although standing there among the senator's staff was not the most appropriate place for me to be having that conversation, the emotion in Clifford's voice prevented me from stopping him. He was very strong and steel-willed, but he was also very sensitive, even if he didn't show it much. I'd seen him drop his stoic facade a few times before—there were occasions when I saw a kind of sensitivity in him that seemed so intimate I almost felt like I had intruded on a private moment—and as I stood there in the middle of Inouye's staff office, with the official business of Washington swirling around me, I pictured Clifford on the other end of the line, letting his emotions overtake him, and I imagined him with tears in his eyes. It's that image of him I remember more than the actual content of the conversation.

We had come a long way together, and it was a special moment for us both. But it also felt like this was the end, that what we had shared and fought for together was ending at this moment, that he understood I was moving beyond him from here. His world was San Francisco, and my world was now Washington and the rest of the country that lay beyond. It was as if he kept talking as a way of holding on to what we both knew was already the past we had created together. It was beyond bittersweet: it was a mixture of joy at what we had achieved and sadness in knowing we were on different trajectories now. I'll always remember that moment we shared.

THE FIRST CONGRESSIONAL HEARINGS

I think I was like most Americans in that my impression of congressional hearings came from either movies or television, and in my case it came from the gripping daily drama of the Senate's Select Committee on Presidential Campaign Activities, better known as the Watergate Committee hearings. I knew almost nothing about the organizing processes for hearings, including who determined who appeared on witness lists, or how hearing agendas were constructed—in other words, none of the things that mattered.

In some ways, we at the JACL felt we had ownership of the commission bill, but, of course, that was nonsense. Once the bills were introduced in the House and Senate, their fate was completely out of our hands except for whatever lobbying we could do to help influence votes. This was my first experience with legislation and hearings, and because teaching was still my professional obligation and my work on redress was done as a volunteer, I depended on our Washington office to advise me on matters like this that would help us prepare for hearings. They apparently assumed that my close relationship with Inouye provided a direct source of information, and perhaps I should have asked more questions, but I didn't know beforehand that a hearing date had been scheduled, and I never knew that a witness list was being put together. I assumed that since the JACL was the organization that initiated the bill, not to mention that it was the only organization in the entire Japanese American community that had advocated for this federal commission concept, we would be invited to testify. Much to my surprise and irritation, that was not to be the case. While the committee staff should, as a courtesy, have invited us to testify, I learned that you sometimes had to *request* to be on the witness list with new issues like ours because the staff may not necessarily know who the players are and who can best provide useful testimony.

The first hearing of a redress bill in the United States Congress took place before the Senate Committee on Governmental Affairs on March

18, 1980, and didn't include an advocate or witness who was actively part of the JACL's campaign. The list of seven witnesses included Jim Wright, House majority leader and author of the House's companion bill; Norm Mineta; and Bob Matsui. Curiously, neither Dan Inouye nor Spark Matsunaga were listed, and I found out later that it was because neither of them had requested to be witnesses, feeling their testimonies would not be particularly useful given that they were Hawaiians and had not been directly victimized by the government's policies against mainland Japanese Americans. As I would learn over time, on issues of such personal nature, both Inouye and Matsunaga tended to defer to those for whom this issue was the most relevant and important. Besides, they had other, more private ways to let their views on such matters be known.

The noncongressional witnesses included Mike Masaoka, who identified himself as a representative of an organization calling itself the Nisei Lobby; renowned civil rights advocate Clarence Mitchell, Jr., chairman of the Leadership Conference on Civil Rights (an organization Masaoka had helped found as the JACL's Washington representative) and a thirty-year veteran of Washington so well known that he was often referred to as the "101st Senator"; history professor Roger Daniels, author of *Concentration Camps USA*; former JACL president (1966–70) Jerry Enomoto; and Diane Yen-Mei Wong, executive director of the Washington State Commission on Asian American Affairs. The real shock was the inclusion of William Hohri, a computer programmer and social activist who seemed an odd choice since he was one of the most vocal and angry critics of the commission strategy. I wasn't sure whether to consider him a total hypocrite or just an interloper for having found his way onto the witness list, but it became clear from his testimony that he was there to criticize the Senate committee for considering a bill that would do nothing more than create a study; he thought the more honest action would be to simply acknowledge the injustice of the internment and then provide compensation to the victims of the government's policies—basically the option we had passed over in favor of the commission strategy. As much as I was sympathetic to his position— it was, after all, my own preference at the start of all this—I couldn't understand why he was speaking out against us now. If he were able to scuttle the formation of a federal commission, what would we have left?

As far as hearings go, there was nothing remarkable about this one, and it was pretty obvious that the bill would meet with no objections among the committee members. On May 21, 1980, on a late afternoon when senators would have gotten an early start on their evening, Sparky made a motion on the Senate floor to accept the bill on the consent calendar, a procedural move that would slip a bill through without debate or extra attention drawn to it. With Matsunaga and Inouye present, and perhaps one or two others, and with Scoop Jackson presiding, the bill to create the federal commission was approved by the Senate by unanimous consent. We were one step closer.

I would have loved to see the bill debated in the Senate, but in the end, it doesn't matter what parliamentary maneuver you use to get a bill passed so long as the result is the same. The important thing is that it succeeds out of its chamber, and in some cases it's far better to slide a bill through if there is any chance at all that a full debate would result in its defeat. No other bill with which I was later involved—not civil rights, not environmental, and certainly not redress-related—would prove to be as easy or as quick as that commission bill in the Senate.

As elated as I was with the success of the Senate bill, I was equally concerned about the lack of communication in our network. I was the chair of the national committee, and as such, my responsibility was to oversee the entire redress operation, which meant I needed to be kept informed about any major aspects of the campaign. It turned out that Ikejiri was reporting regularly to Nobuyuki, his boss, but the breakdown was from staff to volunteer, Nobuyuki to me. To remedy this, we agreed that Ikejiri would report to both Nobuyuki and to me—a nuisance, perhaps, but an important change.

And no sooner had we implemented this new arrangement than Ron called to inform me that the House Judiciary Subcommittee on Administrative Law and Governmental Relations would convene a hearing to consider two bills: the commission legislation (H.R. 5499) and the so-called Lowry bill (H.R. 5977), a revival of the Seattle Bootstrap Plan that asked for direct compensation. The committee was chaired by George Danielson, a California Democrat with strong sympathies to our cause, and we expected smooth sailing through the hearing. House majority leader Jim Wright, the author of the commission bill, would be the first to testify, followed by Mineta and Matsui, and then Mike Lowry (D-Washington). Stuart Schiffer from the U.S. Department of Justice's Civil Division was also listed, as were Masaoka, Hohri, and me (at last!), plus two new additions to the battle, Mike Zacharof and Philemon Tutiakoff, representing Alaska's Aleut people, whose members had been taken off the Pribilof Islands in the Bering Sea and sent to harsh, unforgiving locations in the Alaskan wilderness during World War II. Eight hundred eighty-one Aleuts were taken from their villages on the Pribilof Islands and left at abandoned canneries in locations so isolated that there was no need for guards or fences. The story of their brutal treatment added another dimension to the government's cruel actions against segments of its civilian populations during the war.

I arrived three days before the hearing, at Ikejiri's suggestion, so I could make courtesy calls to the Japanese American members of the House, but whether due to miscommunication or simply lack of preparation, the JACL had nothing prepared for me ahead of my testimony. Since the D.C. office had all the information about the hearing and I was following their lead, I assumed *they* would prepare the testimony. They, on the other hand, assumed I would prepare my own testimony. With two days to compose a statement, I could fairly easily have written a five- to ten-page document that would do the work of attacking the core arguments commonly used to justify our exclusion and imprisonment. But I wanted something more comprehensive, something that would tell the entire story of our incarceration.

Feeling the pressure of so little time to prepare the testimony, we put together a team of four people to write our presentation in the next twenty-four hours. We would cover four topics: the history of anti-Asian sentiment on the West Coast that contributed to the wartime policies; a refutation of the "military necessity" argument as promoted by the army to justify its actions; a narrative about the contributions of Nisei soldiers during World War II; and a legal analysis of the U.S. Supreme Court decisions in *Hirabayashi*, *Korematsu*, and *Yasui*, long considered among the worst decisions ever rendered by the Court.

For me personally, the hearing was especially memorable because it was my initiation as a witness at a congressional hearing. For veterans of

D.C., this was an unremarkable hearing except perhaps for the unusual subject matter. Wright, Mineta, and Matsui testified, and then Lowry spoke to his bill. Stuart Schiffer spoke on behalf of the Justice Department against H.R. 5499, defending the government's wartime decisions, and then Masaoka, who seemed on friendly terms with each member of the committee, undercut Schiffer's testimony. Hohri repeated his oft-voiced objection, and then I testified. I was followed by the two representatives of the Aleuts, Zacharof and Tutiakoff. After the hearing, I introduced myself to them and was taken aback by how Japanese they looked. To both be Native and also resemble the Japanese? No wonder they had been treated so harshly during the war.

With the hearing behind us, we finally had a chance to relax. It had been a long three days. I wasn't pleased about our last-minute scramble to pull everything together, but I was glad it was done. And yet, I couldn't shake the sense of uneasiness I felt about how our testimony had turned out. This was not a great way to be introduced to the process of congressional hearings, and, as I would learn, there's always a price to pay for sloppiness.

OUR DAYS OF INFAMY

We hardly had time for a sigh of relief before, suddenly, things went bad. I had returned to San Francisco and was sitting in my office at the JACL headquarters, catching up on work with Carole Hayashino, when I received a phone call from Yosh Nakamura, who was married to my wife's cousin. Yosh lived in Orange County and was a friend of Michi Weglyn, author of *Years of Infamy*, the 1976 landmark exposé of the government's WWII policies against Japanese Americans. As old friends, Yosh and Michi talked regularly about the goings-on in the West Coast community, and while on a call with her earlier that day, he had found out that she was furious with me and with the JACL for plagiarizing from her book.

I had no idea what Yosh was talking about, so he explained that the section of my House testimony on the 442nd Regimental Combat Team had been lifted straight out of her book. She was angry for several reasons, including our never having asked permission (which she said she wouldn't have given us) and also that we had put a major part of her book into the public domain (because it was now part of the congressional record), both of which situations, she claimed, would hurt future sales of the book. I was shocked to learn about this and called Clifford, who was also a friend of Michi's, to discuss the seriousness of what had been done.

One of the things we were curious about was how Michi had heard about this in the first place. We wondered if Bill Hohri may have informed her, but then we both agreed that wasn't his style; he would have been more likely to contact one of us directly. We then figured it was more likely Aiko Herzig-Yoshinaga, an acquaintance of Hohri's and the principal researcher for Michi's book, who would have easily recognized any plagiarism. It didn't really matter who it was, though. The fact was that we had screwed up, and done so in a very public way. Michi had achieved heroic status in the community, and of all people to offend, she was the one person in our community about whom we should have been the most careful.

Clifford and I called Frank Iwama, the JACL's legal counsel, to inform him that we would probably need to negotiate a resolution, ideally before Michi filed a lawsuit. She was that mad, we explained. I brought Carole into the meeting because she would have to be involved as our principal researcher. We all knew this was a major crisis, a disaster. To do this to Michi, of all people: she and Clifford were friends, and Michi and I had talked and corresponded for over a year about a myriad of topics of mutual interest.

The problem seemed insurmountable, and there was no easy solution. I offered to call Michi to discuss this matter with her one-on-one, but Clifford said that as the president, it was his responsibility. He knew Michi well and felt she would understand and be reasonable. Unfortunately, Clifford couldn't appease her. When I called to apologize, I was met with her seething anger. She insisted on knowing who had plagiarized her book (and had asked Clifford as well), but I told her that it didn't matter because, ultimately, I was responsible for whatever made it into the testimony.

Over the next few days, Iwama negotiated with Michi's attorney, and the final resolution, approved by the JACL National Board, ended up being costly, and in more ways than one, but it was a resolution to which both we and Michi could agree. Surprisingly (to me at least), Clifford was noticeably unhappy with Michi's demands and would not approve the agreement at first but was eventually convinced. A couple of board members thought we should expose the person who had caused the problem in the first place and let him deal with it, but neither Clifford nor I would allow that. I agreed with Cliff that the cost was beyond what we could afford, but the reality was that we had screwed up and it was our responsibility to make things right, whatever the price.

It was a costly mistake and unfortunate, but some good did come out of it: copies of *Years of Infamy* ended up in the hands of every member of Congress and in the office of all cabinet members and countless other political leaders throughout the country; I hope they had the good sense to read it. Yosh later informed me that, when all was said and done, Michi was satisfied with the resolution, which was gratifying to me personally. We had done her wrong and needed to make up for such a stupid mistake.

As it turns out, I would learn much later that our screwup with Michi was even worse than we understood at the time. At the Senate hearing on S. 1647, at which the JACL did not testify, there was apparently a similar rush to compile testimony, which was submitted under the JACL's name and appears to have been presented as part of Jerry Enomoto's testimony. Contained in that work was a section on the 442nd, apparently the same section that had been included in our written testimony. It was the same mistake twice! As far as I'm able to determine, someone had decided at the last minute that the JACL should provide written testimony, which would be submitted by Enomoto, who apparently was considered a JACL witness, despite our not even knowing he was there. As we prepared our testimony for the House hearing two months later under similar pressure, the individual we had asked to secure writers for the last two sections of our testimony instead provided us with the same sections from the Senate hearing testimony. In his 1988 book *Repairing America: An Account of the Movement for Japanese American Redress*, Hohri castigates the JACL for its breach in the Senate hearing testimony but only chides us for the House hearing, which I find curious because, in my view, having it happen once was inexcusable, but having it happen a second time was appalling.

CHAOS

During the two months we were distracted over the testimony fiasco at the JACL headquarters, the House bill was approved by the subcommittee and was expeditiously reported out of the full Judiciary Committee by chairman Peter Rodino and sent to the full House for consideration. The House approved the commission bill by a two-to-one margin, and after a brief conference on the bill to reconcile the addition of the Aleuts on the House version—that is, to ensure that the commission's examination would include the Aleuts—the bill was finally approved by both chambers and sent to the White House.

We now awaited President Carter's signature on the bill to give it legal authority, but there was no telling when that might happen. We knew that there would be no hitch with Carter because he and Inouye were close, and in fact Inouye had breakfast with the president most Wednesdays when the two were in town. He was surely going to sign the bill; it was just a matter of when.

This was the summer of 1980, and although the end of the school year freed me from my obligations on campus, meaning it was the opportune time for me to be in D.C., there really wasn't much I could do there. It was an election year, and Congress was on a long summer recess while virtually every House member was in his or her home district campaigning for reelection. I could still work the legislative staffs while things were more relaxed on the Hill, but I decided instead to stay in the Bay Area to be with my family. I also took the opportunity to prepare for the new academic year, something I had ignored up to then. I felt I needed to become a dedicated teacher again, even if only for a while.

In mid-May, the National Board held its traditional pre-convention meeting, and that year, it was both a good and bad session. I was able to report the happy news from the Senate hearing and convey our optimism in advance of the hearing in the House. The Weglyn troubles hadn't yet fallen on our heads, but the meeting got bogged down in negativity when we reported the final numbers from the fundraising dinner, and the focus narrowed down to a lot of finger-pointing. The event had been a success insofar as it had brought people together and raised $75,000 for the redress cause, but board members argued over the finances and the net results.

By the end of the weekend board meeting, Nobuyuki resigned as the organization's top staffer, partly, I suspect, because of the lack of appreciation the board gave him in return for the nearly full year he had spent planning and working to pull off the "American Testimonial" dinner. After Nobuyuki's resignation, a sense of gloom hung over the national headquarters, and no one on staff seemed to know how to react. His office stayed vacant, as if to remind us that things were not good.

It was around this same period that Ikejiri had begun communicating directly with me about all matters in D.C., and with Karl's departure, Ron informed me that I would be his link to the headquarters there. He and I didn't talk much about what had happened at the board meeting or why things had happened as they did. I felt like we were in survival mode—things happen, there's some collateral damage, but you go on and continue the fight. This was the new order in the JACL, and both Ron and I had no choice but to get on with whatever we had to do to push our cause to the next stage of this monumental challenge.

Foremost in everyone's minds at the headquarters was the biennial convention, scheduled for just three weeks later in San Francisco. J. D. Hokoyama, who had served as the associate director under Nobuyuki, now assumed the interim director title and was responsible for running the organization, which included the responsibility of planning the convention. All was well until the San Francisco hotel workers' union went on strike, and the JACL, being a civil rights organization, could not and would not cross any of the picket lines set up at the major hotels in town. With delegates from across the country already booked on flights, their vacation time already dedicated to the convention, J. D. had to scramble for whatever options he could find in the area. With just two weeks left, he managed to switch the venue from the San Francisco Hilton to the SFO Airport Hilton, which actually ended up being a better choice for those flying in, despite the chaos and logistical nightmares it created for JACL staff.

I wasn't part of the convention staff, so I was free from this particular scramble—all the better because it left me to concentrate on what I had to do, knowing that redress would be the highlight of this convention and that the accomplishments of the campaign would overshadow everything else, including any potential internal political disasters that might be lying in wait for us.

FULFILLING THE PROMISE

If I were to highlight the key points from my first year as chair of the redress campaign, one of the best would be announcing to the delegates at the JACL convention that the House and Senate bills had both been approved in their respective chambers and were awaiting the president's signature.

This was the first time a JACL-sponsored bill had passed since 1952, when Mike Masaoka had led the effort to override President Truman's veto of the Immigration and Nationality Act. Overriding a veto doesn't happen often, and to have a small group like the JACL lead a successful civil rights coalition against a presidential objection to a bill was even rarer. That achievement always stood as the JACL's shining moment in Washington, D.C.

We were understandably thrilled about the passage of the commission bill, but we also knew we couldn't rest on our laurels for too long. It was a mixed bag. On the one hand, it was the culmination of a successful legislative campaign that had been accomplished quicker than anyone could have predicted. On the other hand, we hadn't yet put to rest the question of whether the government would acknowledge its wrongdoing. This was just the first step, and while it was an important and critical step, certainly, we hadn't achieved our ultimate goal of redress.

As I announced our accomplishments to the delegates at the JACL's 1980 convention in San Francisco, I was certain that if things fell into place as we hoped they would, the commission legislation would be one of the most important achievements in the entire process. It was a nice moment and I enjoyed it, even as I knew we had a lot of work ahead of us. What followed would involve finding a way to make all the elements of our campaign come together in just the right way, or the whole thing would fall apart in our faces. If that happened, the commission would end up being exactly what everyone feared: an obscure body stuck behind musty document files producing a report no one read or cared about. We would have lost two or three years during which hundreds of Issei would have passed on. And the JACL would once again crawl into a dark hole to hide itself in shame and ignominy.

My convention report, which would normally have been scheduled for the middle of the week of the convention, was placed early in the agenda because it was the most anticipated report of the event; it was what the delegates had come to hear. On Wednesday, after I had done my scheduled workshop (where detractors of the commission strategy had their one last shot at me), I was on the floor of the convention talking to a group of delegates when one of our office runners interrupted to tell me that Senator Inouye was on the phone waiting to talk to me. She was excited and nervous, and I suspected that Inouye, as was typical of him, had engaged her in a nice bit of conversation before asking to speak to me. She was thrilled to have spoken to the legendary Dan Inouye.

He had called to tell me that he had been at breakfast with the president that morning and had been able to schedule a bill signing ceremony, as I had requested, and that it would happen the following morning. He told me to jump on a red-eye and be at the West Wing entrance to the White House by 10 a.m. sharp. I could bring three others as my guests.

I interrupted Clifford at the podium in the middle of a plenary session to tell him the news. He wanted me to make an announcement to the delegates as a full body, but I preferred that he do it, so I left the stage and sought out Hokoyama to inform him of what to expect. During the next break, I huddled with Clifford, J. D., Yoshino, and Hayashino to talk about who I would take with me to the signing ceremony. There was no question Clifford and I would go, but who should the other two be? Clifford left that decision to me, and I chose Bill Yoshino and John Saito, directors of the JACL's regional offices in Chicago and Los Angeles, respectively. Bill was an obvious and easy choice, and I included John because he had stood loyally by for two years, taking a lot of crap on my behalf from the L.A. community, who largely disagreed with the path I'd chosen for the campaign.

The scene that played out following the announcement of the White House signing ceremony was interesting. An individual who earlier in the day had scolded me for dishonoring Japanese Americans by pushing redress demanded *he* be invited to join me at the White House because, according to him, he was an important person. Another individual, part of the old-guard leadership, told me he had been to every White House signing ceremony relevant to Japanese Americans since the end of the war and should therefore be among those attending. A number of people approached me with stories about how much they had done or were doing for the campaign, some with their own sense of self-importance, some who saw themselves as political players, and still others who felt they deserved to go by virtue of their stature. I listened patiently to each of them and then told them they weren't going. I knew my choice of Yoshino and Saito would cause a ruckus, so I kept that information to myself.

I had been to the White House a few times in the course of my dealings in Washington, but this would be different. I wanted to hear the president talk about the injustice and the need for this bill to uncover the real truth behind the internment. I wanted to see this fifteen-minute ceremony with my own eyes, as I stood just down the hallway from where, thirty-eight years earlier, our rights had been signed away.

Finally, on July 31, 1980, after almost two years from the day I had launched the redress campaign in Salt Lake City, President Jimmy Carter signed our bill into law, creating the Commission on Wartime Relocation and Internment of Civilians (CWRIC). We had taken another step on the long journey of our fight for redress.

Following the White House ceremony, we four boarded a late-afternoon flight to return to the convention in San Francisco. Early the next morning, Friday, the last day of Clifford's term as president, he took his place at the podium, called the council to order, and then announced to the convention delegates that our bill had been signed into law by President Carter. Despite all our conflicts and disagreements of the past two years, we had achieved something remarkable and set the stage for the final battle.

As I watched him up there, I was proud of him, deeply moved by his humility. Over the two years we had worked together, I had come to understand him as a gentle soul, a fierce warrior, and a person with an unmovable moral center. He was tough as nails and yet the kindest man I had ever known. Here was a great man, someone for whom I had the deepest affection, someone who had changed my life, someone who would always be a part of who I was and would become.

It meant a lot to me that I had been able to live up to my promise to him and give him this moment, now two years after he had stood before the delegates at the Salt Lake City convention to announce my appointment as the JACL's redress committee chair. Under his presidency and with his support, I had not only launched a successful public affairs campaign that had swept across the country, but I had also fought in support of our friends in Congress for a bill that was enacted into law. We had taken on the American public and the United States Congress and had proven that we had the strength and determination to succeed.

I don't know if anyone truly realized then—or realizes even now—the magnitude of what we achieved during Clifford's term of office, in part because later achievements overshadowed them, but it was a tremendous triumph for not just him and the JACL but for the entire Japanese American community. And we had accomplished it all within a particularly hostile atmosphere. It was a time when Asian American issues were not regularly covered on the news, a time when Asian Americans had little status in this country, a time when Japanese Americans were falling victim to the growing anger and distrust engendered by the strong Japanese economy and its imports into the United States. It was a time when hardly any schools, at any level, acknowledged the internment as part of America's history, and a time in which equality and civil rights for Asian Americans did not exist as we know them today. It was a time when public protests by Asian Americans were totally ignored. It was a time when Asian people were disparaged and mocked on the air almost daily, a time when mainstream Americans found Johnny Carson's "Chinaman" comedy skits and others like it acceptable. It was a time when many of the JACL's Nisei members (and some Sanseis as well) distrusted Clifford because they saw him as too radical, too bold in demanding, as he always did, that the truth be told.

Clifford became the JACL's president because he believed in

the seemingly impossible dream of justice and equality for Japanese Americans. He became president because he believed that being truthful in the face of hatred was not courageous but simply necessary. He became president because he was willing to stand up and demand justice and then do whatever was necessary to make it happen. He knew that we would be taking positions that were not popular within the organization and in the community, but he stood strong from the beginning, ready to defy the odds and the criticisms, ready to say that we were going to do what was right, no matter the cost. As for our professional relationship, I always appreciated Clifford's willingness to give me a wide path to make the decisions in my committee's best interests. I didn't make life easy for him, because practically every decision I made was controversial, but never once did he question my judgment and never once did he abandon me, even in some of our toughest moments. I simply couldn't have done what I did without Clifford in my corner.

THE NEXT PHASE

The delegates at the 1980 San Francisco convention elected Jim Tsu-jimura, an ophthalmologist from Portland, Oregon, as the JACL's president to succeed Clifford. I thought Jim's election would occasion my termination as the JACL's redress chair, but much to my surprise, he asked me to continue and assured me I would have his full support, especially in dealing with his district, where my popularity had taken a nosedive. Apparently, they felt that I had had something to do with killing their Lowry bill, particularly since I had not been shy in expressing my views that, in submitting it to Congress, they had been in violation of JACL policy. Jim assured me he would take care of the district, but I had my doubts.

Fortunately, Jim felt that what I had achieved in my two years as chair was unparalleled in the JACL's history, and so rather than remove me from the position (which I assumed some of his supporters had urged him to do), he reappointed me as chair for another two years. A strong supporter of redress, Jim told me he wanted *his* legacy as president to be highlighted by whatever I could achieve in the two years of his term. My focus now would be ensuring that the commission didn't become just another useless body issuing a useless report. The future of the redress campaign was still at stake, and I still wanted a role in it.

I accepted the position of redress chair for a second biennium, knowing full well that it meant I would have to make a decision about my career at City College. In the past year, I had already run into problems—needing to be in D.C. at times I couldn't leave my classes, and yet doing it anyway—and I knew another two years of that would mean both my students and the campaign would suffer. I had eleven years of tenure and the financial security for my family that comes with it, all of which would be at risk if I continued on with the campaign. I knew I was risking perhaps more than I had a right to do; even if we won the redress battle, would it come at great personal loss?

I could pretend that it was difficult to get perspective on this decision, but even then I knew that the campaign would prevail. I knew choosing the campaign was not the responsible or sensible choice for someone with a family to support. I knew I *should* continue teaching and spend the next ten years enjoying the classroom as I worked my way toward retirement and the post-teaching adventures that would come with it. But throughout my life, I was always inclined to go after the new, the different, the challenging. Redress was all of those things. And of course it was so much more than just a mountain to conquer. I was dedicated to the principle, to all those things I had told audiences across the country we were fighting for: honor, dignity, the Constitution, democracy, our rights as Americans. My life had always been guided by what my father had told me: Live by your principles, fight for them, and if you must, die for them; for if you don't live by your principles, what then are you?

The principle was driving me still, and for as much as I had already done to bring us this far in the redress campaign, I knew I had a responsibility to continue. There was no choice for me, really.

———————

Things were different at home now too. Carol had gone back to teaching, and I was spending more time with my kids. It bothered me to see how much I had missed in their lives, with all the travel to D.C. and long days at both the JACL office and City College. I felt like I finally had the time to learn about them and enjoy their company in the way a parent should. It was hard to realize that they were now at ages when their attention was turned more toward their friends than their parents, but we were still a family and I was glad to be around.

Being back in the Bay Area full time also afforded me the luxury of talking often with Clifford. We still gravitated naturally and frequently toward each other, and it was exciting to see him focus his attention to new issues both inside and outside the Asian American community. Clifford was a true social activist, a humanitarian who always found ways to help victims of injustices. He still cared deeply about the redress campaign, of course, and worried about how disruptive the campaign work had been on my life, including that it was jeopardizing my tenure at City College. He told me more than once that I shouldn't feel this campaign was my responsibility to carry; I had done more than my share, he said, and neither the JACL nor the community had the right to ask more of me.

Even after two years as its president, Clifford still harbored distrust for the JACL, and when he spoke about the organization, there was a kind of bitterness in his tone that surprised me and made me wonder if something had happened to him that I didn't know about. Or was it that he merely understood the nature of the community better than I and lamented its failings? He thought it brought out the insensitivity of the Japanese American community, even turned the community against itself, as with redress and the redevelopment of San Francisco's J-town, and he had seen it come down hard on the very people that worked so tirelessly on its behalf, including Edison Uno and Ray Okamura. He thought that many in the JACL and the wider community took for granted what we had accomplished with the redress campaign and had no appreciation for what it had taken to get us to this point. We're a community that seems to value its heroes only when they're gone, he once said. I didn't care about recognition or credit, and he knew that and agreed that only damn fools craved such things, but he was saying all this because he knew how much I had already sacrificed, and he said I wasn't being fair to my family. I was risking too much; I needed to think of them.

———

As the last days of summer approached and life began to fall back into its busy patterns, Ikejiri and I kept in contact to discuss our next steps in Washington, even though we weren't yet sure what they should be. I remember that period as one of a kind of quiet stasis. I was in contact with Inouye's office, and Ikejiri with Mineta's, but there was no sense of urgency to get things done, to make things happen. It was a time of waiting, a time to cool our heels. It was nice to bask in the glory of our major accomplishment, but after the rush of the last few years, doing *nothing* felt uncomfortable, like something was out of alignment. We had new sense of commitment and enthusiasm, further enhanced by the network news airing stories about Carter signing our bill, and we wanted to keep the momentum going. We hoped to capitalize on the publicity and make it a springboard for furthering the media's interest.

By this point in the campaign, our members who, as grassroots lobbyists, had helped push the commission bill through their congressional districts were busy bringing news of the bill's signing to their local media outlets. Just as our members had begun to hone their skills as citizen lobbyists, they had also become much more experienced in talking to the media about the issues surrounding the internment and redress. We had learned from experience that news cycles are very short and so once you get an item on the air, you had to take advantage of every opportunity to keep the issue before the public. The signing of the bill was a huge opening to talk about the internment and redress, and on the local-news level, it was also the perfect place to work the human-interest angle of stories. Make it relevant, I'd always tell our chapters, and make it real.

CHANGING THE ODDS

When the Fall 1980 semester began at City College, I had a weird schedule, by my request. Because of overcrowding, the administration had decided to experiment with 7 a.m. classes as a way of easing the daytime rush, and to see if any students would show up. Figuring a morning schedule would mean a lighter class load and being able to leave campus by noon, I opted for the early classes. My office partner Gerry Coletti thought I was crazy. A brilliant man but ever a cynic, he howled with laughter when I told him I had requested the sunrise schedule. But what I didn't tell Gerry (not at first, anyway) was that because I counted on those classes to have lighter attendance, I would feel less guilty cancelling on them when I needed to be in D.C. It would be an odd student indeed who would object to not having to get up while it was still dark in order to make it to class to discuss the likes of Aldous Huxley or the subjunctive case or the use of subordinate clauses in compound sentence structures!

Although I would enjoy some reprieve from my cross-country trips between home and Washington, I knew it wouldn't last long. Even though we didn't have a bill in the hopper at this time, we needed to keep building support in the House. But it's difficult to lobby an issue without a corresponding bill because congressional staff members are already overworked, so the idea of having to meet with a nonconstituent over a nonexistent bill wasn't at all enticing unless you had already developed a friendship. It made getting appointments difficult, but Ikejiri's office always managed somehow to arrange the meetings I requested on my occasional trips to the capital. Flying to D.C. on the Sunday redeye and then taking the last plane back to the West Coast on Tuesday night, I could spend two full days on the Hill.

The schedule worked for me, and I felt I was making headway in Washington, keeping bodies warm and gaining support, or at least breaking down some opposition, little by little. It was a long haul and a slow process, but we had time. We had shifted the campaign's focus back to education about the internment, in part because we had seen the value of that effort in converting congressional votes. My early mantra —convince the public and you can convince the Congress—had proven right, and never was it more important than now.

As redress chair for another two years, my main concern was the timeline of what was to come. Thanks to the Big Four, the commission bill had sped its way through Congress, and Jimmy Carter, obviously sympathetic to our cause, had proven to be the right president for this particular issue. He was in his fourth year in office when he signed our bill, and we were counting on his winning reelection; in the best of all worlds, we would have a money bill for him to sign before he left office. But we were on the commission's timeline now, with two years to complete its work and a termination date of ten years. Once the commission issued its report and recommendations (and it was my personal mission to ensure those recommendations would be acceptable to the Japanese American community), we hoped to introduce our redress bill and then lock in votes during the final two years of Carter's second term, in a race to have him sign the bill as one of his final acts as president. It was, I thought, a great strategy! With the momentum established by the first bill's success, I was confident we had a good chance at getting a compensation bill through the House if we began working on it immediately.

If that seems overly simplistic (which it was) and overly confident (which it wasn't, really), it was because we had already seen so much success in breaking down so many barriers. Although the House bill's success was due largely to the work of Mineta and Matsui, our grassroots lobbyists had contributed to the effort, and we now looked to the next legislative challenge with confidence.

By my account, we had changed the odds from impossible to at least fifty-fifty, and I thought things were beginning to tip in our favor. But our strategy to have the redress bill through Congress and ready for President Carter's signature before he finished his second term, in January of 1985, was thrown into chaos when Carter lost his 1980 reelection bid to Ronald Reagan, the fiscal and social conservative from California.

RONALD REAGAN, THE UNKNOWN

The election of Ronald Reagan threw the entire civil rights and environmental communities into turmoil and sent shock waves through the inner leadership circle of the JACL. Even worse for us, the Republicans had taken control of the Senate, and any hopes we may have had of getting a redress bill through Congress were suddenly dashed. A Democrat in the White House might have given us a fighting chance with a Republican-controlled Senate, at least in those days when politics were not guided by uncompromising partisanship, but Reagan's election cast a cold chill on our plans.

Memos went back and forth among the JACL's leaders about how difficult this would make our situation and how unlikely it now was that we would be able to get anywhere with redress for at least the next four years, and maybe eight if Reagan served two terms. The civil rights community across the country feared that Reagan would undermine much of what had been accomplished during and since the civil rights movement, and those fears were realized as Reagan began to dismantle much of that earlier work by reducing or ending funding for many of the 1960s "social change" programs, a term that became, for conservatives, synonymous with budget waste and irresponsible spending. With the backing of the conservatives who had taken control of the Senate, Reagan set about to transform the face of America once again, and if they could not change it to the image of the America they held dear—an America before the social revolution that brought more equality and diversity into the mix—they would stop the further erosion of that America they once cherished. Ronald Reagan ascended to the presidency on a platform of economic reforms that appealed to conservative, white Americans, and that did not bode well for our cause.

I had seen firsthand how destructive (from my perspective) Reagan had been as governor of California, and I was just as concerned as anyone. He had been especially hard on the University of California system, which he seemed to loathe as a sanctuary for the radicals and social activists who had created so much upheaval in the 1960s with the free speech movement and anti-Vietnam protests. As America's voice during the Cold War, he articulated the fear of communism, from both outside and inside our borders, and I could see in him a certain kind of demagoguery that viewed the world in an unnuanced dichotomy of good versus evil. I often marveled at how Reagan, like so many conservatives, could hold worldviews that ignored the complexities that define us as human beings and shape our various cohorts, whether ethnic groups, workforces, societies, or nations. Reagan and his conservatives rejected the idea that social change that brought about equality and integration was *good* for a society and a civilization, and for the United States in particular—a country that has always thrived on the influx of immigrants. I was a lifelong Democrat who became more liberal through my Berkeley experience and then returned from living abroad leaning strongly toward socialism, and I longed for America to embrace the European social programs I had seen manifest a profound sense of decency and a recognition that the moral measure of a nation was in how it cared for its most deprived and needy. The United States, in contrast, seemed to care little about its poor and underprivileged, and I was appalled by the hardened attitudes of so many of its citizens.

But while Reagan's conservative side may have been good reason for those of us at the helm of the JACL's redress program to become momentarily catatonic with panic, we were able to rationalize other parts of his administration that might work in our favor. Reagan brought into the White House with him his staff from Sacramento, and as governor of such a large and diverse state, he and his people already had experience with the wide diversity of California citizens. In the few meetings I'd had in the Jimmy Carter White House, by contrast, I could almost count on being asked (in a Southern accent) where I was from (which always meant "What *country* are you from?"), and sometimes I was even congratulated on my fine English! Many of the Carter staff had never met an Asian American before, and virtually all of them thought the color issue in America did not extend beyond a black/white calculus.

The Reagan staff, on the other hand, knew race issues were larger than that; they had seen Latino politics pushing at the edges of state issues, and they knew the Asian American community was coming out of its silence and demanding acknowledgment. I knew he was familiar with internment history because it was during his term as governor that opposing factions fought over whether the site of the former Manzanar War Relocation Center should be designated as a historical landmark. The Manzanar camp, in California's Inyo County, was the focus of a controversial debate that drew public attention to, among many important issues, the use of the words "concentration camp" to describe the wartime internment locations.

So whereas at times we wondered if Carter's White House staff knew anything about the world beyond Georgia, we at least knew Reagan's staff would be familiar with some of our issues. Maybe, just maybe, Reagan's presidency would not be devastating for our redress efforts, and maybe Reagan himself would be sympathetic to our causes, and even hold some influence over his fellow Republicans in the Senate. It would be up to us to cultivate that relationship.

I wrote a memo to the JACL leadership and shared my thoughts about Reagan, stating that we might actually be in a better position now than when we began our legislative effort. With the success of the commission bill, we had turned a lot of JACL naysayers—among both the leadership and the rank and file—into believers, and with their backing across the country, we could begin the process of educating and gaining the support of a new majority Republican Senate. The loss of Democrat seats in both chambers of Congress had changed the political landscape, requiring us to begin anew the process of educating and convincing a new body of legislators that the incarceration of American citizens during World War II was a constitutional injustice. We had a year or two to get the new members on board while the commission went about its business of investigating the circumstances of the internment.

Our immediate task would be to ensure the commission was filled with all the right people.

5
THE COMMISSION

(1981 - 1983)

FORMATION

As a strategy, counting on a commission to resolve a controversy is high risk and fraught with obstacles and potential failures at every step. It's one thing to get a bill passed to create an investigative commission, but it's quite another to find a way to make sure it amounts to more than a token gesture.

One thing I learned in Washington is to never leave anything to chance, especially if I could find a way to influence or arrange or—to put it more bluntly—manipulate situations. This was my plan regarding the selection of individuals for the commission; we all wanted to do what we could to ensure that the best names—the best known, the most prestigious—were announced as commissioners of this body. If the commission itself wasn't strong, our efforts would have been for naught; a commission with a bunch of no-names would have virtually no credibility.

On one of my few trips to D.C. in the months after the JACL's San Francisco convention, I met with Mike Masaoka, who had invited me to join him for lunch. He had been on the mailing list of my Reagan memo and agreed with almost everything I said about Reagan and his experience with the Nisei in California. I was the only one in the JACL inner circle list who expressed a positive view of Reagan, and this, coupled with the fact that I had thought to include Mike on my mailing list, was probably what had prompted him to seek me out. Mike had always kept his distance from my work on the commission bill, even though he was, in his own way, very much involved and concerned with the state of things, especially given Reagan's election just as the process of selecting commissioners was about to begin. I knew little about how this sort of thing was done and was happy to have him share his expertise. Mike told me that to fill the nine seats on the commission, the Senate, the House, and the White House would each submit three names. If we wanted to weigh in on the list (which of course we did), we could submit our nominees through the White House and then hope that at least one of our recommendations would make the cut. Fortunately, the House and Senate lists would receive considerable input from the offices of Mineta, Matsui, Inouye, and Matsunaga. When I wondered out loud to Mike whether these types of decisions were ever left to the goodwill of those responsible, meaning it didn't take a good deal of backroom negotiating to get a fair shake, he just laughed full-heartedly. He said nothing—absolutely nothing—should ever be left to chance and goodwill in Washington!

Masaoka had a number of names in mind, including the popular and highly respected *New York Times* journalists James Reston and James Fallows; former U.S. Supreme Court justice Arthur Goldberg; Arthur Flemming, a former cabinet member under President Eisenhower; Milton Eisenhower, brother of the late president and director of the War Relocation Authority for three months before resigning in disgust; and former senator Edward Brooke (R-Massachusetts). I asked Mike if he knew these people personally, and he said he'd met Flemming a couple of times, had lobbied Brooke when he was in the Senate, and was an acquaintance of Reston's. But how in the world could he nominate them if he didn't know them? I asked. "Know them? We don't have to know them, we only have to trust them," was his response.

Mike suggested I arrange for a conference call with key JACL leaders to discuss who should be included on our list of recommendations to the White House. The individuals on that call were Mike Masaoka, Clifford Uyeda, Ron Ikejiri, Min Yasui, Jim Tsujimura, J. D. Hokoyama, and me. Mike and I stated that our overarching purpose was to get at least one Japanese American on the commission, especially since, as Mike informed us, neither the House nor Senate lists would include any Japanese American names. I wanted to submit at least five Japanese Americans so the White House would have some options, but Masaoka advised us to narrow our selection down to one name only, saying that if the White House were presented with only one Japanese American, it would be obliged to go along with our recommendation.

We discussed various individuals, including Clifford and me, but we both declined. Min Yasui's name came up, but Mike said he would be rejected because of his reputation in Washington as a hell-raiser, which I interpreted to mean he was too honest. Min muttered something like, "And I ain't gonna change." We all agreed Mike would be a good choice, but he eliminated himself because, given his close ties to the JACL, Inouye, Matsunaga, and Mineta, he thought he could have greater influence working behind the scenes.

We then began to look outside our group. We discussed whether the person we chose should be active within the JACL, and while Clifford strongly objected to this criterion, Mike insisted on it. On this point, I agreed with Mike because I had grown to distrust those who had not supported the JACL redress effort (not to mention that I couldn't think of a single person among our critics or detractors who had the kind of stature or credibility that would qualify him or her for this type of appointment). Mike's reason was political; mine was pragmatic. The only other criterion I insisted upon was that the individuals we considered had to have been imprisoned during the war.

For the next hour we struggled to name at least ten prominent Japanese Americans suited for the commission. It was an inherently challenging task, and we weren't making it any easier on ourselves; just by virtue of who we were and the dynamics of how the call was working, a single objection was enough to immediately eliminate any suggested individual. Obvious names like George Aratani, an entrepreneur (owner of Mikasa china) and philanthropist (Mike: too kind-hearted for the tough politics expected of this type of commission) and Togo Tanaka, a journalist and businessman (Clifford: he was one of the JACL leaders removed from Manzanar because of the insinuation that he had been a snitch against other incarcerees) were mentioned and eliminated, and this went on and on.

After it seemed we had rejected practically every individual of any prominence in our community, it occurred to me that we hadn't considered a single woman in our deliberations. When I mentioned this fact, the only person we could think of that might have the necessary credentials was Cherry Tsutsumida, the Director of Congressional Affairs in the Health Care Financing Administration at the Department of Health, Education, and Welfare, and the highest-ranking Asian American woman in the Carter administration. We could think of no other woman who might be an appropriate and effective commissioner. It was a sad commentary on both us and the community, but there we were.

Our final list included all of Mike's suggested names from outside the community plus one Japanese American: William Marutani. We opted for Bill instead of Cherry because Bill had a legal background and a proven record of civil rights involvement, and he had argued before the United States Supreme Court in *Loving v. Virginia*, the famous anti-miscegenation case of 1967. Mike also questioned whether it would be a conflict of interest for Cherry to serve on the commission as an appointee of the former president. So we went with Marutani and hoped for the best. If he made it onto the commission, we counted on Bill to not just speak for the interests of his fellow Japanese Americans but be our inside contact and keep us up to date about what was going on, especially when it came to deliberations on the commission's final recommendations, assuming it got that far.

Bill had a well-established reputation. He was a sitting judge in Philadelphia and had gone on one of the Freedom Rides in the South during the civil rights protests of the 1960s. He had participated in the April 1978 JACL meeting at which we had developed the Salt Lake City Guidelines, and he was on my committee when we made the decision to pursue the commission strategy over the compensation bill. Beyond that, I hadn't been in contact with him other than a few brief encounters at JACL conventions over the years. I knew that Clifford was bothered by what he thought of as Bill's self-righteousness, especially since Bill had never spoken out to defend the committee's decision to pursue the commission strategy, but neither had any of the others.

As it turned out, our choice of Marutani turned out to be both good and bad: good in the sense that he was the most conscientious of the nine commissioners, always maintaining a high level of integrity and intelligence throughout the hearings, but he was also bad in the sense that he refused to talk to anyone in the JACL about the goings-on within the commission. And that was a serious problem for us.

Masaoka and I had lunch with Marutani in D.C. shortly after we were informed that he had been offered an appointment to the commission. Marutani informed me that after this lunch meeting, he would cut all communications with me as the JACL redress contact until the work of the commission was complete. There wasn't much I could do to protest, but Mike complained to Bill that one of the main reasons he was on the commission at all was because the JACL had recommended him. He explained that we wanted an inside contact so we could know what the commission was thinking. He even joked with Bill that he wasn't our choice because we thought he was such an important guy. Bill didn't get the joke and said simply that he didn't want his integrity as a commissioner questioned and he would no longer communicate with Mike, me, or anyone else connected with the redress campaign or the broader hierarchy of the JACL.

Once again, the best laid plans of mice and men...

It took half a year after the bill was signed by President Carter for the Commission on Wartime Relocation and Internment of Civilians (CWRIC) to be formed. In January 1981, we finally received word that the White House had announced the appointments of what turned out to be truly a blue-ribbon commission. The nine members were: Joan Bernstein, then general counsel at the U.S. Department of Health and Human Services; former U.S. senator Edward Brooke of Massachusetts; Arthur Goldberg, former associate justice of the U.S. Supreme Court and former U.S. ambassador to the United Nations; Arthur Flemming, Secretary of Health, Education, and Welfare (now Health and Human Services) under Eisenhower, plus holder of various other governmental posts under four former presidents; Representative Daniel Lungren, a conservative Republican from Southern California and an odd choice because he was a known opponent of redress; Father Robert Drinan, a Democratic congressman from Massachusetts who was also a Jesuit priest and one of the most progressive members of the House; Hugh Mitchell, a former Democratic senator from the state of Washington; Father Ishmael Gromoff, representing the Aleut people from the Pribilof Islands in Alaska; and Bill Marutani, the lone Japanese American commissioner.

Shortly after the White House's announcement, the nine commissioners met in Washington and, in a closed-door meeting, chose their chairperson. We expected Arthur Goldberg, a constitutional expert with a high-profile, distinguished career, to win the seat and were surprised to learn that Joan Bernstein had been selected instead, with Lungren as vice-chair. All I knew about Bernstein at the time was that she was a strong advocate of environmental protections and was the general counsel of Health, Education, and Welfare, which meant she was a Washington insider. Over the course of the commission's life, she held tight command of the body and kept it from getting pushed into that infamous dark corner where commissions go to die.

I met with Bernstein soon after her selection as chair to discuss the objectives of the commission. After all we had done to get the issue to this point, I felt we should have some say about the workings of the commission, but of course that was naïve. The commission's work was out of my hands, and Bernstein was not interested in the history of what it had taken to get to this point; none of that was relevant to the task at hand. She was now in control; I was a mere bystander. I hoped she would be politic and include the JACL in some of her considerations, but she could also shut us out completely. It was up to her.

I found Bernstein to be a very tough, no-nonsense woman who was not afraid to make demands. In a city known to chew up neophytes, she had not only survived but excelled—no small achievement in a place where women were often seen primarily as secretary material. In just over a decade in Washington, Bernstein had worked as acting director at the Federal Trade Commission, and as general counsel for the Environmental Protection Agency and then for the Department of Health, Education, and Welfare (which became Health and Human Services in 1979). Jodie, as she was often called, was a force to be reckoned with, and against her career in Washington, I knew where I stood. She welcomed my input and said she would consult with me if she ran into political matters involving the Japanese American community, and I was reassured to know she understood the enormity of the commission's responsibility.

That first encounter with Bernstein exorcised any worries I had that the commission process would be an exercise of futility. I liked Bernstein, I liked her straightforwardness, and I appreciated the confidence she exuded as she talked about guiding the commission's work, regardless of the controversy that may spring from its eventual findings. I liked that she understood that a possible indictment of President Roosevelt's policies lay at the heart of the deliberations, and I appreciated that she had studied the *Hirabayashi* and *Korematsu* cases, understood the gravity of the dissenting opinions in both cases, and seemed intent on seeking out the truth. She was determined that this investigative study would show the internment for what it was, and there would be no sugarcoating the actions of those involved, which included both the government and Japanese Americans.

Once the commission was filled, my next concern was who Bernstein would hire as the body's principal researcher. She mentioned someone had recommended Aiko Herzig-Yoshinaga, who I knew had worked with author Michi Weglyn. I was more familiar with Aiko's husband, Jack, an attorney who had been one of the harshest critics of the redress committee's commission strategy. How ironic, I thought, that Herzig-Yoshinaga had applied to be a researcher for the very commission she and Jack claimed was a typical JACL sellout of the community. I assured Bernstein that if there were concerns that the JACL would try to influence the commission's research, the hiring of someone who disliked the organization as much as Herzig-Yoshinaga did would surely eliminate that possibility!

That said, I informed Bernstein that unless I was legally or ethically forbidden to do so, I intended to lobby the commissioners about what recommendations we hoped the body would ultimately make. She was well aware of the JACL's Salt Lake City Guidelines and asked if those were the demands I would bringing to the commissioners. Of course, they were exactly what I was going to advocate for—unless I thought I could get better, by which I meant more reparations money.

In the early months of the commission's operations, Bernstein and I had several conversations about how long it was taking to establish the commission's operational staff, which included all the personnel and functions outside the research staff, which had already begun its work. This task fell under the direction of Paul Bannai, most recently a Republican legislator in the California State Assembly, who had been appointed executive director of the CWRIC as a concession to Dan Lungren. I was told that Lungren had appointed Bannai as a way of assuring his Republican colleagues in the House that this would not be an exclusively Democrat-run commission. That said, Bannai seemed a strange choice given that he had little experience handling the day-to-day tasks for which he had always had an office full of secretaries and legislative staff. The demands of the job left him feeling lost in a foreign and even hostile climate, and the situation soon became untenable. By the time the commission began preparing for public hearings in early 1981, Bannai had left the commission for an appointment as Chief Memorial Affairs Director (now Under Secretary for Memorial Affairs) of the National Cemetery System, a part of the Department of Veterans Affairs.

———

In the late spring of 1981, the commission finally announced its hearing schedule, which would begin on July 14 with a two-day hearing in Washington, D.C., that would set the stage for the commission's work. The D.C. hearing would be a political unveiling of the story of the internment and would feature an array of speakers who would provide various perspectives on the internment. Among those who would appear were individuals who would present (that is to say, defend) the government's rationale for its actions; historians who would draw a social and political picture of the internment as well as provide analyses of the government's policies; and, of course, Japanese Americans who would share stories of the personal impact of being victimized by the government's policies. It was there in the nation's capital that the full force of the commission's role would be felt. Bernstein would make sure of that.

Following the D.C. hearing, a series of public community hearings would be held in cities considered the major Japanese American population centers: Los Angeles (August 4–6), San Francisco (August 11–13), Seattle (September 9–13), and Chicago (September 22–23). It was at these regional hearings that Japanese Americans from the community would finally have an opportunity to provide personal accounts of their experiences during World War II. In between the Seattle and Chicago dates, the commission would conduct three days of hearings in Alaska with witnesses from the Aleut community.

We had welcomed the inclusion of the Aleuts onto our bill because their wartime experiences paralleled ours, and because we counted on the state's Senator Ted Stevens to do much to persuade his fellow

Republicans to support first the commission bill (which he did) and, more importantly, the money bill that would inevitably follow, and for which we expected to encounter stiff resistance from Republicans.

Following the community-based hearings, there would be one additional hearing in Washington, D.C., on November 2–3, to include any significant individuals the commission wanted to hear from who had not testified at the first hearing. The schedule would conclude at Harvard University on December 9, at which only constitutional scholars would be invited to provide testimony. I anxiously looked forward to the Harvard hearing because, in my mind, that day would be a distillation of expert analyses of the most critical issues pertaining to the internment, including the rights and protections of citizens and legal residents of the United States; the value and viability of the Constitution, and whether the exigencies of a national crisis justify the abrogation of its most sacred tenants; and, pointedly, whether race matters in the Constitution's application of law. That day in Cambridge, I knew, would be the culmination of thirty-nine years of unanswered questions.

A GAMBLE

In early 1981, the JACL National Board announced it would begin a search for a new national director and invited applications for the job. Several board members encouraged me to apply, since they were invested in the redress campaign continuing to enjoy the status it had built up over the past few years. Given my achievements as chair of the Committee for Redress, my selection was a virtual guarantee, I was told, and so I was urged to apply.

The two main problems were that I wasn't too keen on the position, which was largely administrative, and I preferred being able to focus all my work on the redress program itself. Also, in order to work full time for the JACL, I would have to resign my tenure at City College and lose the current and future financial security it promised. I had toyed with the idea of giving up teaching, but I still didn't feel ready to make that leap. On this point, it also didn't help that the JACL board would not make its decision until after the spring semester had begun on campus, which meant I would have to resign my tenure simply to apply, and then what if I didn't get the job?

Leading the redress campaign was already overwhelming and demanded more than I could continue to realistically offer as a volunteer. With the success of the campaign and all the press it had generated, my work in D.C., not to mention the travel I did for the near-constant speaking engagements I was invited to, made it virtually impossible for me to continue as both a teacher and the volunteer chairman of the redress campaign.

Carol and I discussed the matter for days, and our biggest concern was that resigning my tenure would put our family's financial future at risk. On the other hand, working with the JACL was certainly one of the most profound experiences of my life, and the redress effort was one of the two most important moments in the collective lives of Japanese Americans—the other being the internment itself. The work of the campaign would be the legacy of Japanese Americans forever, and I was playing a part in that legacy. I couldn't imagine anything to come in my life would equal the symbolic enormity of this effort.

After days of deliberation, I at last accepted my fate and resigned my tenure as an instructor at City College, walking away from a career I had chosen and toward a career I could never have dreamed of.

I expected my next move to be stepping into the role of national director of the JACL, but it wasn't to be. What had been described to me as a virtual guarantee turned out to be anything but: instead of me or the other candidate, J. D. Hokoyama, the board selected Ron Wakabayashi from Los Angeles, someone I didn't even know was a candidate. Ron, it turned out, had been persuaded by board treasurer George Kodama to apply for the position, and the JACL made him their new national director. Even up to the weekend of the board meeting, I was still being assured by board members that I would be selected for the job, so when the decision was announced, I was caught completely off guard. Kodama had somehow convinced the board that his guy was the best choice for the organization and, in many ways, I think George was right.

Admittedly, Ron was much better suited for the position than I. As national director, he would find ways to keep tight fiscal control of the organization, and he was streetwise, tough, and fearless without being foolish. He was part of the original redress group of young activists in Los Angeles in the 1960s who had raised the issue of camp and was best known to me as someone deeply involved in the community, though I hadn't known he had been associated with the JACL. He was a capable, bright, and very strong-willed individual and I'm glad he was the person who led the JACL into the next phase of the redress battle.

I, however, suddenly found myself in a difficult situation. I had resigned my tenure at City College, with no option to return, and although a few colleges in the area had begun to increase the diversity of their faculties, meaning I would be a good candidate for hire, the semester had already started, so that wouldn't be an option for a few months at least. Carol had gone back to teaching a couple of years earlier, but the fact remained that I had gambled with the security of my tenure at City College and had lost.

Some people would have called it irresponsible and stupid to have put so much at risk at this point in my life, especially for what many still considered a lost cause, and I guess I would have had to agree. And in an ironic twist, I now found myself with more than enough time to continue as the volunteer chair, but because the work was unpaid, my more pressing need was to find a job to provide for my family. I now had no choice but to resign as chair of the redress committee.

Clifford heard the news and arranged to meet with me at the JACL headquarters the following Monday. He was, of course, sympathetic, but he also told me he never thought the national director position was the right job for me, that my strengths were in other areas. It struck me for a moment that as much as I talked with Clifford about so many things, I was stupid not to have consulted him about this. He was as shocked as I was that I hadn't been selected for the directorship, but he also said I shouldn't feel any obligation to continue as the redress chair when I obviously needed to concentrate on finding a paying job. No one was irreplaceable, he said, and despite what I had accomplished as chairman, perhaps it was time now for someone else to take over the responsibility of the campaign. I had sacrificed more than was fair, he said, and no one would have the right to accuse me of abandoning the campaign.

I wrote a letter of resignation to Jim Tsujimura and then, as my final responsibility as redress chair, flew to Washington to take care of the transition of my duties to Ron Ikejiri until a new chair could be appointed. My main purpose, though, was to make the rounds on the Hill to inform my contacts that I was leaving. It was just a formality, a courtesy to make various congressional offices aware of the transition—people come and go all the time in Washington, and I was just another person passing through—but I wanted them to know that the JACL would continue to push the redress issue until, and after, the commission finished its work and we had another bill—the redress bill—in the works. Political issues, like people, also come and go in congressional offices, and I didn't want any of my personal contacts to let this issue slip away. We needed to keep the internment in the minds of those with whom we had made gains.

That would hardly be a problem in the offices of the Japanese

American members of Congress. This was their issue, and their staffs understood how important it was to each of them. Senator Matsunaga was the most demonstrative among the four about my leaving the campaign; Inouye talked about how much of a difference my work had already made toward the eventual redress bill; and Matsui's and Mineta's sentiments were basically, "Oh well." As I said, people come and go in Washington and life moves on.

I ended up spending most of that trip talking with lobbyists I had come to know, especially our Republican backers. (Funny how that works.) Many of them had been surprisingly helpful, whether through lobbying members of their party or sharing useful information and opening doors. In a strange way, I was going to miss some of them the most; maybe it was because, as one of them told me, we actually enjoyed the arguments and banter.

Tsujimura, distraught at my loss and plagued with guilt for having encouraged me to apply for the directorship by all but guaranteeing me the position, began exploring the possibility of having the JACL hire me to run the redress campaign as a full-time employee. There was a vacant slot for an associate director, and Tsujimura proposed I be hired in that slot with a title change to redress director. It required the board's approval, and I doubted Kodama would agree to it since I was sure he'd feel that my presence would undermine Wakabayashi as the new director. The thought of working on redress full time appealed to me, though, even as Carol and Clifford both expressed not only skepticism but a sense of foreboding. Carol especially felt that I had taken a lot of criticism and was concerned that if being a part-time volunteer chair had caused that much turmoil in our lives, how much more grief would working full time bring?

Within a couple of weeks, the board approved Jim's request and Wakabayashi agreed to bring me back to run the JACL's redress campaign. My title would be national redress director, and I would be charged with running the campaign from both San Francisco and Washington. I would continue my work as before, except I was now a full-time, paid director. Wakabayashi said he would give me full rein of the redress program, and I would work with him on related budget matters. Ron was much more understanding and supportive than I imagined he would be, and than he needed to be.

So with a break of about a month, I returned to the campaign. I already had the staff I needed in Carole Hayashino, her assistant, and my secretary. Wakabayashi also agreed to let Bill Yoshino continue as the assigned regular staff to the program, working with me on Midwest strategies and directing the JACL's overall grassroots lobbying effort. After long discussions with Wakabayashi and Tsujimura about the most efficient way to run the campaign now that I was full time, they suggested that I move my base of operations to D.C. Since this would be a temporary move, Carol and I decided that I would make the move to D.C. by myself. And with the approval of the board a few months later, I set out for Washington and opened an office there adjoining the JACL's D.C. office.

Moving to D.C. transformed my life. Not having the constant pressure of return flights back to the Bay Area felt like luxury; there was always tomorrow to take care of what I couldn't get done today. I rented a flat in the city, the monthly cost of which was less than the cost of one week in a fairly inexpensive hotel room, and from my base on the East Coast, I was also able to travel more quickly and cheaply to various other destinations that had been a long haul from San Francisco. Living in D.C., however, had more than its share of downsides.

Just as I was finally situated in Washington, my father, who lived in Los Angeles, became gravely ill. I took every opportunity I could to visit him during the year before he passed away, often taking a late Friday flight out of D.C. and the redeye back again on Sunday night. When D.C. emptied out during congressional recess, I also headed back to California to see my family; the coastal travel pressures of my life had reversed.

This was also the time when Carol became involved with a program at UC Berkeley that would eventually transform her career. My kids were now eight and eleven years old, and I saw them less and less during my trips home because they were busy with their own lives and interests. All of us, I realized, were moving in very different directions, even compared to where we were only a year before. It seemed everything was in transition: from teaching to full-time redress director, from West Coaster to East Coaster, from a private existence to a public one, from someone who loved the life of the mind to learning the game of politics, from trying to broaden the minds of my students to trying to broaden the minds of politicians, from the solitary act of writing and reading late into the night to the social game of playing politics.

When things like this happen, when changes of this type occur, you learn how difficult—and maybe impossible—it is to go back to the way things were. I thought about that sometimes when I was in a reflective mood, and more than once I wondered if I should go back to whatever I could do to recreate a normal life. I hadn't set out to become a campaign director and Washington lobbyist; it was only serendipity that I had happened to be at that 1975 district council meeting that landed me as the chair of my district's redress committee. And yet, this was the path I had chosen. I thought often about my father and the life lessons he had taught me, especially the one about fighting for your principles. It wasn't easy, but I knew this was where I belonged.

THE HEARINGS BEGIN

It was during this transitional period in my life that the commission began its series of hearings in the major population centers for Japanese Americans. To underscore the significance of the commission's purpose, the first hearing would be held in the Caucus Room of the Russell Senate Office Building, site of the Senate Watergate Committee hearings under the leadership of the venerable Sam Ervin. Inouye, who had sat on the Watergate Committee as a junior senator, had discussed this venue with me in our earliest conversations about pursuing a federal commission. No one who was here in the 1970s could ever forget the images of those hearings as, day after day, one of the most intriguing political dramas of our times unfolded. What better venue for the kind of hearing we sought? And, of course, the object wasn't just to put the hearing on display but for the content of the hearings themselves to make the profound statement that the political machinery of this country found it worthwhile to examine a historical event in pursuit of the truth. If we could leverage the hearing location into increased publicity, so much the better.

Joan Bernstein hired the Washington-based media and public relations firm of Wise and Wren to help with strategy. Bill Wise and Sue Wren, both experienced operators in D.C., had worked previously with Bernstein as contractors and were familiar with the ins and outs of Washington politics and especially the intertwining relationship between politics and the media. The plan was for Wise and Wren to turn the commission hearings into something not only newsworthy as a sidebar but compelling enough to land on the front pages of newspapers across the country and as the top story on nightly news programs.

By any standard in Washington, a hearing by a governmental body with the somewhat inaccessible name of Commission on Wartime Relocation and Internment of Civilians would be of only moderate interest to most people, and perhaps not much more than a curiosity even to those who saw it on the congressional schedule. As we had encountered in all our prior redress efforts, the majority of people would consider the hearing as just one more investigative study of some unknown and inconsequential episode that nobody really cared about.

But to seasoned reporters, there was something about the press announcement by Wise and Wren that piqued their interest: the straightforward fact that an entire segment of the population had been forcibly removed from their homes, often at gunpoint, by the U.S. Army and forced into American concentration camps. This was no small matter, however long ago it had happened and how much it had been ignored and forgotten. Not only did that wartime event raise serious constitutional questions, but it was shocking that the group now bringing forth an unprecedented demand for reparations was a segment of the population that had always been stereotyped as docile and even subservient. The Wise and Wren press releases presented a compelling picture of the hearings to come, and it proved to be enough to draw the interest of the media in ways I never expected.

For that first, historic hearing on this subject in Washington, D.C., the media came out in droves. Network television cameras lined the back of the room, and news photographers crowded an area on the floor in front of the dais where the commissioners sat. The hearing room was packed with Japanese Americans, many of whom had come from different parts of the country to witness this momentous event, and staffers, other Hill employees, and people who were just plain curious about the proceedings filled the space. There was also a group of detractors seated around Lillian Baker, the most passionate opponent of redress and defender of the government's internment policy. I had encountered several of Baker's grunts at the House congressional hearing at which I had testified on the commission bill, as well as at every other internment-related event at which I had spoken, whether official hearings or public events.

Regretfully, I never had an opportunity to debate Baker directly. I did, however, encounter her minions on several occasions both in Los Angeles (where Baker resided) and in the Bay Area. After one of the House hearings, a man in a clerical collar had rushed up to me. Eyes glaring like a madman's, teeth bared and with spittle at the corners of his mouth like a rabid dog, he had angrily accused me of being a liar and traitor. He had then condemned me to hell. So much for Christian charity, I thought.

There were many people who opposed our efforts and felt we were besmirching the good name of the country, but this particular group was different. They spewed hate toward Japanese Americans and Japanese immigrants, and they seemed to believe the war was of our making. They condemned us for creating what they considered to be theatrics of guilt mongering, claiming it wasn't right for us to challenge the U.S. government when we were the ones causing the problem. I was curious to know if they had come all this way to disrupt the hearing, but I also wondered if they might be genuinely interested in the outcome of the commission. That was the point, wasn't it? To see which side was right?

Among the witness at the top of the agenda were the Big Four Japanese American congressmen. Dan Inouye and Spark Matsunaga, and Mineta and Matsui provided a written statement, which was read by Bernstein. All four testimonies focused on the important work that lay ahead for the commission, and Inouye and Matsunaga specifically enjoined the commission to ensure their examination of the facts was honest, thorough, and completely neutral on the matter of final recommendations (the last of which many Japanese Americans took as a not-too-subtle statement of opposition to the idea of reparations).

The day included testimonies from other Japanese Americans, a handful of representatives from the JACL, NCJAR (National Council for Japanese American Redress), and NCRR (National Coalition for Redress/Reparations); individuals such as former assistant attorney general James Rowe, who found fault with the government's claims; and Lillian Baker. But for us, much of the focus was on Inouye and Matsunaga, who, although they had both fought in the war, had not experienced life in the camps. And yet their testimonies were important because they essentially outlined the purpose of the commission and the duty it had to uncover the truth.

The coverage of this first hearing by the national media was, as Dan Inouye had predicted, beyond anything any of us could have imagined. If the major television networks didn't lead with news of the hearing that evening, they gave it high priority on their telecasts, which were then picked up by affiliate stations across the country, and especially in areas with significant Japanese American and Asian populations. Prominent coverage appeared in the *New York Times* and the *Washington Post*, and D.C. bureau reporters from the *Los Angeles Times* and the *San Francisco Chronicle* filed substantial, in-depth articles that detailed the hearing and the background of the internment. All of these ran on the wire services and were picked up and run in papers throughout the country. Where there were Japanese American communities, reporters in both television and print media included original interviews to give their pieces a local flavor. The coverage was incredible, and for once the Japanese American community was united on an issue of great importance: everyone recognized the value of the public attention now being given to the story of the internment.

THE COMMUNITY SPEAKS

As the hearing schedule began, I traveled between Los Angeles and Washington, where I dealt with the commission operational staff and with Bernstein on issues that kept arising relative to the upcoming community-based hearings. Bernstein informed me that she was getting demands from the Sacramento Japanese American community, which was upset that Sacramento had not been included on the commission's schedule. They argued the significance of their city in the history of the internment, since it had been struck hard after Pearl Harbor with incessant calls for the removal and permanent banishment of the entire Japanese American population from the state. It was from there that Earl Warren, then attorney general of California, had voiced his intense dislike of the Japanese and then lied and manipulated to effect the removal of every person of Japanese ancestry from the state.

Bernstein was frustrated with the Sacramento community for not realizing that the hearing scheduled for San Francisco could easily accommodate the views of the Sacramento community. True, it was only a couple of hours' drive to San Francisco, I told her, but she would save an awful lot of headaches if she relented. Besides, even if a hearing in Sacramento added little, factually or historically, to the overall proceedings, it would be advantageous for the commission to keep the Sacramento community on its side.

Of course, it wasn't that easy to add a hearing. It cut deeply into the commission's budget, involved a lot of extra planning and time, and was, frankly, unnecessary. Bernstein remained adamant on her position, and it seemed we had hit an impasse, until Bill Marutani volunteered to travel to Sacramento to hold a one-day hearing. He would cover the cost of his travel out of pocket, and the Sacramento community would arrange and pay for the venue themselves. All that was left was composing the witness list, which I said the JACL's regional director could handle with assistance from the leaders of the Sacramento JACL chapter.

When we put out the call to the entire Japanese American community for witnesses to share their stories, the response was overwhelming. The people who spoke up defied the stereotype of the patient, polite, and accommodating Japanese American and were in many cases quite the opposite: they made constant demands, including a fair number of unreasonable ones, and this level of assertion wasn't coming just from the more outspoken Sansei but from the Nisei as well. I actually liked what was happening; it was the sleeping tiger waking up and finding its voice at long last.

In no time at all, the number of people demanding a place on the witness agenda had climbed into the hundreds, and I knew we had a problem. Even in the best of situations, the commission would only be able to accommodate perhaps twenty or so witnesses each day. The unfortunate commission staffer in charge of it all was completely unprepared for the flood of demands, and particularly from so many individuals who insisted they themselves were especially important and needed to be heard from. She tried as best she could to be accommodating and understanding, but many of the individuals had no patience with what they thought were excuses, and they demanded their names be added to the witness list.

Meanwhile in Los Angeles, Sue Wren, the commission's press expert, had arrived in the city a week ahead of the hearing date there to begin working on the local media, but she soon found herself wrapped up in the logistics of the hearing itself. As in Sacramento, the community was upset that the witness list was not able to accommodate everyone who wanted to testify, and they were demanding additional days be added to the hearing. Wren became the voice of authority and did much to calm the situation, and then John Saito, director of the JACL's Los Angeles office, became an additional buffer between the commission staff and the community, working closely with Wren to keep things in order. As much as many people still didn't trust the JACL, John was highly respected in the community, as was his wife, Carol, who was the assistant in the office and the point of contact with the community.

This problem of overwhelming numbers of requests to testify was partially solved when Bernstein issued a directive stating that testimonies presented before the commission at each hearing would be limited to three minutes and that, once the witness list was full, individuals not selected could submit written statements, limited to ten pages. The selection of in-person witnesses would be based on the type of information they could contribute at the hearings, with some deference given to political figures and individuals with special stature in the community, as was common practice with this type of public hearing. I was surprised not only by how many people wanted to testify but how unselfconscious they were about demanding to be put on the witness list. This attitude was totally contrary to the cultural constraint traditionally valued by the community; Japanese Americans were not known for drawing attention to themselves, and especially not by boasting of their self-importance. Maybe we had become too Americanized? I was shocked and amused by the lack of restraint.

In time, the witness list came together for the three-day Los Angeles hearing, with Commissioner Bill Marutani presiding, and on August 4, 1981, the first of the series of community hearings began.

I hoped it would do some good to heal the anger of all those who had been opposed to the idea of seeking redress through a federal commission investigation. If the hearings went well, I truly believed that that animus would subside, if not disappear, and maybe we would feel a sense of solidarity within not just the JACL but also the wider community. At last, almost forty years after their incarceration, the Nisei would finally have an opportunity to tell their story to an official body of the U.S. government, and perhaps free themselves of the burden of guilt and shame they had carried so deeply for so many years. If the hearings achieved what I thought they could, I knew it would be worth all the repercussions we had experienced in the wake of our decision to run the campaign as we had.

But of course not everyone was on board with what was happening. While the majority in the community welcomed this opportunity to expose the truth, a number of Nisei now accused me of forcing them to speak out publicly about matters that were personal and that had been purposely pushed into the corners of their minds. The angry reaction to the commission paled in comparison to the vitriol that erupted among these particular Nisei, and I was bothered by this reaction. Whatever provoked this anger, whatever was happening to the Nisei, troubled me.

What their anger revealed was how deeply mentally and emotionally wounded the Nisei were, so much so that it seemed that the mere thought of talking about their wartime experience—not to mention doing so in front of the public and a governmental body that would judge them for their words—posed a threat to their sense of psychological equilibrium. In late 1970s, we as a community were still reticent about our wartime experiences, in part because we had not resolved the myriad issues that festered in our hearts and psyches. The Nisei were the most affected and were therefore the best suited to describe the impacts of that experience in the commission hearings, but it was they who were often the least able to articulate just how damaged they were, how betrayed they felt by the country to which they held, still, such devoted loyalty. Beneath the facade of silence lay so much shame and guilt for having been labeled traitors to the country of their birth, the only country they knew. This experience would have been difficult for anyone to talk about, and it was compounded within a cultural tradition that demanded *gaman*.

And yet there was so much to talk about. So much to say about the war. The war: it was always the war upon which we measured our lives—how far we had come since those days, what we had accomplished since our departure from the camps, where the future lay for us and our children. Even those who had acted heroically—those who had volunteered from their imprisonment to join the army, those who had resisted, who had railed against our treatment as it was happening—even those heroic deeds were overshadowed by the shame they felt for having been locked up for no reason other than who they were. Being proud of their cultural heritage did not serve them, and being proud they were Americans did not save them.

The word "camp" became almost like a code word for keeping silent about all the memories it signified. Japanese Americans did not talk to each other about camp, did not tell their children born after the war about the camps. What internal dialogues did they have when they thought about the war years and their imprisonment? For most, it was easier to not think about it, to move on with their lives and let the past be the past. *Shikataganai.*

What good could come from unearthing memories buried under decades of silence? That was what the federal commission would decide. And now it was coming to town in search of the personal stories of travail and sacrifice and pain. The psychological walls behind which those memories had remained hidden for so long were now threatened by the commission's call for witnesses, and the Nisei understood that they held the stories the commissioners wanted to hear. But was this an intrusion, an invasion of privacy, or something different? Many Nisei were caught between the silence they had committed to for so long and an undeniable desire to talk about their camp experiences. For some, it didn't matter that they were being invited to share their thoughts and feelings, rather than ordered to talk. Either way, it threatened the relative comfort they had found in silence.

The majority of Nisei, however, did not feel this way, and the public hearings came as welcome news. People wanted to be part of them in some way, wanted to experience this historic event firsthand. Could the process of this federal investigation finally bring to a close all they had been made to suffer during the war?

At each of the hearing sites—Los Angeles, San Francisco, Seattle, and Chicago—hundreds of individuals from the Japanese American community began to prepare for the commission. Those whose names made the witness lists wrote and rewrote their testimonies, while others—thousands of them—recorded their life stories to be submitted as written testimony for the records of the commission. Groups like the JACL and the community-based National Coalition for Redress/Reparations (NCRR), primarily a Los Angeles–based organization that was established as a reparations-focused group, lent their help as people gathered in community centers, churches, and meeting rooms to work on their testimonies. NCRR members, more deeply embedded in communities than the JACL, did a great job of helping the Nisei prepare their statements. Whenever I was invited to speak, giving guidance and answering questions, the rooms were filled beyond capacity. I stayed largely on the West Coast as we prepared for the hearings, and wherever

I went, it felt like everyone was writing something for the commission. I sometimes imagined the dismayed looks that would be on the faces of the relatively small commission staff when thousands upon thousands of written testimonies started arriving at their office in Washington.

It was during the buzz of the pre-hearing period that I was contacted by Dale Minami, a civil rights activist, San Francisco attorney and cofounder of the Asian Law Caucus. Like me, Dale was originally from Los Angeles but came north for school (the UC Berkeley School of Law, commonly known as Boalt Hall) and settled in the area. We would later become good friends, but at the time Dale contacted me, we were only acquainted with each other. He was a younger, postwar Sansei, so there was a gap in our experiences of growing up Japanese American, but we had a lot of the same values and he was fast becoming an effective advocate for Asian Americans in the Bay Area.

Dale asked to meet with me while I was at the JACL headquarters in San Francisco to discuss a draft of testimony on the World War II Supreme Court cases he and his colleagues were preparing for the upcoming commission hearing. After reading the draft, I suggested to Dale that we try to schedule a meeting when Min Yasui would be in town. Min was an integral part of the JACL's redress campaign, came often to San Francisco, and made himself readily available whenever I requested his presence. I suggested to Dale that Min, as one of the defendants who was heard in the Supreme Court in the context of wartime legal challenges, and as a civil rights attorney himself, would be extremely useful to Dale's group in assisting with their testimony.

Min and I met with Dale and his Asian Law Caucus colleagues Lorraine Bannai (daughter of Paul) and Dennis Hayashi. In a two-hour meeting, Min and I offered our suggestions and corrections, and Min waxed eloquent, as he was often wont to do in the presence of young admirers. Min could also be brutally honest, even to the point of being oblivious to how crushing his comments could be, and true to form, he was all of this with Dale and his colleagues. I'm not sure how much they appreciated it, but they survived!

After the group had left, Min wanted to know more about the individuals in the group. Overall, he saw them as attorneys who were young and innocent and wet behind the ears. "But that Minami kid," he said, "with the right grooming, he might turn into something one of these days!" And indeed, Dale did turn out to be something, far beyond Min's imaginings!

What we didn't know at the time was that this group would later become part of one of three legal teams that would challenge the Supreme Court's ruling of *Hirabayashi v. United States* and *Yasui v. United States* (both 1943) and *Korematsu v. United States* (1944). Collectively, these teams would challenge the decisions that gave legal credence to the wartime policies we were trying to discredit.

————

By the time the commissioners flew to Los Angeles for the first of twenty days of community hearings around the country, Sue Wren had been there for the better part of a week, initially to do the lead work for the hearing, but then, given the chaotic situation in the community, to settle things down. Wren took charge, made decisions, and generally helped save the day. Only after things began to calm down did she turn her focus back to the job she was there to do. Watching her at work, I realized why it was important to have a professional working the media, which also explained why we had received such broad coverage for the Washington hearing. Nothing was left to chance; Wren had received commitments from every news outlet in and around the Los Angeles area to have reporters and cameras at the hearing.

Inouye had told me as we considered the commission strategy that, if done right, the commission hearings could generate the kind of national publicity that the JACL could never afford, and he was right. Wise and Wren had made the internment front-page news following the D.C. hearing, and I was eager to see what they could do for the next four. It seemed to me that it would be harder to get coverage of the community hearings, far from the weight of the nation's capital and its big personalities, but I hoped that wouldn't be a problem.

The media response to the Los Angeles hearing removed any doubts we may have had: the coverage once again hit the front pages of papers across the country, and the network evening news programs made the hearings the top story. What television audiences saw and heard were Japanese Americans describing their tragic wartime experiences and, despite their feelings of betrayal as American citizens, their continued faith in this country. Whatever the responses of the viewing audience may have been—sympathy, incredulity, anger at us, hatred even—they couldn't ignore the fact that the United States Congress had found this issue compelling enough to order an official investigation. Based on that alone, we were laying claim to our rightful place in this country.

———

All the problems we encountered going into the Los Angeles hearing were magnified as we prepared for the three days of hearings in San Francisco a week later. Individual members of the Bay Area community were even more emphatic about their right to testify, and we worried things would get crazy again. Fortunately, Carole Hayashino had control of the situation. By the time the commission reached Seattle and Chicago, things were well under control, and the chaos in the communities preceding those earlier hearings had disappeared. In total, the commissioners heard over seven hundred Japanese Americans testify at the hearings and received thousands of written testimonies that told personal stories of individuals and families affected by the government's actions. All are now part of the government's records.

For me, monitoring the hearings was the most emotionally difficult experience I had gone through in all my years with the campaign. The first hearing in Washington, D.C., was, in essence, what I thought of as a dress rehearsal; we weren't yet hearing stories, we were getting kind of an outline of what was to come, and the focus was on individuals with status and recognition voicing their support for or criticism of the commission. In other words, it wasn't substantive in nearly the way the community hearings would be. Those testimonies would get to the real heart of the community's pain, and for many of us they were as emotionally draining as they were exciting.

The hearing in Los Angeles was highlighted by S. I. Hayakawa's appearance and the subsequent jeering of the audience, which was made up of almost all Japanese Americans. He was called out and ridiculed and made to see just how much the Japanese American community had come to despise him. The L.A. hearing was also marked by the presence of our nemesis Lillian Baker. It wasn't Baker's testimony that evoked the biggest reaction, however, but that of a 442nd Nisei veteran, Jim Kawaminami, who read from his prepared statement about his experiences fighting in Europe. He directly refuted Baker's claim that Japanese Americans did nothing for this country during the war, and as he read, she suddenly rushed to the witness table and attempted to tear his testimony from his hands. The audience was on its feet, shouting at her as she and Kawaminami wrestled in the front, this rather prim-and-proper woman with hate in her eyes tussling with this slim, aging veteran who had fought in some of Europe's bloodiest battles. Two marshals were called to escort Baker out of the hearing room, which they did to a bevy of cheers. As she was led down the aisle, a small cadre of her followers accompanied her out of the hearing room to the sound of jeers and catcalls.

With the drama of Lillian Baker over, the hearing was brought back to order, and for the rest of that first day and the following two days, witness after witness told his or her personal story and described the hardships of the internment years. Each story was heartbreaking, sad beyond words. It was the only time I've ever seen Nisei men cry in public, and just about every one of them who spoke broke down at some point during his testimony. It became so emotionally taxing to sit there that I had to leave the hearing room periodically to get some relief.

The San Francisco hearing was absent of the disruptions that characterized the days in Los Angeles, but there were plenty of heavy emotions. In some ways, the three days in San Francisco proved even tougher to endure. It might have been because I personally knew more of the witnesses, as I did, for instance, Wilson Makabe, who had lost a leg and received multiple wounds in Europe and was not expected to survive but then beat the odds and returned to the States only to learn that same day that his family home had been burned to the ground. Story after story, I heard friends break down as they told of their personal travails. For me, the emotional power of the witnesses' stories at the San Francisco hearing was at times almost unbearable.

————

After three days of gut-wrenching testimony in San Francisco, the commission headed to Seattle for another three-day session, with Marutani stopping off in Sacramento to conduct his one-day hearing with the Japanese American community there. Even though the Sacramento hearing was minor and an afterthought, Sue Wren recognized that it was important if for no other reason than we could get coverage through the *Sacramento Bee*, the flagship newspaper of the nationwide McClatchy Publishing Company. The *Bee* was the main source of news throughout the Central Valley of California, a stronghold of Republican conservatism, and it was, in fact, McClatchy, along with Hearst Newspapers, that played a major role in creating the groundswell of fear following the attacks at Pearl Harbor. The front pages of these papers were plastered with jingoistic headlines, their editorials screamed for the ouster of Japanese Americans from the coastal regions, and their reports spread an endless supply of false stories about the untrustworthiness of any person of Japanese ancestry in this country. They played into the racist psychological pillaging that Earl Warren and his cronies had instigated with their warnings about Japanese Americans diluting the purity of the white race in the coastal region. The McClatchy papers in particular raised the alarm that resulted in the public outcry for the removal of the Japanese American population after the bombing of Pearl Harbor. Wren understood this history and had the *Bee* in her crosshairs to ensure that it covered both the San Francisco and Sacramento hearings, which it did; the day following the one-day session in the state capital resulted in stories about the hearing. I found this all very gratifying, especially when I thought about those long-ago headlines and photos that shrieked hatred against us. We were changing the narrative.

By the time the commission reached Seattle, I had experienced just about as many testimonies as I could endure, but, feeling personally responsible for my part in creating this situation, I sat through each day's proceedings and listened to each witness's personal tragedy. The stories were all variations on the same theme but made poignant by the unique circumstances in each tale. We heard about families losing their homes and businesses, careers destroyed, college educations ended. We heard about the bewilderment as the government began its program of exclusion and then the fear as families were shipped off to the desolate prisons in barren lands. We heard about how hard life was in the camps, how men joined the armed forces to prove their loyalty to the nation, the tragic sense of loss parents felt when they received notices from the army that their sons had been killed, how difficult it was after the war, whether families returned to the coast or tried to start somewhere anew. We heard how so many lives were utterly destroyed by those years behind barbed wire, left in shambles by an uncaring government and hostile public, even after the war's end. Each story was heartbreaking, no matter how similar it sounded to every other story. Maybe their similarities made the collective effect even more devastating because it emphasized how widespread the tragedy was. The collective pain of a community is always ultimately measured by individual experiences, and now it was on the record.

And yet, still we were criticized for making what others felt were unwarranted demands. Sure, they would say in letters to editors across the country, they lost sons in the war, but so did we and you don't see us trying to get money for that. Everyone suffered during the war, some more than others, but that's the cost of war and we were all willing to pay that price to preserve a way of life. Don't blame us for something that seemed necessary at the time.

The backlash was to be expected, but it bothered me how those who resented us tried to turn the personal stories of our tragedy into a spectacle. In some cases, the editors of papers who understood the greater meaning in our experiences made sure to run a balance of letters and stories that gave a fuller picture of the landscape of the issue. Sure, these editors would say, we all suffered during the war and we all sacrificed and many of us lost sons in battlefields abroad, and we are all proud of our sacrifices and our pain. But the difference, they would point out, is that white America was not forced from their homes. White America did not lose their businesses and careers and livelihoods, they were not imprisoned for who they were, for the color of their skin. The U.S. government did not let their women and children languish in prisons because of how they looked. As a nation that offers hope to the world,

America must recognize our past mistakes so that we might do better in the future.

As those editorials ran, I knew we had turned the tide, and that the commission, by giving the Nisei an opportunity to tell their stories, was serving an invaluable purpose. It was giving voice to the Nisei's personal and collective deepest heartbreaks and, in doing so, was changing the way mainstream Americans saw us.

After the Seattle hearing, the commission journeyed to Alaska to hear the wartime testimonies from Aleut Natives, and then returned to the lower forty-eight for the final scheduled community-based hearing in Chicago. It was interesting to note the change in tone between the witness testimonies given on the West Coast compared to those shared in the Midwest. The Midwestern Japanese Americans were guided, as we were, by the same cultural values of *shikataganai* and *gaman,* but they also felt the influence of what I can best describe as Midwestern pragmatism, a sense of moral certitude that Joan Didion once described as "wagon-train morality," an emphasis on doing what it took to survive. Even so, in Chicago we heard more of the same stories, and emotions remained high. When the last community witness spoke on September 23, 1981, we were all exhausted.

———————

Although the stories shared in each of the cities on the commission's tour were all personal variations on the same theme, the mood was noticeably less solemn in Chicago. Whether it was that Midwest grit or something else, I can't say, but I sensed a particular determination in the messages of the Chicago witnesses, a kind of challenge to the commissioners to take action, to make things right. It seemed as though the witnesses at this hearing understood that this was the last opportunity for us to emphasize what this entire campaign was about. They emphasized the larger picture, which was to ensure that what we had experienced was never again visited upon any group. As witnesses poured out their personal histories, they impressed upon the commission and the public that we were doing this for the future of the nation.

While the testimonies were still serious, there was also sometimes a touch of humor in the exchanges between witnesses and individual commissioners. The pragmatism of the Nisei mixed with their American sensibility often brought out a brand of humorous irreverence. It's the slightly off-color joke in church or at a graveside funeral service. It's the humor that makes the intolerable more tolerable, that allows us to survive unpleasant circumstances. That sense of lightness was present at all of the hearings to some degree, but nowhere as much as in Chicago. I found myself, along with the audience, frequently laughing at some comment or another, even as the witnesses were unburdening themselves of their darkest memories.

At the close of this, the last of the public hearings and the last time the voices of the Japanese American community would be heard by the commission before it made its official determination, Chairwoman Bernstein allowed each commissioner a final comment on the proceedings. One by one, each commissioner expressed how deeply he or she had been affected by the expressions of sorrow and pain, as well as by the profound urgings of the witnesses to recommend measures to right the wrongs inflicted on them, in part so that what they experienced during the war would never happen again in this country. I was heartened by the comments and felt this was a fitting end to the hearings.

And then Commissioner Bill Marutani spoke:

> These are some closing comments on my part, as a member of this commission. I want to tell you in all candor that much of the testimony I find very gut-wrenching for me.
>
> I am up here keeping a straight face, fighting lumps in my throat, fighting back any tears welling up in my eyes, especially when I hear testimony about young children, like Ms. Ige, Ms. Murao, being hauled off without parents.
>
> I can just understand what is happening. I also recall the testimony of Tom Watanabe and Sam Sato, where you have a wife and two children buried somewhere in an unmarked grave or your mother is dying and they will not let you go to see her.

I am hoping that in our final report, the depth of inhumanity that was inflicted upon the Nisei will be conveyed to Congress so that they will do the right thing.

I also must tell you, in all candor, as I sit and listen to the testimony, various emotions well up—anger, rage, frustration, sorrow, despair. I must add to that, however, that there is an element of hope.

And with those words, the commission returned to Washington, D.C., where it would hear, from November 2 to 3, from two principals who had carried out the president's orders when EO 9066 was implemented at the beginning of World War II.

KARL BENDETSEN

The commission returned for a second hearing in Washington, D.C., and this time the star witnesses were not senators or camp survivors but two of the principal figures responsible for the government's wartime policies against Japanese Americans: John J. McCloy, assistant secretary of war from 1941 to 1945, and Karl Bendetsen, the attorney liaison between the Provost Marshal General's Office and Western Defense Command's General John L. DeWitt, who had been charged with implementing the president's executive order. As the assistant secretary of war in 1942, McCloy had fashioned the government's exclusion policy once the war with Japan broke out. He was the chief architect of that policy under Secretary of War Henry Stimson and was instrumental in transforming the racial politics of the West Coast into a national policy. Bendetsen, an army major who was promoted to full colonel and put in charge of implementing the exclusion and internment policies, was the individual who established the concept of "military necessity" as the rationale for carrying out the racist policies that could not be justified by the facts, war or no war.

McCloy and Bendetsen weren't the only two witnesses on the list, but they were the ones everyone was curious to hear. I had waited years for this moment, to hear from the two men who had so efficiently and determinedly carried out the policy that sent us into those desolate prisons and destroyed our lives. They were living history. I had seen hundreds of memoranda and documents bearing the names of these two men, had seen in words how they had shaped the circumstances that had resulted in the violation of the Japanese American community. For the two years I had worked the Hill and the airwaves, I had picked apart the thinking and reasoning of these two men and had tried to prove to the nation that these key players of the government's wartime policies never thought about the human consequences of what they were doing. To McCloy, we were pawns in a calculation of political wins and losses. We were an inconvenience, a stumbling block in the way of the ambitions of a president who viewed us through a racially tinted lens. To Bendetsen, we were less than chattel, and he thought we should pay a price because of who we were. Scouring through the many recorded conversations he had with DeWitt, I saw a man who was possessed with a hunger for power, a man who manipulated the truth to conform to his obsessive need to validate his view of us as a threat to everything America stood for. I was convinced as I read over these documents that Bendetsen never saw us as anything more than abstractions, not human at all.

And now, with the members of the Commission on Wartime Relocation and Internment of Civilians sitting there, charged with uncovering the truth, I waited anxiously to hear Bendetsen and McCloy explain what it was that had driven them to their decisions and how they now viewed their roles in one of the most profound violations of constitutional rights of American citizens in the history of this country. I wanted to hear how they justified what they had done.

Bendetsen, in my mind, should have been the main target of the investigation because it was he, as assistant to Provost Marshal General Allen Gullion, who had argued so adamantly that the entire Japanese population should be removed from the West Coast, if not gotten rid of entirely. Transcripts of his conversations with DeWitt and all of the documents bearing his name reveal a man who was undeterred by constitutional considerations because he had one purpose in mind: the exclusion and imprisonment of every Japanese American within reach of the Pacific coastline. Time and again, he convinced DeWitt to acquiesce to his thinking; the general, his superior, was doing his bidding. I never read anything that showed Bendetsen to be a brilliant thinker, but DeWitt clearly was no match for him. When politicians including Earl Warren raised their racist cries on the West Coast, John McCloy heard and understood the politics of that clamor, but it was Karl Bendetsen who designed the plan and twisted the facts to meet the ends he sought. And it was Karl Bendetsen who rationalized those actions, in violation of the basic principles of democracy, as both necessary and right.

His actions show that he saw the Japanese as some kind of insidious plague on the sanctity of the whiteness of the West, just as Earl Warren did in provoking his brand of hatred against us. In all the research I had done on the internment, it was Bendetsen's manipulations and insistence on carrying out the president's orders that I found most disturbing: the cold calculation, the emotionless rationalizing, the view of this segment of the population on a strictly racial basis, his grim determination to expel us from the West.

As the truths about the WWII treatment of Japanese Americans closed in on Bendetsen over the course of the redress campaign's reach across the country, he attempted to remake himself, seeking distance from his former persona as the proud author of the draft that became Executive Order 9066 and as the principal mastermind of the exclusion and detention policies. Now in his seventies, his once immodest pride over how effectively he had designed and executed the enormous undertaking that resulted in the complete removal of every single person of Japanese ancestry from the exclusion zone was reduced to a man who claimed only limited knowledge of what had been ordered by others of superior rank with less sensitivity than he to the victims of an unfortunate policy.

Bendetsen, always the lawyer, hid behind words and played the bureaucrat during his testimony before the commission. His responses were steadfast and defiant, even when pushed by any of the commissioners. He was stoic and seemed unmoved by anything or anyone who challenged his views or comments. What bothered me most about Bendetsen was his coldness; he seemed so detached, as if none of this was in any way related to him—except for the fact that he defended his decisions and rejected any suggestion that he had acted improperly or had formulated policies based on questionable information. His response was always along the lines that he had just been working with what he was given. The decisions he made in 1942 that had affected the lives of the entire Japanese American population were not his. "I was just a pretty junior guy on the staff," he told Commissioner Flemming. According to Bendetsen, he was little more than a soldier doing his duty, echoing the inevitable and consistent response soldiers made to reckon for their actions, a response that echoed the words of German soldiers at Nuremberg and American combat troops defending their actions in Vietnam. Bendetsen insisted that he was doing nothing more than following orders but also said he did not regret anything he had done because he had never thought any of it was wrong.

Bendetsen defended his arguments from 1942, insisting that military necessity had driven the orders to remove and isolate the Japanese population from the West Coast. Yes, it was done in part because the government could not determine the loyalty of Japanese Americans, but, and to a greater urgency, he said, he was guided by a concern for the safety of Japanese Americans who would suffer at the hands of angry Filipinos who had lost relatives in the Philippines to the brutalities of Japan's armies in the Pacific. Sitting there listening to him, I only became more certain that here was a calculating and determined man who, in 1942, had done everything in his power to ensure that the exclusion policy was fully implemented.

Bendetsen had been handpicked for the responsibility and seemed to relish it. He had begun as an emissary for the army's racist provost marshal general, Allen Gullion, but Bendetsen became his own man once let loose to carry out the program. He was, in many ways, the perfect choice for the job: he was smart enough to understand how to manipulate the system and knew what had to be done and how to get it done. By creating the argument of "military necessity" for the implementation of an exclusion policy, he established a rationale for an action the nation's leaders knew was unconstitutional and unwarranted. Bendetsen's tactic was, in many ways, a stroke of genius: it played on the fears of an unknown that could not be knowable and presented a scenario of a constant threat—at least so long as the threat was allowed to remain. Bendetsen warped the truth and shaped those fears into a convenient reality.

As I listened to Bendetsen recount all of this in his own terms, I could see not only how he had created the logic of the internment for others but how he justified, in his own mind, everything he had done. He had convinced himself that we were dangerous. Is this how Nazi soldiers in postwar Germany had protected their own sanity even as they carried out the horrors of the Holocaust? Or did he really think we were dangerous? How could he say that even I, not yet three years old at the time, was a threat to America? As the commissioners barraged him with questions and tore apart his logic, Bendetsen refused to crumble, even as they gave him an easy opening to admit his mistake: it was easy enough to recognize the error of such thinking in hindsight, they said, and would he agree that this might be the case here? This perspective, however, did not ring true—or perhaps just did not seem of value—to Bendetsen.

It was interesting to me to see how the commissioners responded to Bendetsen, especially considering they were charged with conducting an unbiased investigation. As Arthur Goldberg questioned him, not always kindly, it was apparent that the commissioner, with his vast experience as a career statesman and a leading jurist in this country, felt no need to show deference to someone like Bendetsen. Marutani also challenged Bendetsen, and when the latter stood his ground, Marutani became visibly frustrated. Bendetsen could not, or would not, be broken or convinced to consider that he may have been wrong.

This was someone who felt no sympathy for having destroyed the lives of so many people through his own direct actions. In the end, he just didn't give a damn.

JOHN MCCLOY

And then there was John McCloy. He was a perfect study in contrasts with Bendetsen. Where the latter was very contained and restrained, quietly combative in the way an executive might be, McCloy was an amiable sort, openly friendly to the commissioners with whom he was acquainted, a man full of energy and political poise. He was very sure of himself, even in the face of the hostile grilling he knew awaited him. Even as he walked to the witness table and addressed the commissioners, he exuded the kind of confidence that comes from years of public service at the top levels of government and from having spent much of his political life dealing with world leaders, including the most obstinate and dangerous among them. There wasn't a fine line between his arrogance and confidence—they were one and the same.

There was nothing excessive or flamboyant about McCloy. Dressed in an expensive suit and armed with a sharp mind and wit, he could cross verbal swords with the quickest of the commissioners. He knew about government commissions—I suspect he had created more than his share—and knew he would face tough questions from this body of mostly Democrats. McCloy was an East Coast Republican who in 1940 had taken a top-level position in the Democratic Roosevelt administration, which was made up of other East Coast intellectuals who had built their reputations in the White House by bringing the country, and the world, out of the Great Depression through sheer force of intellectual will and political courage. McCloy had presence, the kind that drew eyes to him in a crowded room, and especially in an environment he knew so well, such as a federal commission hearing. This was clearly a man who understood power from the position of someone used to wielding a great deal of it.

McCloy's presence dominated the room, and it was interesting to see how Joan Bernstein paid deference to him as they parlayed back and forth in an exchange about which of McCloy's many official titles they would use to refer to him during the hearing. She was an attorney who herself had spent many years working at high levels of government, and so she shared McCloy's system of determining who is, and who isn't, important on the Washington scene. He definitely fell into the former category, and they both knew it. That said, her deference was politic: she showed respect but not one ounce of intimidation.

McCloy began his testimony by describing his position and responsibilities within the Roosevelt administration at the outbreak of the war and his role overseeing the exclusion and detention policies under EO 9066. He detailed how and why decisions were made, and recounted the difficulties the FDR inner circle had struggled with as it dealt with the question of what to do about the Japanese American population in the face of the often harsh and unyielding demands of the political voices on the West Coast. At no time did he seem to feel the need to justify or rationalize the decisions or apologize for anything he may have done or caused to happen in relation to the exclusion and imprisonment of Japanese Americans.

I was fascinated by McCloy. Here he was, an eighty-one-year-old man, his mind like a laser, recalling minute details in reports he had read or conversations he had had forty years earlier. His memory was so vast and so defined that the commissioners who tried to challenge him found it difficult to do so.

Unlike Bendetsen, he did not become defiant and defensive or try to evade questions about his responsibilities as assistant secretary of war, and he did not attempt to shift the blame to others by stating that he was only following orders. McCloy was combative and never contrite: he was sure of himself and did not shirk responsibility for the role he had played in the internment. Although it was FDR who made the final decisions and Henry Stimson to whom McCloy was accountable, it was he who was responsible for formulating the policy that changed our lives forever.

During questioning, he refused to acknowledge Marutani's characterization of these camps as prisons, detention centers, or concentration camps, despite Marutani's reminder that the camps were surrounded by barbed wire and there were soldiers posted in guard towers to make sure no one got out. McCloy continued to insist that he had intended the camps as temporary sites in which Japanese Americans would be kept safe and from which they could depart for destinations in other parts of the country. In his mind, these camps were never intended to become long-term residences or prisons.

McCloy never once dodged questions from any of the commissioners. He responded directly, sometimes with a hard edge to his responses, and he did not seem to object to being kept at the witness table for lengthy exchanges. He seemed almost eager to confront the questions that he knew were really accusations, and he seemed completely undaunted by even the harshest of them. When a commissioner dared cast doubt on his president, the man whom he ultimately served, McCloy answered with a steadfast faith that transcended the forty years since those dark days when the nation went to war. It was clear that the years had not diminished his admiration for and belief in Roosevelt, and at times it seemed he was at the witness table as much to defend the honor of his commander in chief as he was to defend his own actions.

In many ways, it was a remarkable display by a man who would not let the memory of the president he had served and most admired be tarnished. There was no mistaking that McCloy viewed Roosevelt as the great American hero who had brought the nation out of the depths of the Great Depression and had the courage and vision to lead his country in a world war that tested the soul of America. McCloy refused to accept that the internment was a mistake and insisted that it was a sound policy for the time and circumstances in which it served—a time when we faced the despotic threats of enemies in Europe and the Pacific, and when the devastating attack at Pearl Harbor fueled the confusion and hysteria of a nation catapulted into war. He maintained that even if, through the lens of forty years, the internment was decided to have been a mistake, those who had created and enforced the policies of exclusion and detention could not have known that at the time. And if mistakes were made—*if* mistakes were made—he was there to take the verbal bullets for his president.

As a witness, McCloy was skillful in shining facts through the prism that shaped his perspective of history, and the result was often convincing. He was especially skillful at articulating the confidence with which he or Stimson or Roosevelt made difficult decisions at a time when outcomes were so uncertain. It was clear that he believed that if he had made misjudgments, they could be judged only from the perspective of that time and not from a distance of forty years.

In the long hours I had spent at the National Archives going over hundreds, maybe thousands of documents, including memos and correspondence from McCloy himself, I had developed a sense of the man and why he may have done what he did. But watching him there as a witness before the commission told me something much more about him: he held an unwavering belief in what America stood for, and every action and decision he had made was wedded to that belief. He was, in a true sense, a patriot built from the mold of our Founding Fathers— unlike today's self-declared patriots with their perverted sense of devotion to the country. I didn't agree with how he interpreted history and his role in it, but I couldn't deny that he was impressive. This was the man I had wanted to see and get to know.

During a break following McCloy's testimony, Mike Masaoka introduced me to McCloy, whom he had first met as an adversary when he, Mike, was sent by the JACL to Washington during the war to lobby for the release of Japanese Americans from the concentration camps, as well as for the opportunity for Japanese Americans to serve this country in the military. McCloy said something about having known Mike for over forty years, and he described Mike as a great man and a close personal friend. Half-jokingly, Masaoka told McCloy that if any Japanese Americans found out they were friends, he would be in serious trouble; then he told McCloy that I was a national JACL leader and the head of the redress campaign and that I, especially, was not someone who should be told such things! McCloy said that was "nonsense" and, looking at me, said, in complete earnest, that Japanese Americans *should* realize just what a great man Mike was. "He bugged the hell out of me to create the 442nd, you know," McCloy said. And then he followed with something about having given the Nisei the opportunity to show this country just what great Americans they were, as if he hadn't needed Mike to convince him to allow the formation of the all–Japanese Ameri-can combat unit.

I replied with something along the lines of, "If you hadn't taken away our lives and forced us into those camps, we wouldn't have had to prove anything." I don't recall my exact words, but I remember I was seething with anger, barely managing to keep it below the surface. There was something maddening about how detached this man could be after spending a couple of hours talking before a federal commission about his role in destroying our lives and implicating the entire Japanese American population as disloyal to this country. And yet here he was making light of the circumstances that had hurt us so profoundly.

Then he said to me, "But Mike knows I'm one of the good guys." What happened next surprised me. Mike's response to that was, "I never said you were a good guy, John, just a good friend." McCloy was taken aback by that and didn't seem to know how to take the comment. Mike had said it with a touch of humor, but it was hard to know his intent. I don't know if Mike was posing for me, if this was his "cover-your-ass" attempt to distance himself from McCloy, but the moment seemed to have significant impact on both men. It seemed to cross the years between them.

The awkwardness lifted almost as quickly as it had descended, and the two men verbally jostled a little while longer, before McCloy again turned to me. It was a hard look. Dead serious. "You have no idea what we had to deal with in those days after Pearl Harbor," he said. "Those were awful times."

I should have merely acknowledged what he'd said and walked away. I had worked in Washington for two years by then and knew how this sort of interaction worked; some things you just count as losses. If you want to survive in that town, you learn to let certain moments go and just move on, especially in the face of someone who's more powerful than you.

But I didn't let it go. I don't remember the exact words I spoke then, but I remember exactly how I felt, how he looked at me, how I understood who this man truly was. "I know those were awful times, Mr. McCloy," I said, "but you put this man"—meaning Mike—"through a lot of shit he never should have had to go through, and you destroyed our lives. It was all so unnecessary, and you were the one person who could have stopped it. So I'm not so sure that you're the good guy you think you are."

I then told him I appreciated his willingness to testify before the commission and offered my hand. As he shook it, he said something curious: "I hope you win this fight. Good luck to you, young man." The way he said it made me feel there was some sincerity behind the words, but then again, he was a cagey old political animal who had dealt with some of the most powerful politicians in the world for over forty years. How could I trust a thing he said?

I've often thought about that moment with McCloy, and most of the time I regret not having said more, not having had the courage to tell him in ways that would hurt or bother him what a horrible man he was and what he had done to all of our lives. The funny thing, though, is that I felt no hatred toward him as we stood there talking. He was amicable enough, and a very quick-witted, almost funny guy. In talking with him, you would never get a sense of the kind of power he once had, or what he might have been capable of doing.

Still, I was taken aback by his parting words to me, and even more surprised at myself that I believed he meant what he said about the campaign's success. I was having a hard time reconciling the two years I had spent getting to know McCloy so intimately through his words and writings, and learning to dislike and distrust him, and then suddenly having him profess sympathy with our cause in this final accounting of right and wrong—a wrong for which he was largely responsible. The incongruity threw my equilibrium off kilter, and I didn't know what to think. I reminded myself then who John McCloy was and decided to take his comment with a political grain of salt.

I later ran into Mike in the corridor outside the hearing. I felt I should apologize for having possibly embarrassed Mike and burned one of his bridges by confronting McCloy in the way I had, but he said I shouldn't worry because McCloy needed to be told the truth as I had told it to him. I asked Mike if McCloy could have meant what he said when he wished the redress campaign well. Mike said he didn't know for sure but would remind McCloy of that if we later decided we could use his help and influence to lobby our eventual compensation bill. It could be worth having him make a call or two on our behalf, Mike said, and maybe even go visit a few offices together when the time came. Mike also said that McCloy had personally gotten to know every president since his days with FDR, something we should keep in mind if our bill ever made it to the White House.

CAMBRIDGE

Shortly after the Chicago hearing, Bernstein informed me that the Japanese American community in New York City was demanding a hearing there, and so on November 23, the commission convened a one-day hearing at the Roosevelt Hotel in Midtown. (The hotel was named after Theodore, not Franklin Delano, but the irony didn't go unnoticed.)

Two weeks later, the commission traveled to Cambridge, Massachusetts, for its final hearing, on December 9. I had arrived two days early along with Sue Wren, and while she did her magic and laid the media groundwork for the one-day event, I took care of my business and spent the off hours exploring Cambridge and the Harvard campus. For a Californian like me, the biting cold, snow-covered streets and half-frozen river were delights rather than inconveniences.

This was not my first time in the Boston area—I had been there to give speeches in the early days of the redress campaign—but on this trip the historical significance of the city weighed heavily on my mind, no doubt because I hoped we would soon be making history here too. The Cambridge event would be the culmination of the previous hearings and all the work that had come before, and it would reduce the complex issue of internment to one essential question: Do the protections guaranteed by the Constitution apply to all individuals in this country— whether citizens or not, whether white or not, and even whether under a cloak of suspicion, real or imagined, during times of national crisis? It was my expectation that the views of the constitutional experts and legal scholars called upon to testify on this question would ultimately refute the government's arguments and rationalizations that had stood for forty years.

The hearing began with opening comments by Bernstein, who framed the day's discussion around the constitutionality of the government's wartime policies. What followed was not so much a hearing as it was a series of presentations by scholars, beginning with Peter Irons, a visiting professor at the University of Massachusetts and someone who would later play an important role in the legal challenges of the wartime Supreme Court cases. Irons was followed by Professor Henry Monaghan of Boston University's School of Law, and Christopher Pyle, a law professor at Mount Holyoke College, whose area of expertise was civil liberties and constitutional law. All three legal scholars focused their presentations on the constitutional issues surrounding the wartime policies aimed at Japanese Americans and ultimately reflected the popular view of colleagues across the country that the Supreme Court rulings in *Korematsu*, *Hirabayashi*, and *Yasui* were some of the worst decisions rendered by the high court.

The evidence and arguments presented by the scholars was nothing new or startling. We had been saying all the same things from the beginning—at JACL meetings and conventions, at community events, on the air, on speaking tours and in meetings with members of the House and Senate. There at Harvard, however, the argument had been granted more legitimacy. Our critics could say all they wanted about the supposed necessity of the government's emergency wartime policies and actions, but the overwhelming message that day in Cambridge was a reiteration that the internment was wrong, and for a number of reasons. It was unnecessary; it was racist; it was political; it was stupid politics. Most of all, though, the internment was unconstitutional and illegal. If America continued to insist that the internment as a policy was excusable regardless of its unconstitutionality, then we would have to examine whether the rule of law meant anything at all as a principle in this country. The application of constitutional law could not be applied selectively or only when it was convenient; to say otherwise would be to say that the fundamental basis for governance and order in the United States was illusory and meaningless.

So then, what does the nation do when it is proven to have been so unjust and so abusive against a group of its own citizens? Do we just forget it and say, "It was a difficult time"? Do we shrug it off and say it was a mistake but one that seemed necessary? Do we say that the exigencies of war demanded measures that were regrettable but also unavoidable under the circumstances? Do we say that the Constitution doesn't stand for the same things for all people? Do we say this was the best we could do with what we had?

Do we say that some people matter and others don't?

COMMISSION DELIBERATIONS

Once the hearings were completed, the commission settled in to do its work. The staff continued its research in the National Archives and the files of the government's World War II holdings, kept in repositories all over the country. The staff also began the laborious task of reading the transcripts of the 750 testimonies presented at the hearings, plus the literally thousands of written testimonies that had been packed and shipped to the commission's research office in Washington. There, staffers would mine each testimony for details that would serve the investigative needs of the commission. It was a monumental task, but one that was maintained faithfully over two years, before it culminated in the drafting of the report by commission director Angus Macbeth and its subsequent review by Bernstein and the other commissioners.

In the year that it would take the commission to complete its work following the hearings, I had two main jobs: one was to lobby the commissioners to include in their final recommendation a provision for individual compensation, and the other—the one that would take up the majority of my time—would be to liaise with congressional offices. Dan Inouye had been right that laying the groundwork for redress through the publicity generated by the commission hearings was crucial to our ultimate strategy of seeking a reparations bill, and although we had raised the baseline of knowledge about the internment overall, we still had to convince enough members of Congress to vote in favor of full redress should such a bill come their way. We knew the majority of congresspeople were still opposed to the idea of reparations, but it helped to know that at least we wouldn't have to work so hard to convince members that we had been treated unjustly during the war. My job was now to begin to chip away at any remaining resistance.

On the matter of lobbying the nine members of the commission, my work had started in observing the effect the personal testimonies were having on the individual commissioners. I could not fathom that any one of them hadn't been affected enormously by the stories they were hearing, but my interest was not their reactions to the stories, per se; I needed to try to measure how much impact the stories would have on the deliberations that followed. Would it be enough to compel the commissioners to recommend reparations? I knew by this time that all nine commissioners considered our wartime treatment unwarranted, even Daniel Lungren, who had made it clear that he opposed monetary compensation. My assessment was that the commission as a whole would concur that the internment was not justified, and I expected (based on conversations with some of the commissioners themselves) that we could expect their recommendations to include monetary compensation, although we didn't know how much and in what format, whether individual compensation or trust fund. My main challenge was to persuade them on the amount of the individual compensation figure—$25,000 per person—as well as the amount of the trust fund, which I had decided with Inouye and Masaoka, on separate occasions, to be $50 million. I felt our demand for a formal apology from the U.S. government was already a given, so I left that alone and concentrated on the details of compensation.

Another major concern was whether the commission's recommendations would include some kind of mechanism that would help prevent future administrations from acting so precipitously in the future. I figured they would have to be ingenious indeed to come up with any such proposal because these commissioners, being who they were, knew better than any of us that all the proper and necessary safeguards against such injustice already existed; the Constitution, with the individual protections enumerated in the Bill of Rights, is an eloquent declaration that guarantees the rights of all citizens, and so it was not the frailty of the law itself but the fallibility of our nation's leaders that had accounted for the violation of those rights, and no manner of legislation could protect American citizens against circumstances yet unknown.

In drafting the legislation that had created the commission, Glenn Roberts in Mineta's office had left the consequences of the commission's investigation completely open ended: that is, if the investigation resulted in a conclusion that the government's policies had been warranted and justified, so be it. If, however, the conclusion found the government's

arguments unacceptable, it would be up to the commissioners to determine if there was enough cause for remedy. If so, they would have the
latitude to evolve the recommendations to such effect as they deemed
appropriate. What I already knew about the character of these nine individuals as commissioners gave me full confidence that they would let
the facts speak for themselves and rule in our favor.

The one commissioner who strongly opposed the monetary compensation issue was, we all knew, Dan Lungren. I talked to him several
times about this—two or three meetings in his D.C. office with Ikejiri
and once at his district office in Long Beach, when I was accompanied
by George Nakano, a constituent and at that time a council member
for the city of Torrance—and I knew he was inflexible on the matter
of reparations. While there was no ambiguity about his opposition to
monetary payments—not just for Japanese Americans but for anyone,
as a matter of principle—what was lost in the Japanese American community's assessment of him was the fact that he voted with his fellow
commissioners in what turned out to be a unanimous agreement on the
findings and conclusions of the federal investigation. This was important because it proved once again that, while we might disagree on the
issue of remedies, there was no denying the truth of the facts of history.

———

As for the other commissioners, I had little doubt that four of them—
Bernstein, Goldberg, Drinan, and Marutani—favored monetary compensation, and among that group, my guess was that Drinan and Goldberg would be the strongest advocates of individual compensation. I
also knew that Marutani favored individual compensation, but his position on this issue was nuanced. Bill had a long history of social activism.
Many JACLers thought his now-famous Freedom Rider trip was done
on behalf of the JACL, but I knew he went because he felt a deep personal conviction in the fight against that particularly Southern brand
of racism and injustice. He preferred to keep that to himself, however,
and brushed it aside whenever anyone asked him about it, in much the
same manner that he brushed aside mention of his having served with

distinction in the Military Intelligence Service in the Pacific during the war. He was an enigma to many of us who knew him through the JACL, but I did know from my encounters with him at the organization's meetings that he was so deeply tied to Japanese cultural values that our seeking monetary compensation was repugnant to him because he, like many in the old guard of the JACL, believed it dishonored us. Asking for money as compensation for the loss of our freedom and dignity was not something that could ever be culturally reconciled.

And yet in the April 1978 meeting when we created what would become the Salt Lake City Guidelines, Bill and I were the ones who advocated the sum of $50,000, his position being that as long as we were going to do so, we should not insult ourselves by asking for too little. That $50,000 figure was one of the few things about which Bill and I were in complete agreement.

Between Father Drinan and Arthur Goldberg, I thought the former would be the strongest advocate for individual payments, but it turned out that Goldberg thought our suggestion of $25,000 was too modest, timid, and conservative. He thought we should have set our figure at $50,000, probably the maximum we could realistically push through Congress.

It was encouraging to have Justice Goldberg, one of the most informed and significant individuals in the country at the time, express such confidence on this point, but while the commission could make whatever recommendation it wanted to, ultimately we (meaning the JACL) would have to fight for the actual compensation bill, and we didn't want to overshoot and then fail. While $50,000 was a nice thought, I had been in Washington long enough to know that, despite what Goldberg said, it was totally unrealistic. We hadn't yet done any hard analyses on the projected numbers of Japanese Americans who would be eligible for compensation, but I calculated approximately sixty thousand still living, which, at $50,000 per person, would put the total amount over the $3 billion range. The United States was at this time still rebounding from a Carter-era recession, and the first two years of Reagan economic policies didn't hold much promise of a quick recovery, if any, so raising the ante on our compensation package felt risky at best and self-defeating at worst. I took Goldberg's encouragement more as cheerleading than serious advice.

In a separate conversation I had with Father Drinan, one of the most progressive members of the House and certainly the most progressive of the commissioners, he indicated that even the $50,000 suggested by Goldberg was far too inadequate if we hoped to make a statement about lost freedoms, but he also realized that we would never be able to get a bill passed that reached into the $3 billion range.

Edward Brooke and Arthur Flemming were probably the most realistic in their assessment of what amount we might hope to get. Neither had yet committed to recommending individual payments, but both thought the amount the JACL had decided on—$25,000—might be doable.

When commission director Angus Macbeth and I talked, the most he was willing to tell me was that individual monetary compensation *was* part of the discussion about recommendations, but he wasn't free to discuss the deliberation details themselves. He was of course aware of the JACL's position on compensation.

Although I had very little contact with Angus, I got the sense from Sue Wren that his presence on the staff brought a distinct sense of order, and I could see why Bernstein had prevailed on him to accept the directorship of such an important and massive undertaking. He was an old hand at Washington politics, but more importantly, he had a brilliant analytical mind. He was the insurance policy that the report would be substantive and thorough. Angus was genuinely a nice guy, but he didn't play games, and I liked that about him; any time I asked him for information, he was always forthright with me, even if it was to tell me he couldn't give me the information I was after. Bernstein also flat-out refused to discuss the recommendations other than to say that, yes, compensation was part of the discussion, which at that point was like telling me the sky was blue.

As time passed, however, my discussions with Bernstein became more specific. At one point she suggested that while there was a good possibility that compensation would be included in the package, I shouldn't expect the $25,000 figure proposed by the JACL. When I asked why, she was very frank with me and said that if the commissioners accepted that figure, it would appear they were under the thumb of the JACL. I rather doubted that, but I was willing to go along with her story. Fine, I told her, set the figure at $50,000 and it would be abundantly clear to everyone that the JACL had absolutely nothing to do with the recommendations.

"Come on, John, you know that's not realistic," was her response, reminding me that we would never get a bill through Congress with $3 billion in individual payments, not to mention a possible educational trust fund on top of that. "Okay, how about $30,000? That would send a clear message that the JACL's not in control," I replied. She gave me a hard took and said, "So would $20,000." I argued that the right thing for the commission to do was recommend an amount higher than the JACL's demand for $25,000 in order to send a message to both Congress and the nation about the magnitude of the injustice. It was an important message, I argued, because we had already let it be known publicly what our demands were, including the monetary amount we had in mind. Here was the chance for the commission to make an impact not just on the Japanese American community but on the nation. Our overarching intent, I told her, was to send the strongest possible message that this type of prejudicial action would have serious political and economic consequences in the future, if repeated. The amount had to be high enough to make that statement loud and clear. Otherwise, why not make the amount merely symbolic, as Senator Orrin Hatch (R-Utah) had suggested to me previously and would do so again: as a mere gesture, the commission could recommend a payment of $1 per individual. But to do so would be a mockery of the Constitution and an insult to Japanese Americans, and so, I argued, would be recommending less than the amount sought by the JACL. Anything less than $25,000 per individual would send a weak signal and undermine this attempt to correct such a monumental wrong.

Jodie listened to me patiently, but there was nothing I said that she didn't already know or hadn't already thought about, I'm sure. I wonder sometimes if she found it amusing how sincere and insistent I was about things that were completely obvious to her!

Nevertheless, I was able to tell her one thing she didn't know: I told her that if the commission came out with, say, $15,000, the JACL would reject the amount and publicly denounce the recommendation. Our goal, I reminded her, was to seek the introduction of appropriations legislation in accordance with the Salt Lake City Guidelines, which was our official position on the issue. I told her that I had gambled with the future legacy of Japanese Americans by choosing the commission strategy, so if the commission recommended a figure that was unacceptable to us as an organization, to us as a community, I would speak on behalf of the JACL and the Japanese American community to denounce the recommendation as politically timid and insulting.

It was not a threat. You don't threaten someone like Jodie Bernstein. But I wanted her to know in no uncertain terms that anything less than $20,000 would be absolutely unacceptable to us, and if that's what the commission decided on, we would be at war with each other. As I said all this, I was mindful that she had spent her career in government service and had more than paid her dues and knew what she was doing. I had tremendous respect for her and appreciated her candor and especially her sympathetic leanings, and there was nothing I could fault her for as far as the commission proceedings were concerned. Having gotten to know her over the past year, I was happy she had been the commission chair. But I also needed her to know that I would not take things lying down. Ron Ikejiri and I met with Bernstein several times after that, and we kept pushing the JACL's preferences for individual compensation at or above the magic number of $25,000, and although Bernstein was always willing to meet with us and discuss what details she could, she wouldn't ever reveal her hand. We would just have to keep waiting.

I continued having conversations with all the other commissioners, with the exception of Bill Marutani, who, true to what he had told us at the beginning of the process, would not discuss commission business with me, let alone even agree to meet with me. Lungren was willing to discuss the concept of a trust fund, although he still thought it problematic, and I met with little or no resistance from the other commissioners with regard to the concept of individual compensation. At that point, all I could do was make sure compensation was on the table and then I would just have to trust that the commissioners who were on our side would fight that battle on our behalf.

Senator Inouye and I met on a fairly regular basis to discuss the redress campaign in general as well as our more immediate concern, the possible outcomes of the federal commission. During one of my visits to his office, he asked me which of the JACL's demands I most wanted, most *needed* to see become a part of the recommendations: the individual payments, the creation of a trust fund, or the formal apology to Japanese Americans from the U.S. government?

Concerned that by not saying "individual payments" I would be opening the door to possible alternatives to that option, I replied that it was the money for the victims. Unless we sought and received direct financial compensation for the injustice committed against us, and unless the sum total of that restitution was large enough to make an impact and a statement, nothing we accomplished with this campaign would serve as a deterrent against future abuses of this nature. An apology wouldn't do it, and in fact we had already gotten one of those when President Ford issued his "American Promise" statement upon rescinding Executive Order 9066 in 1976. But ask a hundred Nisei about that and maybe you will find five who know anything about it, and ask a thousand non–Japanese Americans and not a one will have a clue what you are talking about. That's how insignificant an apology would be, I said. An apology would be nothing more than words.

Strong words to say to one of the most powerful politicians in Congress, but our relationship by then was built on trust, and I was confident he understood my reasoning and even agreed that the financial cost would be the statement to the future. (Also, as with Bernstein, there was nothing I could tell Inouye that he didn't already know, but I hope he was at least amused by my earnestness and passion for the subject.) Yes, compensation was necessary, he acknowledged, but so was the apology, and, he said, contrary to what I thought, the apology may be ultimately of greater importance and significance. He was thinking from the perspective of his colleagues in Congress. If we hoped to keep the campaign alive, Inouye believed they would need to apologize first, because the apology would be the thing that would open the door for us to be able to launch a drive for compensation legislation.

All along, I had accepted that the apology would be a factor, but only now as we discussed it as a legislative process did I realize it was the linchpin to the entire commission strategy. If Congress accepted the commission's report—and there was no reason for them not to since the facts were irrefutable—it followed that an apology would be an

appropriate response; it would be unthinkable for Congress to acknowledge and admit the wrong without apologizing for it. "You cannot say
you agree that a terrible injustice was committed against Japanese
Americans by the government," Inouye told me, "but then say you're
not going to do anything about it."

I agreed with Inouye's reasoning in theory, but I still saw a seemingly
uncrossable chasm between acknowledging the wrong and agreeing to
provide compensatory redress. We would have to find a way either to
close that gap or to bridge it. But there was also the matter of whether
the apology would be a good first step toward full redress or if Congress
would see that as an end in itself, and even a way around the question
of reparations. My cynicism and distrust of politicians led me to believe
strongly that we, the JACL, should *not* ask for an apology as part of
our official list of demands, lest it become an easy excuse to avoid any
consideration of compensation. Given the choice between offering an
apology or offering monetary compensation, of course Congress would
opt for the apology. And then what?

Throughout the process of my lobbying the commissioners and
attempting to dissect their thinking, my father, whose health continued to deteriorate, often came to mind. I visited him as frequently as
I could, and meanwhile ruminated on what he had always believed
about our responsibilities as Japanese Americans, which was that we
had an obligation to fight for our rights. Even when I was a young boy,
he impressed upon me that if I were ever given the opportunity to do
something about the internment, I should accept the role given to me.
My entire life had changed because I heeded that advice. I had willingly given up much in choosing this course, not because of some stupid
notion of self-sacrifice above all else but because I was my father's son.

It had been important to my father that we Japanese Americans be
granted our rightful place in America, finally, and I was proud that he
had understood the redress campaign was the road that would lead
us there. I had wanted badly to succeed at some stage of the campaign

while he was still alive, but that didn't happen. He wanted to believe completely in America again but never had that opportunity, never saw what we were able to accomplish, never saw the final judgment contained in the commission report. He died in July 1982, half a year before the commission concluded its investigation and issued its report to the nation.

THE CWRIC REPORT AND
RECOMMENDATIONS

In December 1982 the commission published its report, a four-hundred-page investigative study that examined the circumstances surrounding the government's decision to execute an exclusion policy aimed at the Japanese American population and to place under military detention more than 118,000 individuals, three-fifths of whom were American citizens, without trials or any evidence of guilt or wrongdoing. Titled *Personal Justice Denied*, the report stated unequivocally in its conclusion that the decision to exclude and detain was a result of racism, wartime hysteria, and a failure of leadership. In their examination of incontrovertible facts, the commissioners concluded that the arguments of national security and military necessity were not reasonable or credible, and they found that President Roosevelt and other leaders in the administration had accepted, without question, the racist rationale of politicians and military leaders in the West Coast at the outbreak of the war.

On February 24, 1983, Bob Matsui, from the floor of the U.S. House of Representatives, began:

> Mr. Speaker, today the Commission on Wartime Relocation and Internment will deliver to Congress and release to the public its report setting forth the facts and circumstances surrounding Executive Order 9066 and the impact of the order on Japanese American citizens and resident aliens.
>
> The report, entitled *Personal Justice Denied*, sets forth the circumstances surrounding the initiation and implementation of orders from the highest authorities of our land to evacuate and intern American citizens and resident aliens of Japanese ancestry.

...It is a report that for the first time sets forth the tragic and shameful chapter of our history that is unknown to millions of Americans.

(Congressional Record, 98th Congress)

Having been in close contact with the commissioners in the several months after the hearings ended, I had a fairly good idea of what to expect when the report was finally released. Ikejiri and I had discussed the possible outcome, but Japanese Americans across the country were stunned when they watched the news broadcasts that summarized the unanimous report that found the government culpable of an egregious racist policy. The phones in Ikejiri's office rang for days, many of the callers JACL members hungry to get a copy of the report so they could read through the entire four hundred pages and see for themselves an official government document that declared they were the victims of a racist policy.

The media response exceeded our expectations, surpassing even the wide coverage of the commission hearings. The story appeared on the front pages of many if not most of the major newspapers around the country, and all of the network news programs began that evening with, "Today, the Commission on Wartime Relocation and Internment of Civilians released its report..." The story ran on local news outlets practically everywhere, even in areas where there were no substantial Asian American populations. As far as I was concerned, this was a slam dunk, an absolute confirmation that our decision to follow the commission strategy had been the right one.

———

In June 1983, six months after the report was published, the commission issued its formal recommendations, which included monetary compensation that would, in part, signal to the nation and its future leaders that there was no place for national policies based on bigotry and hate, that such actions are odious to the ideals of American democracy and to this nation's sense of morality. It was a strong message.

And it was stunning.

The commission's recommendations included five measures, of which the first three would form the core of our redress legislation: First, the commissioners were unanimous in urging that a joint resolution by Congress, signed by the president, acknowledge that "a grave injustice was done" and offer an apology to the victims of the government's actions. Second, Congress was advised to appropriate funds to create a trust for humanitarian and educational purposes. And third, Congress was urged to set aside $1.5 billion from the fund to provide individual payments of $20,000 to each of the surviving victims of the actions taken under the aegis of FDR's executive order. Further, noting in its report that the commission had neither the authority nor means to rectify the legal judgments against Japanese Americans relative to the government's policies of exclusion and detention, the commission included in its recommendations that the president formally pardon those convicted by the courts for refusing to obey orders that led from the military proclamations at the outset of the war. In this last recommendation, it was obvious that the commissioners sought a way to mitigate the Supreme Court decisions in *Hirabayashi, Korematsu,* and *Yasui,* as well as lesser-known cases.

In this singular document, Joan Bernstein and her commission colleagues had taken an extraordinary and courageous step to do what no governmental body in the United States had ever considered: redress for the victims of a governmental injustice.

In the midst of the cacophony of reactions to the commission's recommendations, there were those who understood that the recommendations were just that—recommendations and not mandates. The campaign was not yet a *fait accompli*. There would still be a legislative battle to implement the recommendations, and that was just what we had been preparing for all along.

Although we at the JACL expressed our public disappointment that the commission's recommendations had not met our demand for $25,000 in individual compensation, our statement was only political posturing and, I'm sure, not unexpected. We even discussed with Bernstein and Macbeth that we would need to express our displeasure at the figure, even though we were ultimately pleased with the amount. They, of course, understood; it was politics, after all. In the end, we accepted the final recommendations and appreciated that the nine commissioners had been so diligent in bringing this matter to a close with a report and recommendations that, for the first time, unilaterally made an official statement that the WWII internment was unjust. This was enormous and profound in the hearts and minds of Japanese Americans, and we were, more than ever, prepared to move forward in our efforts to bring those recommendations to fruition. Again, however, taking that next step wasn't in our hands alone; it was up to Representative Norman Mineta to decide when the redress bill would be introduced to Congress.

————

It's worth noting here that Bill Marutani, the lone Japanese American on the commission, stayed true to his word: not once did he allow contact between himself and the JACL or its representatives throughout the deliberations of the commission, even as every other commissioner accepted my requests for meetings. I also want to point out that Marutani was the only one of the nine commissioners who attended every single day all eleven hearings of the commission—the nine originally scheduled plus the two additions, Sacramento and New York City. He listened to more than 750 testimonies, always sitting there stoically, the image of an impartial and fair jurist. I found it difficult to hear so much pain and suffering in the words of the Nisei, but Bill never once wavered, never showed his personal reactions, stayed always strong in order to give the witnesses who appeared before him the courage to continue their testimonies.

That wasn't to say he didn't have his moments, though. His anger showed as he questioned John McCloy and Karl Bendetsen, and when he admonished a witness who claimed the Nisei Military Intelligence Service (MIS) soldiers were traitors because some of them had not returned from scouting missions, the implication being that they had joined the Japanese forces. Marutani, himself an MIS veteran of distinction, his voice seething but controlled, said, "I'll tell you why they never came back. It's because if they were captured by the Japanese, they were decapitated." His anger was palpable. His personal connection to the community was underscored during the Seattle hearing when he responded to an older Nisei who had shared details about his work as a foreman at a cannery in Alaska prior to the war. "You know that young boy you mentioned in your testimony, the one who worked for you at the cannery?" Bill asked the man. "That was me! I was that young boy!" If not for decorum, Marutani would have gone over and hugged the witness right then. It was the only time Bill broke ranks from his judicial propriety, and it was good to see him so happy.

And finally, it is very much worth noting that Marutani never once asked for or accepted reimbursement for any of his expenses. He paid entirely out of his own pocket for his airfare, hotel costs, ground transportation, meals, everything, and he was the only commissioner to do so. He did not spend any of the commission's allocated $3 million. Not a single penny. Bill Marutani and I may not have seen eye to eye on many issues, and certainly there was no affection lost between us, but there were a lot of things to admire and respect about him. Even though I was disappointed to learn that he wouldn't act as the JACL's inside man on the commission, I needn't have worried. Bill wasn't there to represent the interests of the JACL but to represent the interests of all Japanese Americans, and I think he did a great job.

HOHRI V. U.S.

In the months between the publication of the commission's report, in December 1982, and the announcement of its recommendations, in June 1983, we had been hearing talk that the National Council for Japanese American Redress (NCJAR), led by Chicago Nisei William Hohri, was going to file a lawsuit against the government for an amount that would far exceed what we expected the commission would recommend for reparations. Even more troublesome was that the lawsuit was planned before the recommendations would be released. Also during this time, Representative Mervyn Dymally of Los Angeles introduced a compensation bill on behalf of the National Coalition for Redress/Reparations (NCRR), calling for $25,000 in individual reparations, and in January of 1983, Mike Lowry would introduce his own bill on behalf of the Seattle Japanese American community, demanding $20,000 in reparations. Matsui was upset at the timing of both bills; Mineta thought they were inconsequential and was more concerned by the NCJAR lawsuit. Neither bill gained any traction and would eventually die while the JACL awaited the introduction of its redress bill.

William Hohri, et. al., v. United States was filed in March 1983 and left no doubt as to its convictions about the pernicious intent of the government's wartime policies. The plaintiffs charged that the government unjustly forced Japanese Americans from their homes at the outbreak of World War II and imprisoned them in concentration camps without justifiable cause.

I was intrigued that the lawsuit contained information only recently unearthed by the commission research staff, a curious circumstance pointed out to me by my research assistant, Carole Hayashino. It wasn't surprising, since commission researcher Aiko Herzig-Yoshinaga was one of the Washington, D.C., plaintiffs for the *Hohri* case (along with her husband, Jack), and it was pretty much assumed that information from the commission's research was finding its way to the community, and especially to individuals affiliated with groups like NCJAR and NCRR, as well as independent academic researchers. This raised some eyebrows in D.C., but I thought, "To hell with propriety and ethics, the cat is out of the bag and there's no going back." I figured we *all* deserved to know *all* the facts.

The *Hohri* complaint cited twenty-two causes of action against the government, with damages totaling $23 billion. It was a huge figure, but in my mind, that amount was more realistic in terms of providing some reasonable measure of relief to make up for the magnitude of the government's callous disregard for the Constitution. And the catch in *Hohri* was that it would be decided straight up or down: he either wins his case or doesn't, as opposed to the more fluid terms of nonbinding recommendations from a federal commission. On its own terms, I did not find the suit necessarily objectionable. The timing, though, would create a problem because it overlapped with our final effort to get a monetary compensation bill through Congress.

With the commission in the final stages of discussing its recommendations, there was nothing more we could do to influence the outcome, and so we had shifted our attention to lobbying the Hill in advance of our own redress bill. I had set my sights on House members who were either on the fence or opposed to redress, and now that the subject of compensation was officially on the table, I found that those who were not sympathetic to the subject put up stronger walls than ever before. Most were just plain stubborn, but some turned downright hostile, and it soon became apparent that it wasn't worth the time or effort at this stage of our lobbying to waste time on the hard opposition. It was more productive to call on those House members who at least sidestepped the issue by claiming they wouldn't make a decision until they had read the commission's report once it was issued. The new complication, however, was that there were now representatives who hid behind the NCJAR lawsuit, saying they thought it prudent to stay undecided until the Court had rendered a decision on *Hohri*. My counterargument was that if *Hohri* succeeded, it would cost the government much more money than what we were estimating as the likely amount of the commission's recommendations. Our estimated $2 billion wasn't an unreasonable request, and it paled in comparison to *Hohri*'s $23 billion. That said, if *Hohri* succeeded, I certainly wouldn't mind because, in my opinion, the larger amount more accurately reflected the cost of the freedoms that had been lost. Take away my freedom and put me in prison for no reason other than your own racism, and this is what it will cost you. I saw it as a win either way.

For us the case provided an interesting cross-sectional insight into the Japanese American community. Many assailed the filing as excessive and therefore not in keeping with the Japanese sense of social decorum and honor. It was "too *hakujin*" (that is, too white) and inappropriate for a community that has historically never sought solutions through litigation. Others in the community, however, responded positively, saying that *Hohri* had a more realistic take on how significant our lost liberties were as Americans. It would take a big action to undo a big action.

The response from many in the JACL leadership was predictable, if for no other reason than because the principal in the class-action suit was one of the JACL's harshest critics. Hohri and I would often come to verbal fisticuffs over redress strategies in the *Pacific Citizen* and other vernacular newspapers, and he was among those most strongly opposed to pursuing the federal commission strategy. Some saw Hohri's suit as a kind of frivolous stunt, no more than a futile exercise to gain attention and win favor among the anti-JACL segments of the Japanese American community. I had always thought Hohri as one of the more intelligent and articulate of our critics, and I admired his writings even though I didn't agree with what he wrote. We ultimately agreed on the larger philosophical ideas of the issue, but we differed on strategy.

I had no reason to dislike Hohri personally because, up to that point, we had never met face-to-face, and as much as I may not have liked the harsh criticism he directed at me, I let it go as the discontent of someone whose proclivity to dislike the JACL made him misjudge our intent, and the sincerity of it. When we heard the rumors about a possible lawsuit by NCJAR, Min Yasui called me to suggest that the JACL go to court to stop Hohri. Min was worried that Hohri's class-action suit could jeopardize our legislation, or at the very least would become a distraction. He was right, of course, but we had no grounds for filing a lawsuit to stop Hohri, which Min, as an attorney, must have known. Instead, he made it a point to rail against Hohri and his lawsuit as often and as vehemently as Hohri spoke out against the JACL, and I suppose he thought it did some good, or at least made him feel better. As for me, I started to see how maybe the NCJAR lawsuit could be used to our favor, and I intended to exploit that as much as possible.

One thing was certain: the NCJAR case could not be ignored (one doesn't just set aside a potential $23 billion suit against the government!), and since we couldn't make it go away, I would find a way to leverage it on behalf of our cause. The commission report had set the stage, *Hohri* was laying some groundwork, and now we were ready to jump into the final stage of our fight for justice.

6

THE FINAL STAGE

(1983-1988)

ONE VOTE AT A TIME

We had made it at last to the final drive on this long journey for redress. We had been down this road once before, when we got the commission bill passed in 1980, and now we would make one last loop toward the finish line. We knew that trying to pass a bill with an award amount of $2 billion would be met with resistance, and we were right. We also saw the resurgence of some of the old arguments against redress, from the hand-wringing excuses about decisions made in wartime, to "you deserved what you got," to the full spectrum of insults from the more racist, hardline reactionaries (which in some ways seemed more honest, even if more distasteful).

Experience had taught me that we would also encounter arguments that would range from brooding injunctions against taking corrective actions *now* for decisions of the past to the complexity of assigning guilt and redemption. Once you go down that path, where do you begin to draw the lines to determine a single standard of morality even as social mores change over time? The obvious examples of paying reparations for victims of slavery and tribal genocide were for many an impediment to even considering the idea of rectifying a single past misjudgment, lest all of the others come back to haunt us. It was a can-of-worms defense, but also, it seemed to me, more than that. And it was more than money too. It meant having to admit to guilt for things past. It judged the moral conduct of the United States and questioned its claims of greatness in a time when we were engaged in wars for our very survival as a nation. Good and evil were not so easily defined when it came to looking inward at ourselves, and some thought that to open those chapters of history could only harm the legacy we had built as a nation emerging victorious from a great war.

The success of the commission report and recommendations, it would seem, should have been enough to help us move a reparations bill through Congress. But nothing is for sure when it comes to legislation, and the safe assumption had to be that many of the congresspersons who supported our previous bill would harbor serious reservations about voting in favor of an appropriations bill on the same issue. Of course, logic would suggest that those who accepted the facts the commission had presented would also support action to rectify the injustices brought to light by the investigation, and yet logic isn't always the natural order of things, and especially not when it comes to politics.

In a way, we would be starting over. We would start with our list of 435 members of the House and determine each individual's position on the issue of compensation. We would once again have to call for support from our friends, including national civil rights organizations, public interest groups, environmental groups, and religious and theological communities. Often, our unlikeliest of allies were the professional lobbyists from the large and influential law firms that represented commercial and corporate interests, a group with whom we had virtually no shared concerns except that we had made personal connections with them and they were willing to use their political capital to help us because they believed in our cause.

Now, for the first time, we began to believe—truly believe, not just hope—that we could get a compensation bill approved in Congress. On the House side, we had the support of some of the most influential and powerful members, including Peter Rodino from New Jersey, Dan Rostenkowski from Illinois, Bob Kastenmeier from Wisconsin, Phil Burton from California, future majority leader Don Edwards (D-California), who shared an adjoining congressional district with Mineta, and of course, Majority Leader Jim Wright. It was also a factor that Bob Matsui had by then established himself in the House and would help bring cosponsors on board. By our initial count, we figured we had as many as eighty members who would join the bill, and perhaps even nearly one hundred.

The bill would require a simple majority in both the House and Senate, and our focus would be the House vote, where the magic number was 218 votes. Our goal would be to get the bill introduced with as many cosponsors as possible. We knew that our bill would have to go through at least two or maybe even three iterations in several sessions before it would be ready for a vote, and Mineta was adamant that we secure more than the necessary number of supporters to take the bill to the House floor for debate and a vote. He wanted a comfortable—that is to say, large—cushion of supporters on the bill by the time it came up for debate in the full House.

It would be an uphill battle to get enough votes, but progress was steady if slow. By the beginning of 1983, I figured we had almost 100 votes on which we could rely, another 25 to 30 that looked favorable, and an additional 40 or so votes that were categorized as "possible," for a total of somewhere around 165 votes. That was still a long way from the 218 we needed in the House, and so we hunkered down and focused on the daily grind of lobbying, picking up one vote at a time.

"This feels right," Glenn Roberts said to me as we did our assessment.

"We're going to get there," Inouye agreed.

CORAM NOBIS

When we first began lobbying Congress in the 1980s, it was extremely rare to encounter any members who had not studied and practiced law, the majority having been prosecutors at some point in their careers. It was fair to assume, then, that they had all encountered *Korematsu* (1944) and *Hirabayashi* (1943), and, by extension, *Yasui* (1943), the three most notable cases that challenged the government's wartime policies against Japanese Americans. It was through these cases that the United States Supreme Court established that, in times of national crisis, the president has the authority to suspend the constitutional rights of citizens to maintain the security of the nation. For over thirty years, those decisions stood as dangerous precedents that could be used (and sometimes were) to justify governmental actions that infringed on the constitutional rights of Americans. While the average Japanese Americans may not have fully grasped the legal implications of those Supreme Court decisions until they became part of the debate in the early days of the redress movement, we knew from experience their potential danger in the hands of any dictatorial authority, from the president all the way down to local authorities.

From the outset of the JACL's redress campaign, we understood that we had to find a way to mitigate the decisions in these cases because they might act as legal impediments to our cause. As we began the process of educating the American public about the internment, I frequently heard from lawyers interested in knowing how we intended to navigate around *Korematsu* and *Hirabayashi*. At times, those questions were asked not sincerely but as a hostile challenge, a reminder that even the highest court of the land had found the government's actions justifiable in the specific case of the internment.

It was therefore not a surprise to me that this same argument would be raised by members of Congress who objected to our redress claims or who, reluctant to openly oppose a compensation bill, chose to use the

Supreme Court decisions as an excuse for side-stepping our legislation. On some level, I preferred a bigoted but honest congressperson to one who hid behind the sanctity of a truly bad Supreme Court decision.

Because we had neither the resources nor time to challenge the Supreme Court decisions ourselves, I accepted that the most we could do was to counterargue from the position of legal scholars who called the *Hirabayashi* and *Korematsu* decisions some of the worst ever rendered by the Court. It might not work to change anyone's mind, but it was all we had for the moment.

What we didn't know then was that the resolution to this particular problem would come just as we were in the thick of lobbying our compensation bill, having begun at the San Francisco commission hearings of August 11–13, 1981, when that group of young attorneys from the Asian Law Caucus, with whom Min Yasui and I had met, presented testimony that showed just how flawed the *Korematsu* decision was. While they raised issues about the veracity of the Court's decision in *Korematsu*, the turning point came when UC San Diego law professor Peter Irons (who presented testimony at the Cambridge hearing) introduced the legal procedure called "a petition for writ of error *coram nobis*"—an arcane and then-little-known procedure that, in simple terms, provides a legal mechanism for a court to reconsider a previous judgment based on the discovery of new evidence that might have changed the outcome of the Court's judgment. In this case, Irons knew of a document unearthed by CWRIC researcher Aiko Herzig-Yoshinaga that could be of major significance. Could this legal maneuver be the key to opening the three Supreme Court cases again? The three cases stood out like a cancerous sore on the face of the government's actions during World War II, and aside from their blatant racism, they set dangerous legal precedents that could have far-reaching effects. But to get such important cases overturned was a virtual impossibility. Or was it?

Working with Irons, the Korematsu legal team put together a *coram nobis* case centered on a piece of evidence previously suppressed by the government: a Justice Department memorandum, written during the war years by DOJ attorney Edward Ennis, in which he raised concerns that the government's policies and actions were unconstitutional. The government had suppressed this document at the time of the Supreme

Court examination of *Korematsu*. It was an admission of guilt, a smoking gun, *and* a silver bullet.

On January 19, 1983, the *Korematsu* team filed its petition in the Ninth Circuit of the U.S. District Court for the Northern District of California, with their case assigned to Justice Marilyn Hall Patel, a favorable choice. Similar legal teams filed *coram nobis* petitions for both Gordon Hirabayashi and Min Yasui. In Seattle the Hirabayashi team was led by Rod Kawakami and Kathryn Bannai (daughter of Paul and sister of Lorraine, part of the Asian Law Caucus), and in Portland, attorney Peggy Nagae, who had been a key member of the JACL's National Committee for Redress under the chairmanship of Clifford Uyeda, led the Min Yasui *coram nobis* team in what would be a somewhat convoluted case.

Toward the end of that same year, a couple of months after the summer congressional recess, I was in D.C. while Hayashino, back in San Francisco, kept tabs on the progress of the *Korematsu* case. I had figured that whatever happened in *Korematsu* would probably also be repeated in *Hirabayashi*, with the *Yasui* case trailing closely behind. We all had a feeling that there was a good chance that, finally, the decisions on these landmark cases would be reversed and the dangerous precedents removed from the legal and historical records of the country.

We finally got word in November 1983 that the *coram nobis* challenge in *Korematsu v. United States* had prevailed, followed by *Yasui* in January 1984, and finally *Hirabayashi* in September 1987. It was a huge victory.

With the commission report clearing the way and now the *coram nobis* cases knocking down the legal arguments supporting the internment, the success of our redress bill would come down to which members of the House were courageous enough to set a historic precedent by provide redress for a wrong committed by an earlier generation.

I was in D.C. when I learned of the *Korematsu* decision in a phone call from Carole Hayashino. I had waited for this moment, and now I staked out the course of my lobbying over the next few days before D.C. emptied out for the holidays. I wanted to see the faces of the congressional members who had so smugly put up the shield of the Supreme Court when I broke the news to them that the Ninth District had vacated the *Korematsu* decision and the others would fall with it. I wanted to hear what they would say, now that they could not hide behind the high court's decisions. Just seeing those looks would be an early Christmas present, albeit long overdue. I knew that of course they would find other reasons to deny our legislative effort, but I wasn't going to let that take away the good feeling of yet another undeniable success.

PRECEDENT STRATEGY

As we slipped into the early months of 1983, the JACL was hard at work bringing mini-redress efforts to successful conclusions at the local level, in an effort to create precedents for reparations payments in the United States. The only international example I was aware of was Germany's reparations payments to Jewish people via a worldwide redress program, but the circumstances of that situation demanded we maintain our distance and not venture any type of comparison. There were no examples in this country's history, although one would have thought the victimization of Native tribes and those whose ancestors had been brought here as slaves from Africa would provide some useful historical and legal model, but neither did. Ultimately, there were no cases we could turn to for guidance and legitimacy, so we would have to create our own.

In looking at situations we might take on in lower levels of the justice system, one that stood out was the case of Mitsuye Endo, a California state employee who had been fired at the outbreak of the war based solely on her Japanese ancestry. The details of the circumstance seemed like a good fit for us, but we didn't feel up to the challenge of taking on the state of California at that point in time because so much of our resources were already being expended in the congressional effort. Ron Wakabayashi and I were discussing this when one day he wondered if we couldn't do something similar at a smaller level: "What about Japanese Americans who were employed by the city of Los Angeles and were fired right after Pearl Harbor?" He knew specific individuals in L.A. who fit this profile, and we were certain we could find similar examples in San Francisco. Why couldn't we create precedents at the municipal level and *then* take on the state? It would be a test: we would seek reparations for individual Japanese Americans who had been fired from their city-government jobs after Pearl Harbor for no reason other than their race. The parallel wasn't perfect, but the basis for the termination was precisely what we sought: a race-based discriminatory action and/or policy by a governmental authority.

This strategy was particularly appealing because we already had great political connections in both cities. Clifford Uyeda had close ties to San Francisco Board Supervisor Quentin Kopp, and we knew we would have the support of his fellow supervisor Louise Renne as well as the sympathy of then-mayor Dianne Feinstein. In Los Angeles, JACL National Board member Rose Ochi, a strong supporter of the JACL's redress efforts, was one of the most connected and effective operators in Southern California. She was a known entity in Los Angeles and had proven her value while a member of the Manzanar Committee, which had not only instituted the annual pilgrimage to the former incarceration site but had proposed a memorial plaque using the words "concentration camp" and then engaged in a major fight over this wording with the state of California during Ronald Reagan's tenure as governor. She and Wakabayashi also knew Los Angeles Board Supervisor Kenneth Hahn, a strong supporter of Japanese American community interests.

By the end of 1982, it was evident that both the Los Angeles and San Francisco initiatives would be successful, and although neither affected more than a handful of Japanese Americans and the award amounts were relatively small (up to $5,000 for each Japanese American who was fired from city government following the attack on Pearl Harbor), they nevertheless became credible and legal precedents for redress. A similar initiative by a coalition group was under way in the state of Washington and would also conclude successfully. At this point, we finally felt we could turn our focus to Mitsuye Endo, whose 1944 U.S. Supreme Court case, *Ex parte Endo*, had been decided in the plaintiff's favor—the only one for which that was true among the four Japanese American WWII cases the Court saw during that era. The Endo case had further significance because it was tied to Sacramento, where Endo had been employed. And, of course, it was the city from which California attorney general Earl Warren had led his chorus of racists demanding our removal. Thus, Sacramento had always held a special appeal for us as a target.

The success of the San Francisco and Los Angeles initiatives coupled with a win against the state of California would serve to answer a question often asked of me as I lobbied members of Congress: Why should they support a bill whose intent it is to remedy an action taken by a Congress from forty years ago? Yes, why indeed? The findings at the city level in the 1980s made it clear that the responsibility of acknowledging historical injustices did not end with the passing of the generation guilty of those injustices. The current members of the boards of supervisors in both Los Angeles and San Francisco recognized that they, as individuals then responsible for the governance of their cities, were also responsible for the moral integrity of their respective cities going forward, and that meant righting past wrongs for which their predecessors had been at fault. The Sacramento precedent spoke volumes in response to that question via a bill authored by Assemblyman Patrick Johnston of Stockton. It was approved by the California State Assembly under the aegis of Assembly Speaker Willie Brown, approved by the state senate, and signed into law in 1983.

CAUGHT IN A DOUBLE VORTEX

There are times in your life when one decision, caught in the vortex of other circumstances, can have major consequence, and as it turned out, I would experience that for myself over the next few years. I had been at the helm of the JACL's redress program for five years, and for two years I had lobbied the Hill virtually every day as the full-time redress director. I was prepared to stay to the end of this fight for redress, but I had begun to rethink how I could manage the job for the amount of time it looked like it was going to require. Inouye and Mineta predicted that our bill would need to be reintroduced at least two times before we would have the votes to take it to the floor, which meant that realistically we had to accept that we were looking at another five years before the final bill would be signed into law. With that much time ahead in this campaign, I again considered my responsibilities to my family, who had stayed behind in the Bay Area while I went to Washington. My occasional trips back home to spend time with my kids didn't seem enough anymore, and I worried that the longer I made D.C. my operational base, the less I would feel the need to return home to be the father I had promised myself I would be. Living in D.C. kept me in the middle of the legislative action but outside of my family circle. I was an asset to the campaign, but it came at significant personal cost.

We had taken a pause in our lobbying activities while Glenn Roberts worked out the language of the compensation bill, and I headed to California to be with my family, figuring I could work from the JACL's San Francisco headquarters during this hiatus. I knew I would be back in Washington at summer's end as our bill got introduced. It was on that trip home that I made the decision to base myself in San Francisco whenever the House went on recess, which was at least a third of the year. Some JACLers wondered why I was back in California when logic would dictate that I should be in D.C. while the iron was still hot from the fire of the commission's report and recommendations, but what they

303

didn't know—and I should have told them but didn't—is that the legislative fight ahead would be measured by months and even years, not by days. Congress had adjourned for summer recess, Mineta's office had not yet drafted a bill, and there was no need for me to be in Washington at that time.

Ironically, during this same period there was also growing unease within the JACL leadership that I was spending *too much time* lobbying, possibly exceeding the IRS limit allowed for nonprofit organizations, and was therefore jeopardizing the JACL's nonprofit status. The issue was raised by Inspector General Frank Sato, the board treasurer during the JACL presidency of Floyd Shimomura (1982–84), a Sansei attorney. That Frank was the inspector general for the U.S. Department of Veterans Affairs gave credence to his concerns about our lobbying activities. If anyone knew government, it was Frank, and if anyone understood accounting issues—including the accounting of time and money devoted to an activity such as lobbying—it was he, a kind of governmental super-accountant.

Thus, when Frank raised the question about the number of hours we were spending on direct lobbying—that is, lobbying on specific legislation—Shimomura decided with Sato that I should log the activities of my day, from morning to night, but that did little to ease their concern and they ultimately decided that the JACL needed to create a lobbying arm that could be activated if the IRS cautioned us that we were approaching the limits allowed to nonprofit organizations. To protect our tax-exempt status, we could apply under tax code 501(c)(4) to create a separate subgroup, commonly called a (c-4), whose primary purpose would be to lobby. The JACL filed documents with the state of California to establish the (c-4) organization, calling it the JACL Legislative Education Committee (JACL/LEC). In accordance with California laws, a board of directors was designated, but because the JACL/LEC would not be activated unless necessary, its board was comprised of the same individuals who sat as elected officers of the JACL board.

No one could have predicted that this nonoperational entity of the JACL would one day dominate the board of the JACL and gain control of the redress campaign in a perfect example of the tail wagging the dog.

In the four-month lull that followed the flurry of activity leading up to the commission's final report, some JACL members questioned if the campaign had been beset by stasis and began to wonder what my role was exactly. After Ron Wakabayashi's selection as the JACL's national director in 1981 and my appointment as redress director, my role changed from high-profile redress chairman to full-time staff member responsible for the day-to-day operation of the campaign. This happened at the same time Min Yasui was named chair of the redress committee, the intention being that he would be basically a figurehead; it was a way to provide Min with an official programmatic title at a time when it was important to have a spokesperson. As the redress chair, Min would not have the full set of tasks I had had in that role, and he would serve instead mainly as the voice of redress. Min, always the orator, shone most brightly in front of an audience, and we were lucky to have him. He was never at a loss for words, and his words were eloquent and inspiring. A firebrand and an old hand at politics, it also helped that his name had earned, through *Yasui v. United States*, a highly recognizable association with the wartime experiences of Japanese Americans.

We continued with this arrangement through two biennia—the presidencies of Floyd Shimomura and Frank Sato—but it wasn't without its problems. Min was not satisfied with his role as a mere figurehead and began to take action where he saw fit. He would not be held down by anyone, and as much mutual respect as there may have been between us, he was not about to have me tell him how to conduct himself in the public arena when speaking on an issue he had lived with for over fifty years and understood so well. Min had earned his place in the world and wasn't going to let anyone put a limit on what he could do.

I understood and admired Min's passion, but it was that same passion that sometimes prompted him to take premature action and would sometimes get the JACL in a bind. Several times I received calls from the offices of the Big Four (most frequently Matsui) asking what the hell was going on and why were we jumping the gun on an issue, contrary to what we had discussed? This was more of a problem when, for whatever reason, his action or call to action was contrary to the current strategy. There were other times when I suspected Min just saw an opportune moment to strike and went ahead with it, even if our strategy may have been to sit tight for the moment.

Trying to undo a badly timed political move is difficult if not impossible, and while, on the face of things, Min's action orders may have been reasonable, it was damaging that he was issuing them contrary to strategies Ikejiri and I were developing in concert with the Big Four. Min had great ideas, and it really was mostly a problem of timing. If Min could be faulted for anything, it was his enthusiasm and determination to make things happen. And it was my fault for not maintaining a regular pipeline with Min to keep him advised of our moving targets.

In the end, the arrangement simply didn't work, and in a closed meeting of the executive leadership of the JACL board, a decision was made to officially dissolve the redress committee and thereby eliminate the committee chairmanship. Min had lost his official position, and although he said at the time that it wasn't important, this move ultimately set the stage for an ugly fight that would pit Min and me against each other. We would both end up losing more than just our friendship, and that loss would haunt me for a long time.

Before the end of his term in 1984, JACL president Floyd Shimomura informed the board that the JACL had reorganized its redress operations and formally eliminated the redress committee, placing total control of the redress campaign in my hands once again as its director. The change was made with good intentions, but the management of the entire episode set into motion a battle for power and control of the JACL and its redress campaign.

THE MEANEST LITTLE TOWN IN AMERICA

With a heads-up from Mineta's office that the first iteration of the House bill would be introduced sometime in early October 1983, I returned to Washington to help secure sponsors, and for the time being, I was free of whatever bickering might have been going on.

I tried not to take it to heart anyway, as it was just one of the liabilities in working for a membership-based nonprofit organization. The senior staff were always vulnerable to the scrutiny of the organization's members, and as the JACL's redress campaign gained momentum in its outreach across the country and its successes in Washington, the more high-profile staff in the organization—namely, the JACL's director (Wakabayashi), the Washington representative (Ikejiri), and the redress director (me)—were common targets for criticism. In the organization, as it is in the community and as it is in Japanese American families, there is always room for improvement and no one should be allowed to rest on his or her laurels. Such was the nature of the beast, and those of us who were part of the JACL's professional staff understood this and lived with it.

I knew that Ikejiri was experiencing similar criticism, and with the added pressure that some JACL members wanted him to spend 100 percent of his time on redress, not realizing how many other issues he was dealing with on the Hill. My time was dedicated specifically to redress, which was my main responsibility, but Ikejiri and the JACL's Washington office were tasked with working on a number of other critical issues, such as immigration, the constant attacks on voting rights, and different elements of the agenda of the civil rights coalition of which the JACL was an active part.

In retrospect, we could have handled a number of situations differently, like telling non-JACL members to butt out and mind their own damn business, but that hadn't seemed necessary at the time, in part because it was something that was never done. In the Japanese

American community, it was unheard of that outsiders would try to control an organization they were not members of, and so although we knew this was happening, we just ignored it went about our business, not recognizing that, if left unchecked, it could become more problematic in the future. Perhaps I had gotten too dismissive about what seemed an endemic organizational negativism, because by then I had gotten used to it. A lot was at stake and so everyone felt they had a say in everything about the campaign, whether they were emotionally invested in it or not.

We tried to put this type of drama aside, but it was difficult, and the constant bashing began to take its toll. In late summer of 1984, Ron finally decided he had had enough of all the backstabbing that had become too much a part of our lives and decided to take advantage of what turned out to be a great career opportunity for him. He had been there in Washington from the beginning of the campaign, and I knew I would miss his company; he made work enjoyable, and even in the worst of times, he found a way to bring equilibrium and humor into the mix.

In our last conversation before he departed his position, we talked about what it meant to walk away from something that was so important, and I told him it bothered me that he wasn't going to be there when we finished this campaign.

"It's like a parade," he said. "You're standing on the sidewalk as the band comes by, and you're not out there marching with it, but you know you had something to do with helping that band get there. I don't need to be out there. It's enough to know that I played a role."

———

Ron's official departure was set for fall of 1984, but he was essentially gone long before then, mostly serving to facilitate the transition. His absence changed everything, and it was especially challenging because it occurred during the same period in which I was in the process of reestablishing my home base back in the Bay Area, once again making regular commutes to D.C. for stays of two or three weeks. With Ikejiri's departure, I faced the possibility of having to move back to D.C. since the JACL would need a full-time person to take over the D.C. office responsibilities. We had a secretary to handle administrative matters, but we needed someone at the director level, and I was the most logical choice, at least in the interim. Wakabayashi asked me to carry the responsibilities of the Washington office until we were able to hire someone to fill the D.C. position, and with so much to attend to, there was for me especially a sense of urgency to have Wakabayashi hire a replacement for the Washington office so I could return to the Bay Area and to redress full time. Realistically, I would still be in D.C. a majority of the time, but psychologically, I needed the sense of having my home be on the West Coast. More important than my own needs, however, was the fact that we needed someone in the D.C. office who could maintain our presence there and handle the always urgent need to put out policy fires. Redress remained our priority issue but was not our only concern, and that was as it should be if we wanted to stay a legitimate part of the national Asian American community. To turn our backs on our brethren would be unthinkable.

Wakabayashi shared my concern and felt an even greater urgency than I to find a replacement for the D.C. office. Because the person we hired would have a direct impact on my work, Ron asked me to give him input on the applicants, and together we agreed on the choice of Tim Gojio, a *magna cum laude* graduate from the University of Washington School of Law and the associate counsel of the Washington State Senate Republican Caucus. His policy and legislative experience made him a strong candidate for the job, which, as we have seen, can be challenging because it is, even in the best of situations, a public position that's always vulnerable to criticism, deserved or not. Tim of course understood this and was more than capable of handling the demands of the job.

I was happy to have Tim as a colleague who could step right in and carry whatever responsibilities faced him as the JACL's new Washington rep. While a part of his time would have to be devoted to the other parts of the JACL's civil rights agenda, it was clear that he was hankering for a fight on the redress stage, and that he was more than ready for it. He had an arsenal of skills, not least of which was his knowledge of constitutional issues as well as case studies relevant to our wartime experience. That he was a Republican also proved to be useful in instances where opponents of the bill toed the party line. I knew from friendships I had cultivated with some Republican lobbyists that Tim's party affiliation would help him make inroads with some congressional members, both Republicans and Blue Dog Democrats, who had shut their minds on the redress issue. As we made calls together to some of those offices in his early days in D.C., I was convinced that we had made the right choice in hiring him.

Unfortunately, things turned sour for Gojio within a month of his arrival to D.C. Inouye, Matsunaga, and Mineta welcomed him warmly as a great addition to our team, but Matsui had the completely opposite reaction. In what turned out to be a very public and very heated exchange between Matsui and me, Bob voiced his objections to our hiring a Republican and demanded his removal. I made the mistake of letting it get personal—an ill-advised move, especially for someone with congressional experience and who should have known better—and in so doing, I crossed a line and made trouble for Gojio. Sadly, he was an unwitting victim caught in the cross fire of one congressional member's rage and one redress director's anger and stubbornness. The argument never had anything to do with Gojio's abilities, and in fact, he was the best that office would see in a long time.

I look back on that period and am amazed that Tim stayed for the better part of a year to do the job he was hired to do. He had wanted to be part of something that was truly meaningful to all of us Japanese Americans, and he was made to suffer because of the actions of others. Despite his having been handicapped in the opening volley before he had even stepped onto the court, he did the best he could and made significant contributions to the JACL's mission and most definitely to the redress effort. He proved that his party affiliation made no difference and that his true value was his integrity and commitment to our mission in Washington. It had been unfair to judge him by anything other than his talent and dedication to the post, and I would be less than honest if I ignored the fact that I contributed to Tim's difficulties when I made his fight mine, and made it personal in the process. It made things miserable for Tim during that year, and I've always felt bad about my role in the encounter, which would come to define at least a part of my Washington experience for the next twenty years.

During my time in Washington, I was often asked what it's like to go from being a teacher to working in D.C. and getting so involved in the world of politics. I would often describe Washington by saying that, beneath its veneer of civility, it can be the meanest little town in America, an unforgiving place where memories run long and forgiveness is a foreign concept for many. In a place where big decisions are made daily, it's amazing how petty things can get at times. Generally, common courtesies and politeness are the norm and adherence to decorum is essential (or at least this was true in those days), and most people never experience the underlying meanness. But it does exist, and anyone who becomes a target or victim of it knows only too well what it means.

The entire year of 1984 was eventful in terms of our legislative effort. I spent most of my time in D.C. working on trying to get a hearing on H.R. 4110, the House redress bill, while Mineta and Glenn Roberts worked on Sam Hall, chair of the subcommittee to which the bill had been referred.

On June 20–21, the House Judiciary Subcommittee on Administrative Law and Governmental Relations held a hearing on the bill, authored and introduced by Representative Jim Wright, to implement the recommendations of the CWRIC. Two other similar bills, H.R. 3387 (the Lowry bill) and H.R. 4322 (redress for Aleuts), were also included. This was the first step, the first real movement on a monetary compensation bill in Congress. Norm Mineta and Bob Matsui testified, as did former assistant secretary of war John McCloy. It was at this hearing that David Lowman, a former intelligence officer who worked at the National Security Agency, testified against consideration of the bill and criticized the commission for having minimized secret communications (codename: "Magic") between West Coast consular offices and Tokyo that, according to Lowman, indicted Japanese Americans as agents for Japan. Both Joan Bernstein and Angus Macbeth testified and dispelled the argument put forth by Lowman, as did Jack Herzig, also a retired intelligence officer, who took Lowman's argument apart piece by piece and showed how absurd it really was.

In June and September 1984, a year after the introduction of the redress bills, the House subcommittee held four days of hearings that included major figures from the FDR administration involved in the implementation of the wartime policies, including McCloy and Bendetsen, who testified in September.

In August, Senator Ted Stevens, one of the only Republican senators to cosponsor a Senate redress bill, and definitely the most important of them, held a one-day hearing in Los Angeles. The key witness was our longtime adversary S. I. Hayakawa, who warned that if Japanese Americans were given redress for what he considered beneficial treatment during World War II, it would open the Pandora's box of America's misdeeds of the past, and where would that stop? He claimed and seemed to yearn to be Japanese American, but he was an outsider who had others do his bidding in the community. He may have been a national figure, but when it came to what mattered most, he would never be one of us.

CHANGES

By 1984 the Japanese American community had more or less coalesced behind the JACL on redress. While the commission hearings had exposed the raw pain of the community, they had also revealed our strength and determination to make this a better country. And with the commission's report and recommendations, the community had brought itself together to reconcile differences. Opening the psychological wounds through the hearings was brutal, but in the aftermath, we began to heal as a community.

In the meantime, a fissure was growing within the JACL. The miscalculated decision to dissolve the JACL's redress committee and the consequential silencing of Min Yasui had repercussions that were just beginning to be felt. The old guard and those who had been persuaded to join in the push for a more activist lobbying effort rallied around Min with a determination to take over the redress campaign.

On the other side of that battle, Rose Ochi, a National Board member and friend of Ron Wakabayashi, was determined to stop the formation of what many viewed as a breakaway group. She openly challenged them as they sought to replace the JACL's leadership and to remove the organization's redress team in Washington—that is, Ikejiri (before he left), myself, and Tim Gojio—and replace them with individuals they considered better suited and more committed to the effort.

As the division within the JACL continued, Wakabayashi held the organization together and skillfully walked the tightrope between the two sides, proving himself to be a politically astute operator. I continued my trips to Washington as I had been doing now for five years, working in tandem with Gojio and relieved to be free of the infighting that encumbered us at the headquarters. There was for a time an uneasy détente within the organization as we awaited the next step in our legislative push for a compensation bill.

The JACL was also at this time spreading its reach beyond the redress campaign. In what proved to be a visionary strategy, Wakaba-yashi began quiet discussions with Japan's consul general in San Fran-cisco about the impact of Japan's trade policies on the lives of Japanese Americans and other Asians in the United States. As in World War II, the public wrongly held Japanese Americans responsible for Japan's unfair trade policies, but there was no formal avenue of communication between the Japanese American community and the Japanese govern-ment to make the latter aware of the consequences of their policies. The JACL was well positioned to be that link, and it was clearly in our inter-est to create a means by which both sides could share their concerns. Wakabayashi came to this realization at a time when few others under-stood how important it was, and he had begun a quiet dialogue with Japan to see how it might change things.

Wakabayashi's strategy became public in spring of 1983, when the JACL was invited by the Japanese government to send a delegation of Japanese American leaders to Japan to discuss issues of mutual concern. Without a great deal of fanfare, the delegation traveled to Tokyo, where it met with Prime Minister Yasuhiro Nakasone and then with the minis-ters of Nakasone's cabinet. It was a successful trip that created informal links between the JACL and Japanese government officials and estab-lished a reciprocal open-door policy.

The following year, Wakabayashi asked if I would lead a second delegation to Japan. He understood the possible fallout of my being on a delegation such as this because it would no doubt add fuel to the fire of those who by this time were actively seeking a change in the leadership of the redress campaign. But ever since my first encounter with the pub-lic in 1975, I had been dealing with Americans angered by Japan's trade policies, listening to them accuse us of being nothing more than agents of Tokyo, and so I viewed this trip as an opportunity to share with Japanese government officials the real consequences of their arrogant trade policies. As I examined the potential fallout of this trip in regards to my own position as the redress director, I told Wakabayashi that I would go only if I could speak my mind.

In the spring of 1984, I led the second delegation, which had sev-eral messages: that Japan's trade policies with the United States were having dire consequences for Japanese Americans; that we were being victimized because Americans saw the policies as unfair and unreasonable and viewed us as targets for their anger and frustrations; that the murder of Vincent Chin in Detroit in 1982 was the direct consequence of Japan's policies; that this was not unlike the way we were viewed and blamed after the bombing of Pearl Harbor; and that the simmering anti-Japanese sentiment throughout the United States was serious, both for them and for us. For six days, this was the message we pounded home in all the meetings we had with ministers of the cabinet, heads of political parties, and corporate leaders.

I was, not surprisingly, harshly criticized for having taken the trip, and my detractors within the JACL said my involvement would surely be used against me by the likes of Lillian Baker as clear evidence of our ties to Japan. (It never happened because Baker and her cronies couldn't have cared less about my travels.) My having stepped foot in Japan, the argument went, would destroy my credibility and give members of Congress reason to reject our legislative efforts, further confirming to the bigots in the House and Senate that we were somehow tied to Japan. But not a single member of Congress I met with after my trip to Japan knew about the trip, or cared about it when I brought it up.

With the distance now of thirty-plus years, the argument that my trip would hurt our position seems even more ludicrous than it did then, but in retrospect, I think my opponents in the JACL actually believed what they were saying. They seemed to think I had left the United States as the chief advocate for redress and returned an apologist of Japan's trade policies, a flunky for the nation that had done us so much inadvertent harm. Thankfully most Japanese Americans in the community found the idea laughable, and those who might have wondered about my motives at least had the courage to confront me about it, and I grew to appreciate their honesty in doing so. And interestingly, those who did mention it to me were all Nisei, longtime JACL members who remembered the vague mandate from the past, "Thou shalt not cavort with Tokyo." Whenever confronted on the topic, I would wonder out loud if, say, an American of German or Italian or Swedish or maybe even Russian descent visited his or her ancestral home country, would that be viewed as a betrayal of his or her loyalties to America, and would that cause alarm in the community?

It was an absurd criticism, and one that I knew would be used against me even before I made the decision to take that trip, but it stuck, and eventually became a knife in the side of the JACL. Ultimately, it was one of a number of factors that worked to dislodge the JACL's ongoing strategy to keep a dual focus on both educating the public and lobbying Congress. The JACL was already showing signs of discontent among those who believed we should concentrate solely on the passage of the compensation bill because we had only one shot to make it work. On the other side of the argument were those of us who had brought the campaign this far and were obviously committed to the cause but also sought to maintain the JACL's commitment to a broader civil rights agenda. Our mission was to protect the rights and well-being of Japanese Americans and *all* Asian Americans, Wakabayashi would argue, not just to fight for redress. Ours was a broad and noble mission and Ron Wakabayashi its caretaker.

We continued to work redress on our side of the organizational divide as best we could, and, ironically, Min Yasui was one of the few people who attempted to offer assistance, occasionally suggesting things that needed tending to, offering edits to my documents and possible alternatives to directives I issued. In periods like these, one learns what one's friends are made of, and who will stand by you when trouble calls. Min rose above the differences we may have had and showed me yet again why I had always admired him and the distinguished life and career he had built for himself.

At the next JACL national convention, this one in Honolulu in August 1984, a shift of power and a transformation of the board occurred. Of the six executive positions on the board, three supported activating the LEC lobbying arm, and of eight governors who represented their districts on the National Board, seven were proponents of the LEC. Newly elected president Frank Sato favored the status quo for the redress program, crippling his efforts to guide or protect the JACL's current direction and marking the transition of the JACL's redress campaign into the hands of the LEC, which was not an opposition group: these were all longtime JACL members, or at least most were.

To their credit, the LEC members were dedicated to redress and were eager to do what they could to further our efforts. Its leaders were Nisei members Denny Yasuhara from Spokane, Cherry Kinoshita from

Seattle, and a host of other Nisei who were not involved in the infighting but eventually joined forces with the LEC. Chief among those additions were Grayce Uyehara from Philadelphia, who became the LEC's principal lobbyist; former JACL presidents Jerry Enomoto of Sacramento (1966–70) and Shig Wakamatsu of Chicago (1958–60), plus a number of other old-guard Nisei. Grant Ujifusa, who had been the editor of my book *And Justice for All* (1984), had been unofficially and was now officially the LEC chief strategist.

But most important to me personally was seeing Min Yasui as the group's chairman and chief spokesperson. I was glad to see Min back in the public eye, to know that his fiery and charismatic voice would be heard once again.

I had my disagreements with the LEC proponents, but the one thing I fought tooth and nail against was their decision to make redress the sole issue of the organization and therefore suspend the other programs on the organization's civil rights agenda, a move that I warned would leave the JACL directionless and floundering for years once the campaign ended, win or lose. I thought it was foolhardy and shortsighted, and argued that with the JACL's credibility solidly established through our successes with the redress effort to this point, we had an opportunity to become a significant and effective organization in the civil rights arena. But we had to continue to keep a broad perspective in our vision. To limit ourselves now to a single issue would negatively affect the future of the JACL. What the LEC board members proposed was, in my view, myopic and would be rightly viewed as self-serving at a time when the Asian American community had so many pressing needs.

In the end, though, the LEC won the battle, and what I saw made me worry, both for the JACL's future as a viable and credible civil rights organization and for my own future engagement with redress.

As much as I criticized the LEC's thinking as shortsightedness, I was at least glad to see Min as their spokesperson. It was important to him to be part of this and to be looked upon with much-deserved admiration. Unfortunately, though, we were on opposite sides now and rarely talked. I tried to keep Min informed on important details concerning redress, but we did not communicate very well by then. Whatever close relationship I had once shared with him had been lost.

Even without the support of a likeminded redress committee, Ron Wakabayashi and I tried to maintain the JACL's presence in areas where we
could help the larger Asian American community. Things were in flux in
Washington as we transitioned from the JACL's dual priorities of lobbying and public education to the single focus of lobbying only. Until the
transition took place, I went about my responsibilities, which included
traveling to D.C. to continue lobbying, although my work was complicated by my eroded relationship with Bob Matsui, who seemed to find
my presence in D.C. threatening to the new LEC-led campaign. My public fight with Bob had put us at odds and seemed to be a factor for both
of us for the rest of our relationship in D.C. But as far as I was concerned,
he was a congressman and I was just a lobbyist: there was no contest
who had the most power, especially as he climbed the seniority ladder
on the all-powerful House Ways and Means Committee. I was there to
carry out the JACL's mission as its redress director, and my contacts
were mainly with Mineta's office, not Bob's. I just went about doing my
work whenever I was in D.C. and minded my own business. It was a
challenging time to be in Washington, but it was also an exciting time
because new energy and enthusiasm was coming to the redress movement through the LEC-directed program.

Whatever one might have thought about their strategies, one could
not argue against the LEC's dedication to the issue: their focus was completely on redress and furthering its cause, no matter the cost.

As we transitioned, I had a chance to work closely with Wakabayashi.
Before he became director, I knew him mostly by reputation. Everyone
spoke highly of him. Unlike my friend Ernie Weiner, who had turned
the rough-and-tumble experiences of his life into smooth *savoir faire*,
Ron retained the grit that told you he came from the streets, and I think
he did it, in large measure, because he felt no need to be other than who

he was, a characteristic he wore almost as a badge of honor. I liked that about him; what you saw was what you got, and what you got was someone who was smart, insightful, kind, and, surprisingly (at least for me) gentle. There was in him also a keen political sophistication that could be disarming. He had found his way to the JACL without intending to, but he was no interloper and certainly no outlier. Everything for him was about the community, and that was something I knew he would never betray.

In those days of fighting to preserve the integrity of the JACL, we would sometimes talk about how ironic it was that we should find ourselves here, he as the leader and I as one of the top staff members. We both had our issues with the JACL and we both were critical of much of the organization, but we also believed in what we were doing and what our commitments were.

One of the things that really struck me in this period was how quickly people moved aside when things went awry, and how often they virtually disappeared when things got nasty, but while others ducked for cover, Wakabayashi never did, something I've always appreciated about him. In the time she was there, nor did JACL receptionist Yuki Fuchigami, forever loyal to me, who simply hunkered down and took the attitude that she would be my guardian angel. She never once buckled or even flinched under the pressure. And, as expected, things became increasingly ugly and tense. As much as Wakabayashi and I tried to contain it, it was difficult to do. It felt like the tension had become a pervasive part of each working day.

———

As the 96th Congress drew to a close in the waning weeks of 1984, both the House and Senate had witnessed movement on our compensation bills in their respective chambers. The House bill had 106 sponsors, and the Senate bill 20 sponsors. After these bills were introduced and made the focus of the redress fight, I would take a back seat on the JACL legislative effort.

It was also toward the end of 1984 that the JACL held a redress summit with the major redress groups from the community, including the NCRR, NCJAR, and other groups interested in the campaign, such as the L.A.-based Japanese American Bar Association and the Asian American Legal Defense Fund of New York. Little was actually accomplished except for one item: the JACL announced publicly that its lobbying arm, the Legislative Education Committee, was taking over the legislative effort of the redress campaign, while the JACL's campaign, headed up by me, would continue to work on an education outreach program.

And with that, the LEC had successfully assumed authority over the JACL's redress program, keeping my operation in the loop, as it were, while keeping us at arm's length. The changeover was smooth, but there was no transition to speak of. We never talked about prior lobbying efforts, who the hard targets needed to be, which House members should continue to be given the courtesy of being kept abreast of our progress, etc. In fact, we never had a single conversation about any of it; out with the old, in with the new. The JACL National Board now had a majority of LEC supporters, and they effectively took over the organization and did whatever they needed to do. Frank Sato, newly elected as JACL board president, had two strong supporters in Yosh Nakashima, the JACL vice president of operations, and Rose Ochi but was otherwise outnumbered by LEC supporters. It would be a tough two years for him.

Change was taking place whether I liked it or not, and I can see now that, in some ways, maybe it was time. I've always believed in change, always thought it was good, but I have to admit that when you're part of the old regime that's being pushed aside, there's a degree of discomfort!

H.R. 442

Before the transition took place, my regularly scheduled travels to Washington had been welcome distractions from the internal problems in the JACL. We continued to gain support in the House for our first compensation bill, and it helped that our expectation wasn't to have it pass on the first try but to act as a sort of trial balloon that would tell us whose support we had now that the demand for monetary reparations was officially on the table. Matsui's office was optimistic that we would reach seventy-five supporters by year's end.

On one of my trips to D.C., I huddled with Glenn Roberts, who was in the process of drafting legislation for the second iteration of our bill, and he talked about the specific language he was using, his strategies to keep it out of certain committees, and other criteria guiding what should or shouldn't go into the bill. I told Glenn in all seriousness that I was hoping we didn't end up with a long title like that of the commission bill, with its cumbersome phrasing Commission on Wartime Relocation and Internment of Civilians Act; I was hoping for something short, to the point, something that had the right message, something that got to the essence of what we were fighting for. He was already way ahead of me. We agreed that it couldn't contain the words "Japanese" or "internment" or other similar hot-button words that echoed the CWRIC title. He said the bill had to convey that it was about America and Americans, and I wanted it to include something about the Constitution and the rights of citizens. Glenn had been talking with Mineta on the same subject and asked what I thought of the title Civil Liberties Act. It was perfect.

Mineta happened to be in the office right then, so we went in to talk with him. His first comment to me was that he heard I had gone to Japan and come back brainwashed and was now a secret agent for Tokyo! He was curious about the rumors he had heard going around the JACL's D.C. chapter, so I explained. "What a crock of bull," was his response. He then told me that Matsui was being openly critical of me in D.C.-area JACL circles, confirming what I already knew. There was nothing I could do about that, and I certainly didn't expect Mineta to intervene on my behalf, so I just thanked him for the information. With all that out of the way, Glenn went on to talk about some components of the bill he was drafting and said we were agreed on the title. Norm said he would time its introduction so that it would be assigned the label H.R. 442, to honor the Japanese American combat unit. As I departed Mineta's office, he said with that mischievous look he sometimes gets, "Hey, John, give Hirohito my regards!" It's hard not to like Mineta: he achieved great things, never forsook the community, and certainly never lost his sense of humor.

It was during that trip to D.C. that I had a meeting with Henry Hyde, a Republican from Illinois and one of the most conservative members of the House. Hyde was important to us because he was a member of the Judiciary Committee and was ascending to leadership positions within his party. He was opposed to redress, but he was amenable to discussing the issue, even knowing full well what the ultimate fiscal demands would be.

I know that Mineta and Hyde had at least one intense conversation after Norm's office drafted the second compensation bill and before it was introduced as H.R. 442. I was sitting in the back of the subway tram that goes from the basement of the House office buildings to the Capitol and saw Mineta and Hyde in the front car in conversation, the kind that signals to their colleagues to give them space. It may have been about any number of topics, but it didn't have the look of politics so much as personal matters. And they were not arguing or debating: Mineta was doing most of the talking. I don't know what was said, but whatever it was may explain why, when the redrafted legislation was introduced as the Civil Liberties Act, Hyde indicated his support of the bill.

That was one vote I know we all felt good about, not only because it was a key vote but because logic and reason had won the day and proved that even the bill's strongest opponents could be persuaded to support it. Sometimes getting one vote closer seemed so much bigger than a single vote.

In January 1985, Majority Leader Jim Wright reintroduced the redress bill—now designated H.R. 442 and officially titled the Civil Liberties Act—with ninety-nine cosponsors in the House. In May of that year, Sparky introduced a companion bill in the Senate with twenty-five cosponsors.

As Congress went into the summer recess, we were optimistic that we would be able to get enough support in the House to put the magic number of 218 votes within sight. We were already almost halfway there, and, thanks to Mineta and Matsui, we had a good number of cosponsors, which in many cases had involved smoothing over the rough edges of those who had originally opposed both the commission and the compensation bills (not to mention doubting our position on the internment altogether). But there were still many House members who needed convincing—and I believed they could be convinced with some effort—and these were the people who would eventually get the bill over the top. To them, there was one essential question: Does the Constitution stand for what we say it does, or is it simply a document that can be selectively applied at the whim of whoever is in power?

The last group of House members were those I wasn't sure we could ever convince to see things our way. They stayed in the shadow of reason, on the dark side of this particular issue, and held to the belief that no matter the circumstances and no matter the injustice, monetary redress and an admittance of wrong were not in the realm of possibility. They somehow spelled justice in a different way, and they would not be won over.

The goal of persuading half of the 435 members of the House seemed daunting, especially given that H.R. 442 was introduced with the support of fewer than one-fourth of the House members. But what didn't show in those numbers were the differences between the hard and soft No votes. Counted as our soft opposition were a significant number of House members who had initially opposed the commission bill but kept an open mind and then been convinced to support it; we believed we could persuade them on the compensation bill too. It would take work, but I strongly believed that we would eventually get the votes to see a redress bill approved by Congress.

MOVING ON

Because of the internal changes that had taken place in the JACL, I went to Washington less often in the lead-up to the introduction of the Civil Liberties Act. The lobbying responsibility was now in the hands of Grayce Uyehara, since her role was to work Congress and mine was to support her efforts however I could.

On occasion, I would get a call from Dan Inouye asking me to be in D.C., and I went when possible. In a meeting toward the year's end, he asked about my role with the LEC and said he heard that I had rejected the offer to be the executive director of the lobbying group. I confirmed that I wasn't interested in joining them and that, no, I was not being forced out. I had enough credibility and reputation in the community, and certainly in the JACL, that no one could force my being fired except Wakabayashi, who was my boss. I knew that I could stay if I wanted, but the organization was changing, as all organizations do, and I had already had my share of disagreements with the new board. I was feeling more and more that it was my time to go.

I had devoted the better part of ten years to the campaign and had made sacrifices to ensure the success of our efforts, and I had done it all willingly and without regret because it was all so important. But lately I found myself sitting in my office wondering if it was time for me to move on and take care of my family. I thought about Clifford and what he would advise me to do. I thought about others who had contributed to the redress effort but would never be acknowledged for their work if I wasn't there at the end to acknowledge them. I thought about the deterioration of the relationship between Matsui and me. I thought about whether it was worth it anymore.

And then I decided it wasn't.

I met with Wakabayashi in early 1986 and informed him of my intent to resign sometime in the next few months. Ron was kind to reiterate his feeling that I should stay, that I deserved to stay, but by then I had already spent ten years of long days on redress and knew it was time to go.

I met with Clifford at the office and talked to him about my decision. He, of course, supported my intention even as he said he regretted that others would take credit for what I had accomplished. He knew what had happened and how it had all come about.

I told him none of that mattered anymore. I had done all I could, especially under the current circumstances, and although I knew I would have been able to work with Mineta to get the votes needed, I would now leave that task to others. I had given enough to the cause and had decided, at last, that my time with the JACL was finished. I wanted to get back to my family and have a normal life. But I knew I would continue to go to Washington on my own to lobby the bill because I knew I couldn't just quit altogether. I admitted I didn't know if I would continue being involved with the JACL at any level. I told Cliff I had pretty much had my fill of the organization, even though it had brought so many good things into my life, including my friendship with him.

Talking to Clifford that last day, I resisted the urge to rehash the many ways in which he had encouraged and inspired me over the years, nor did he say much of what he was thinking or feeling about this incredible journey we had taken together. As was typical, we had no great or memorable moment there in that office where we had met so often; I simply thanked him for all his support and told him our paths would cross again. He smiled that awkward smile of his and said yes, our paths would cross again, many times. That was our destiny, he said.

———

Before my final days with the JACL, I took one last trip to D.C. to get my personal affairs in order, mainly visiting offices of fellow lobbyists and advocates I'd worked with for so long. I also went to visit the office of Norm Mineta. It was a short visit, more a conversation with Glenn Roberts than with Norm himself, and then I went over to the Senate office buildings. Since most of my lobbying was in the House, I had spent little time on the Senate side of the Capitol, and of course the two offices I knew best were Matsunaga's and Inouye's. Sparky wasn't in, but I had a chance to chat with Cherry Matano, his administrative assistant and one of my favorite people in D.C. I used to marvel at how someone so kind could last so long in the climate of D.C., but she did it, and with so much grace.

Among all the people I saw on that trip, Inouye was the one I most needed to visit. He of course knew about the JACL's internal conflicts and had encouraged me to hang in there and see the campaign to its end, but I had decided otherwise and was there to let him know. I wanted to thank him for all his assistance and guidance and to assure him that while the campaign was in the good hands of Grayce, whom he knew, I would continue to do what I could to help the effort. When he asked if my departure and the internal conflicts in the JACL were about control, I told him it was to infuse new energy into the campaign, evidence of which was already apparent in the work that Grayce Uyehara was doing. He had seen it all before—in the JACL, in his native Hawaii, and in other communities, including tribes he worked with as chairman of the Senate Committee on Indian Affairs. None of this was new to him, but he figured it was probably a big deal for me.

"After all we've been through, don't you want to be there when we finish this?" he asked. I had already thought about that and decided that, no, I didn't need to be there, I told him. It didn't matter to me who got credit or how success was achieved, only that it *was* achieved. I was confident there were others on board who were going to make sure of that.

In my early days in D.C., I used to drop by Inouye's office to talk to Sabrina Golding, the staff person assigned to handle his redress portfolio, and if Inouye happened to see me there, he would usually tell me to come visit him before I left. For some reason, he trusted me from that first meeting with the Big Four, when he beckoned me to his office for our private talk about pursuing the commission strategy, and for the next six years I had met with him on a regular basis. He always got straight to the point, talking strategy, telling me who needs to be seen, who to ignore, but whenever he had extra time, he would talk with me about other things as well. He was a great storyteller and had incredible tales to share—fascinating stuff about politics, but also so many other things, and usually with a lot of humor. One of my favorite stories was about the time when he was serving on the Watergate Committee and was caught on a hot microphone saying about John Ehrlichman, Nixon's chief domestic adviser, "What a liar!" Outside the hearing room and surrounded by the media, John Wilson, Ehrlichman's attorney, then referred to Inouye as "that little Jap," creating a national ruckus. The next morning, committee chair Sam Ervin, without ever mentioning Inouye by name, opened the day's session by talking about a committee member having been disparaged, and he referred to this member as a great American and a great American hero, words echoed by vice-chair Howard Baker, at which point the television camera switched over to Inouye's empty seat. I told him that, in the weeks following, I was struck by the way Americans across the country had voiced their disgust and anger at Wilson's bigotry. I was surprised that white America would be so sympathetic to Inouye, that there was such a conscious outrage against this kind of intolerance.

In his quieter moods he often talked about his wartime buddies back home, even though he never talked about the war itself. He had once taken me into his private office and shown me some memorabilia, some of which brought back old jokes as well as more serious memories still kept private after all those years. I only recall three times when I heard him talk about the war and its effect on his life, and one was after he had been awarded the Congressional Medal of Honor. At the ceremony in 2000, his Distinguished Service Cross was upgraded to a CMH in a ceremony alongside nineteen other members of the 442nd regiment, making it the most highly decorated unit in the history of the United States Army. It was after that ceremony at the White House that he told me he felt embarrassed to be given this recognition, saying it was a hell of a thing to get a medal for killing people when it should go to soldiers like the medics, brave men who daily saved lives on the battlefield at the peril of their own.

As much as I enjoyed my conversations with Inouye, I often felt I was overstaying my welcome because I knew he had a heavy schedule. There were times when I dropped in to say a quick hello and ended up talking with him for unexpectedly long hours. On many occasions, Sally Watanabe, his secretary, would interrupt our conversations and hand him a note, which he'd glance at briefly and then put aside while he kept talking. Invariably, Sally would come back a few minutes later and give me a look before handing Inouye another note, and then I'd know it was time for me to leave. Whenever this would happen, I would apologize when next I saw him, but he always told me not to worry about it because he never kicks his friends out. I knew this applied to his 442nd buddies and those old chums from Hawaii who could walk in saying, "Hey, Danny." He never forgot who his friends were or where he had come from.

Among my most memorable stories of Dan Inouye, one other will always stand out for me. I once arrived early for a 4 p.m. meeting with him, only to be told by Sally that the senator was conducting a hearing and asked that I wait until he got back. Twice more Sally gave me a similar message and I continued to wait. Three hours later, Inouye finally returned, with apologies, saying that he had wanted to get through all the witness testimonies before adjourning the hearing. When I noted that it was highly unusual for any hearing to last this late, he told me about a time when, as a student at George Washington University Law School, the Veterans of Foreign Wars asked him to testify at a congressional hearing on behalf of disabled veterans. He was the perfect witness: a handsome one-armed war hero and recipient of the Distinguished Service Cross, plus a chest full of other medals. He was honored to be asked and set about to prepare for the hearing, taking weeks to write out his testimony in longhand and then typing it himself. ("Typed the whole damn thing with one finger," he told me, holding up his left pointer.) Maggie, his wife, told him he needed to buy a suit for the occasion, and so on the day of the hearing, he arrived early ("as any good Nisei would," he said), wearing his new suit. He sat patiently with his testimony in his lap, waiting hours for his name to be called as the hearing dragged on all through the morning and after the lunch break. At 5 p.m., the chairman looked at his watch and asked if Mr. Inouye was present. Inouye stood, testimony in hand, and said, "Yes, sir, Mr. Chairman," and was about to make his way to the witness table when the chairman thanked him for his patience and said the committee had copies of his testimony, and then brought the hearing to a close. It wasn't so much the disappointment, he said (and there was plenty of it), but the humiliation he felt. He swore then that if he ever were in a similar position of authority, he would never do that to any witness, especially those who came to present their personal testimonies, even if it meant continuing into the late hours, even if it meant he was the only one on the committee still there to listen.

"Couldn't you have reconvened in the morning?" I asked of the hearing he had just adjourned. The schedule would not allow it, he explained, reiterating that he would have gone all night if necessary. Over the years, I recall having slipped into rooms where he was conducting late-hour hearings, and, true to his word, he was there listening patiently to witnesses, usually the only member of the committee still there. And he wasn't just allowing these witnesses to testify as a perfunctory exercise; he listened intently to the presentations and asked witnesses thoughtful, relevant questions. As I watched, it was almost as if he was showing these witnesses that, despite the emptiness of the room, there was one person in the United States Senate who truly cared and valued what they each had to say, that their personal stories were meaningful.

Without a doubt, he could be just as tough and hard-edged, and even nasty, as any Senate member, but that was not the side of him I ever had to deal with. Nor was it his natural style. In those days of bipartisan politics, when Democrats and Republicans struggled together to pass good legislation, he was one of the few Democrats who would cross over the aisle after a hard-won victory on major legislation to offer Republicans a way to work out some of their differences. There was a lot to respect about the man, no matter your politics.

In that last meeting in my role as redress director, Inouye talked to me about not just our fight for the compensation legislation but the next few steps it would take to get us to the end. He also said he had in mind that the appropriations bill should be authorized as an entitlement, which was "the only way to protect the authorization," he said. I realized even as he said it that he wasn't actually ordering me back for those fights but was just letting me know how far ahead he was thinking. And that he was confident we would succeed.

We had achieved so much since that fateful meeting in 1979 when he had brought up the commission strategy. The story of the internment was part of the national conscience now, and that in itself was pretty amazing. When it's all said and done, he told me, this is what America will remember. This knowledge is what Americans will use as the reference point, the lesson of the internment. You've brought us a long way, he remarked, and I knew he was being generous, since my staying or leaving wasn't all that significant considering there were others to carry on with the battle. I also knew that Inouye was a pragmatist and that, as a politician, sentimentality doesn't count for much in the world of D.C. People come and go all the time, and when one person steps out, another steps in to take over. I'd seen that happen in my time there and knew it was simply how things worked. With very few exceptions, no one plays a role that no other person could fill. We're all called in because we're the best there is for the moment, and to think otherwise would be self-delusional. This thinking isn't cynical or self-deprecating, just the reality of life in our nation's capital.

Besides, whatever happened next was going to be largely up to him in the Senate and Mineta in the House, with Matsunaga playing an important role in hustling votes with his Senate colleagues and Matsui doing the same in the House. The Big Four would continue to play the most critical roles in getting the bill through its last stages of the legislative battle, and the rest of us were just cogs in a machine, working to bring in votes wherever and however we could.

Over the years, I've thought about how prescient Inouye was and how clearly, from the very beginning, he understood the process that would be required to level the political battlefield and ultimately make it possible for us to even consider a compensation bill. While he was able to guide us step by step along the way, he also kept the bigger picture in mind, and his ability to see our work in terms of historical perspectives was ingenious. He had always urged me to not lose focus on educating the public: Change their thinking and you change history. I liked the simplicity of the thought, and although executing the strategy had proven to be much more difficult, it was solid advice.

I remember the first time I walked through the halls of the Russell Senate Office Building and saw the nameplates on the doors of some of the most powerful people in the world, Inouye and Matsunaga among them. The sense of awe I felt that first time was real and profound, and although it had since been reshaped by experience and even some cynicism, I never lost sight of the fact that the people inside those offices had the power to make decisions that affect all our lives.

But Inouye was right: things had changed, things were different here now. This was not the government that had incarcerated its own citizens. For one thing, he, Sparky, Bob, and Norm were now members of the United States Congress, and no one, not even those who opposed the intent of our compensation legislation, could now claim ignorance about what had happened to us during the war. And perhaps that was the biggest accomplishment of all: we had turned the usual story of subconscious guilt because of Japan's treachery into a story about the injustice thrust upon us and the sacrifices we had made to reclaim our rightful place in American society. I knew then that the story of the internment would be part of this nation's history, that it would not be forgotten. I was proud of the role I had played in making that happen, and I was ready to move on.

———

Over a period of several months in late 1985, the JACL's redress program transitioned from the JACL into the hands of the JACL/LEC. While there was tension between the two factions, they were both made up of JACL members, albeit ones who did not share the same views about operational aspects of the redress program. Outside of the leadership, not many people realized there was anything unusual going on until they read Min Yasui's end-of-year report, in which he stated that I had been expected to transition from the position of JACL redress director to that of LEC executive director, but I had declined the offer. That signaled trouble, and more news about the internal unrest came a couple of months later when the *Pacific Citizen* reported that I had submitted my resignation and declined to discuss the reasoning behind what some perceived as an unexpected and sudden turn of events. The hint of the problem was revealed when Yosh Nakashima, the JACL's vice president of operations, was quoted as saying he was "very unhappy with the fact that it has come to this," even as he admitted that it wasn't a total surprise coming on the heels of the September board meeting in which the LEC-controlled board reallocated all of the organization's program resources into redress, essentially making it a single-issue organization, against the wishes of the non-LEC board members.

As Nakashima indicated, things were not well in the organization, and my decision to resign meant that I would be walking away from the campaign when we were so close to the end.

By the time I formally resigned, in January 1986, the transition of the redress campaign into the hands of the LEC had already taken place. I ended up feeling okay about it because, although nothing really changed in the basic lobbying efforts, it brought new blood and new energy into the campaign. Grayce Uyehara was the new key person in D.C. working the Hill, and everyone knew and trusted her. Grayce was a longtime JACL member from Philadelphia and one of the early voices within the JACL advocating redress, and although she stood not quite five feet tall, she was a force to be reckoned with. She was a great advocate for the cause, and I can't remember a single occasion when she let someone get away with a misstatement or a cruel word. She was a peacemaker and a fighter, a good person to know, and always, for me, a trusted friend. Although she was a central part of the LEC operations, I don't think she considered herself anything other than a loyal JACL advocate, and everything she did on behalf of the redress campaign was, in her mind, as part of the JACL (and she was not incorrect, since the LEC was an operational function of the JACL).

Grayce and I talked about Min Yasui and together reflected on the unfortunate circumstances of his role within both the JACL and the LEC. She told me Min was no longer the official spokesperson for the LEC group, but she didn't share more than that. I told her how, as redress director, I had wanted to keep Min on the redress speaking circuit because he loved speaking before audiences and was good at it. I pointed out that Min's removal as the JACL's redress committee chair had been the beginning of the split within the JACL and the catalyst for the LEC's takeover; how ironic, I thought, and how tragic. Grayce informed me that Min had been retired from the LEC for the same reason—being put out to pasture, as Min had described the process to me once—and ultimately, having it done to him a second time had been the final blow. Within a year, Min died of a heart attack.

It was an unhappy end for someone who had been a significant figure in the whole sorry episode, from the internment to redress. I felt sad for Min. He had wanted this so badly, and he would not be around for the final chapter. I took comfort in imagining his reaction as one of amused resignation. He would probably have said, "Ah, what the hell," something I had heard him say often and always with a laugh.

It felt good to be free of the problems of the JACL as I tried to figure out what the next phase of my life would be, even as I was sure I would never be fully divorced from the redress campaign. In fact, in my work as a consultant, the offers that most interested me were jobs that gave me the latitude to stay involved with the Japanese and Asian American communities and even took me back to Washington. I found that being on my own in D.C. gave me a great deal of freedom, and once I had accomplished the task I was there for, I often stole some time to wander through the halls of the congressional offices, ostensibly playing the tourist who just happened to end up at one office or another where I would manage to ask about the redress bill. Redress and D.C., it seemed, had become part of my DNA.

A SUCCESSFUL CONCLUSION

H.R. 442 was reintroduced in the 100th Congress as the Civil Liberties Act of 1987 by Tom Foley of Washington, now majority leader, and the LEC began its work to rally support on the legislation, with an eye on trying to get the bill to a vote that year.

The earlier version of H.R. 442, introduced in the 99th Congress, on the heels of the commission report and recommendations, was dropped in the hopper with 99 sponsors, despite stiff opposition. That was a long way from the 218 votes needed for passage, but no one expected us to get this far on our quest for an impossible dream, and we were undaunted. By the first hearing, 125 House members supported the legislation, and that was where we stood by the time the Civil Liberties Act of 1987 was introduced. Mineta had rightly predicted that the first bill would not pass but the second would be our ticket to success.

In the midst of the progress being made on the 1987 bill, Supreme Court associate justice Lewis Powell announced in June of that year that he was retiring. There had been a good deal of talk that President Reagan's nominee to replace Justice Powell was Robert Bork, a conservative jurist of the D.C. appellate court who had alienated himself from the civil rights community and was most famous for firing special prosecutor Archibald Cox during the Watergate scandal's Saturday Night Massacre. His nomination raised alarm bells across the country even among politically moderate organizations. Senate Democrats vowed they would block the president's nomination of what they considered a conservative ideologue, a reactionary who was hostile to civil rights gains made in the past twenty years. With the Democrats aligned to kill the nomination, the ensuing fight in the Senate turned ugly, with partisanship becoming a strategy that would ultimately turn divisive beyond reason. The entire civil rights community, including every organization that was a part of the Leadership Conference on Civil Rights, the umbrella organization of which the JACL was a founding member, took a hard position against the Bork nomination *except for* the JACL because, the reasoning went, opposing the Bork nomination would jeopardize the chances of H.R. 442 and would draw negative attention to the JACL in the White House. The concern was that the controversial nomination was a political flash point, and so opposing the nomination could jeopardize the JACL's chance of getting a bill signed by the president. Grudges in politics run deep.

At first stunned by this information, I discounted it as a rumor and had serious doubts the story could be even remotely true; and then I talked to contacts I had in the NAACP and ACLU, who confirmed the report. When people asked me what the hell were we doing, all I could say was that I was just as baffled as they, and I also explained that "we" didn't include me anymore because I was no longer a part of the JACL's leadership and decision-making apparatus. The reaction in the Japanese American community was harsh, and some likened the decision to the cooperation deal of 1942; once again, the JACL seemed to be siding with the administration against what was best for the community. As it turned out, Bork's nomination was blocked in the Senate, and Anthony Kennedy was eventually appointed to the vacant seat, but the JACL's actions, whether right or wrong, would linger for years to come.

On September 17, 1987, after a monumental effort mounted by Grayce Uyehara and the JACL/LEC, H.R. 442 was at last brought to a vote on the floor of the House of Representatives. On the fourth roll call, it was approved by a vote of 243 for, 141 opposed—102-vote difference with a 25-vote margin over the minimum needed for a bill to pass. As wonderful as that victory was, it still bothered me that so many members still did not agree that this nation should have the moral fortitude to not only acknowledge its past mistakes but take measures to correct them, and yet the victory was decisive and I couldn't help but feel proud of our success.

With the year-end holiday recess approaching, Matsunaga and Inouye decided to wait until the Senate reconvened in 1988 to try for a vote on the Senate bill, which had been introduced as S. 1009. Sparky wanted to get all 100 senators voting in favor of the bill, or at least close to that number, but Inouye didn't think that was realistic. As the new year came in, Sparky continued to seek additional sponsors, and after discussions with Inouye and Republican cosponsor Ted Stevens, they agreed the time had come for a floor vote.

And thus, on April 20, 1988, the United States Senate approved S. 1009, amended as H.R. 442, by a vote of 69 for, 27 opposed. Interestingly, the first iteration of the Senate bill had 71 cosponsors, but by the time it reached final approval in the Senate, there were 2 fewer yes votes. Also, four senators hadn't bothered to show up for the vote at all. The Senate being a smaller chamber, where relationships are much closer and votes are taken much more personally, I cannot even begin to imagine the fallout for the four senators who snubbed a bill that was so important and personal to both Dan Inouye and Spark Matsunaga, as well to Senator Stevens.

The next step was that members from the House and Senate were selected to a conference committee whose purpose was to reconcile any differences between the two versions of the bill. On July 26, the committee issued the reconciled bill, and on the following day, the Senate once again approved the bill, this time by voice vote. On August 4, the reconciled version of the bill was presented in the House for final approval, and opponents were allowed one last opportunity to defeat it. That was not to be, however, and the House voted 257 to 156 to approve the bill. The final step was sending the bill to the White House for President Reagan's signature.

Word had gotten around very quickly that Reagan was equivocating on the bill and would possibly not sign it or, worse yet, veto it. There weren't enough votes to overturn a presidential veto, so it became critical—if the rumors were true—to convince the White House to sign the bill into law. I was not in the JACL/LEC loop at this point, so I had no way to verify what I was hearing, but I had one direct source: the father of my daughter's best friend was a personal friend of Reagan's. Inouye, called me to discuss the matter but seemed surprisingly unflappable about it, although he did add that it wouldn't hurt if I knew anyone who could reach Reagan and put in a good word for redress. I assumed (but didn't mention it to him) that Inouye was our best hope in reaching the president because he was close with Ted Stevens, who was himself close to the president *and* one of the principals on the Senate bill. And of course President Reagan, an army veteran of World War II, was known for his great admiration and respect for America's war heroes, and prominent among them was Dan Inouye.

But in the Japanese American community, there was grave concern that the bill was about to fail. I was told that the members of the LEC network had put out the word that the bill was in serious trouble and they were scrambling to contact individuals that might help. Among those on the list were the most prominent among the Nisei Republicans, starting with Paul Bannai, who had served in the California State Assembly when Reagan was governor, and Harry Kubo, who had had been a spokesperson for Central Valley farmers against the United Farm Workers and was also a friend of Reagan's. The most significant name that came up was Togo Tanaka, a former journalist and the owner of a real estate holding company in California. He was a Reagan supporter and had been appointed to the board of the Federal Reserve Bank of San Francisco and then of Los Angeles. Tanaka was among the most successful Nisei in the country and the one Japanese American I thought could get to Reagan, if it suited him to.

Ultimately, President Reagan did sign the bill into law, but the reasons for that remain unknown, or, more accurately perhaps, are unknowable. I was not involved in, or privy to, any actions undertaken to persuade Reagan and can only report what I understand to have happened.

It appears that the LEC strategy team had known for some time that there was a question whether the president would actually sign the bill, but it was not until the bill had reached the president's desk that this became an urgent matter. The LEC put out the word through its network to enlist the help and support of anyone who might be able to convince Reagan to sign the bill.

In the course of all the activity, Grant Ujifusa, the LEC strategy chair, prevailed on New Jersey governor Tom Kean to help reach Reagan on this matter, and Kean mentioned he would be with the president in October as the president campaigned in New Jersey for Republican legislative candidates. Ujifusa provided Kean with a letter written by the sister of Kaz Masuda, a 442nd veteran killed in Europe and honored by General Joseph Stilwell in what amounted to a publicity stunt during World War II. Accompanying Stilwell for that photo op was a young captain, an actor by trade, by the name of Ronald Reagan, who, even in a subsidiary role, showed what a great speaker he could be. At Ujifusa's urging, June Masuda wrote to Reagan about that moment, and her letter was accompanied by photographs of the occasion. While some claim the letter and pictures caused Reagan to change his mind, the documentary *Right of Passage* (2015), a detailed and thorough history of the redress campaign, concludes that there was no single catalyst and that the success of the redress campaign, including the concentrated effort to persuade Reagan to sign the bill, was the consequence of many different individuals from within the Japanese American community.

One individual whom Reagan himself acknowledged at the signing ceremony was Rose Ochi, the National Board member who defied the LEC at many turns but ultimately put their differences aside to work for the passage of the redress bill. She was heavily involved in the very earliest efforts in the 1960s to seek public recognition of the injustices of the government's World War II policies, and she was an active member of the Manzanar Committee, was involved in many of the major battles for and on behalf of the Japanese American community, and was one of the earliest supporters and activists on redress. One could safely assume that the ubiquitous Ochi was involved in efforts to convince Reagan to sign the bill, but we will probably never know the truth of it because, as dedicated as she has always been to the community, she has never sought recognition for her many achievements.

One other incident that may have favorably influenced Reagan has not been discussed publicly until recently. As the story goes, in August 1984, future JACL president Frank Sato, as one of only a handful of elite inspector generals for the federal government, had arranged a meeting between the JACL and Jack Svahn, Assistant to the President for Policy Development (which carried with it the responsibility of domestic policy adviser). Sato knew Svahn personally and had met with him numerous times in the White House.

On August 10, just days before the JACL's 1984 convention in Hawaii, Frank, Floyd Shimomura (then JACL president), Ron Ikejiri, and I met with Svahn in the West Wing. Having been raised on the West Coast (Washington State and California), Svahn was familiar with the history of our WWII experience, so we focused our discussion on the salient points, both historical and constitutional, and briefed him on the status of our legislation. We were cautiously confident at that time that the bill would make it through both houses of Congress and would reach the White House for approval.

In his memoir, *There Must Be a Pony in Here Somewhere: Twenty Years with Ronald Reagan* (2011), Svahn mentions the meeting with Frank and the JACL and describes raising the incarceration and redress issues initially in late 1984 and then again in 1985 at what was called the Issues Lunch, at which West Wing assistants to the president sat down for a meal with the president each week. Svahn describes having mentioned the Kazuo Masuda story, which Reagan only "vaguely recalled," and then bringing up the subject of the internment again at an Issues Lunch a year later. Svahn writes, "He seemed to be very interested but also noncommittal," noting that "his natural inclination would be to right the wrong."

Svahn left the White House later that year but notes that it was the president's advisers who opposed H.R. 442 and not Reagan himself. The Office of Management and Budget opposed the bill on fiscal grounds, and the staff involved in foreign relations argued, somewhat oddly, that the bill would adversely impact relations with Japan. It's interesting to note that these strains of opposition to H.R. 442 were *not* based on the need to defend the government's wartime rationale in order to justify the treatment of Japanese Americans during World War II. The campaign and commission had clarified those issues, and those in the Reagan White House understood that.

Svahn believed that, ultimately, Reagan would sign H.R. 442 and said as much to Bob Matsui. When the bill finally made it to the president's desk three years later, Svahn's sense of the president in 1985 proved true, that Reagan's "natural inclination would be to right the wrong," and we can only speculate that Svahn's comments to the president—spurred by information and materials we had provided him on behalf of the JACL—had something to do with his decision to sign the bill. And of course no one knows how much truth there was to the idea that the president was ever conflicted in the first place, a point confirmed by a good friend who had called Reagan and reported that the president intended to sign the bill, despite the rumors to the contrary.

Who deserves credit for convincing Reagan is ultimately unimportant and unknowable. It may have been our meeting with Svahn and his subsequent urging on the issue, or it may have been Ujifusa's intervention with Governor Kean, or his convincing highly influential conservative individuals to prevail on the president, or it may have been the calls made to the White House by various influential Nisei or others, or perhaps it was Frank Sato's meetings with West Wing staffers in his role as IG. Most likely, it was a combination of all of the above. What *is* important is that Ronald Reagan signed the redress bill into law as the Civil Liberties Act of 1988 and entered it on the public books as Public Law Number 100-383.

The measure provided for the following:

- A trust fund into which $500 million would be appropriated each year, and from which restitution payments of $20,000 would be made to each Japanese American claimant who was a victim of policies that emanated from Executive Order 9066;
- A new Office of Redress Administration, which would operate under the aegis of the Department of Justice and would oversee the implementation of payments, including notifying and identifying individuals deemed eligible;
- Under a separate program, $12,000 for each surviving member of the Aleut people who were affected by the wartime policies, plus a $6.5 million payment to a trust fund for the use of their community; and
- For both Japanese Americans and Aleuts, a letter from the president acknowledging the injustice of their wartime treatment by the United States government.

I was with my family driving south through Oregon, returning to California from a vacation in the Northwest, when we heard the announcement on the radio. It came as somewhat of a surprise given that it had been so long since anything about the incarceration or redress had been in the news, but I did know the signing would be that day because Dan Inouye had called to tell me he wanted me to drop everything and be at the ceremony. I thanked him for the invitation but said I was on vacation with my family and wasn't going to leave them. I had done too much of that in my life and was happy to be with them.

And then something occurred to me: I asked him, "How did you track me down on vacation when no one knows where I am?" I could hear the amusement in his voice when he reminded me of the many long years he had chaired the Senate CIA oversight committee. "I could find you if you were on the moon!" he said.

Hearing the news on the radio about the signing was, for me, a moment of relief. I could finally let go of the campaign. We had achieved everything we had set out to do: We had informed and educated the American public about one of the most significant abrogations of constitutional protections in the history of this nation, the importance of which could never have been fully appreciated on a massive scale had we not forced this issue. We had become part of America's history through the CWRIC's official government report on the injustice of our wartime treatment. And we had successfully sought passage of redress legislation on behalf of Japanese Americans who were victimized by the internment. Our successes were monumental and profound.

This moment was also vindication for the Nisei and all they had endured and sacrificed to prove they were worthy of their citizenship. Throughout the campaign, even at the outset, when the majority of the Nisei objected to making the camp issue public, they held on to their dignity, held their heads high because they knew no other way. They were proud Americans, and throughout the decade of fighting this battle, the Nisei, above anyone else, fought not for what they were owed but for what they believed about American ideals. The signing of the bill meant it had all been worth it.

─────────

While President Reagan signed H.R. 442 into law, his fiscal budget the following year did not provide adequate funding to fulfill the intent of the bill. For the next two years in the House, Norman Mineta and Bob Matsui fought off amendments seeking to weaken their appropriations legislation that would, finally, provide redress payments. On the other side of the Capitol, Senators Matsunaga and Inouye fought similar battles to secure passage of their appropriations measure, a fight that would carry on through the first two years of George H. W. Bush's presidency.

The JACL/LEC team coordinated their efforts with the Japanese American members and launched a major campaign to get passage of the appropriations bills. It was a hard-fought battle that I can describe only in summary here, but it is a story well worth telling by those who were part of the LEC's valiant effort, which resulted, in October 1990, with the first redress payments to nine Issei. They were the first of eighty-two thousand Japanese Americans who received a letter of apology from the president and a $20,000 check. In the end, $1.6 billion in restitution was paid to Japanese Americans affected by the government's wartime policies.

JAPANESE LATIN AMERICANS

The JACL faded out of the news cycle once the redress bill was signed into law, but it resurfaced in the rumor mill of the Japanese American community in the early 1990s, after the Japanese American vernacular press reported turmoil in the organization, a symptom of growing pains as it moved beyond redress toward whatever it would become.

I had steered wide of the organization but was drawn back when I was approached to assist with the Japanese Latin American (JLA) issue. This was a redress-related matter that had always been treated as a footnote to the larger story of our wartime internment but was, in fact, a subtext that revealed just how far America's leaders had been willing to step outside the accepted bounds of decency.

Starting in the early months of World War II and up through 1944, a total of approximately twenty-five hundred ethnic Japanese from South and Central America were brought to the United States as part of an American plan to exchange Japanese Latin Americans for American POWs and American civilians held captive in the Pacific. A majority of the JLAs were from Peru, and although the Peruvian authorities were eager enough to banish the country's Japanese population, it took American coercion to accomplish this action when the U.S. authorities dispatched American ships to Peru to transfer—essentially to kidnap—the ethnic Japanese people from Peru and other countries in the region for our use. In the process, U.S. agents confiscated the passports of those abducted and incarcerated them primarily at a Justice Department camp at Crystal City, Texas. A year after the war's end, the Japanese Latin Americans were released from Crystal City, but because they had neither passports (which had never been returned to them) nor visas (which they never had in the first place, because they had been abducted and brought to the United States as prisoners), they were declared illegal aliens and ordered to leave the country. Most scattered; some headed south of the border, the majority went to Los Angeles, where there was a large Japanese American population, and still others went up to Canada, with the hope that they could establish residency there and reenter the United States legally.

While the JACL was sympathetic to the cause and knew that the wartime situation of the JLAs was much worse than that of Japanese Americans, their inclusion on redress-related legislation posed a problem because some House members objected to consideration of noncitizens in the bill. (When I first heard this objection, I thought that by "noncitizen" they were referring to the Issei, whose official status was "legal resident alien" because federal law prohibited them from gaining naturalized citizenship.) Some House members, ignoring for the moment that this country had kidnapped foreign nationals and imprisoned them against their will and without cause, nevertheless found this a credible reason to object to the legislation and refused to sign the bill if it would grant reparations to non-Americans. Regardless of where our conscience fell on the issue, we couldn't deny that the inclusion of the JLAs weakened our argument, which was centered on the government's actions against American citizens and legal resident aliens, a fact that distinguished our experience from any other historical injustice and was the basis of our argument for redress. The Big Four agreed that the JLA issue could jeopardize the bill, but Sparky felt we should keep them on the bill anyway to emphasize how absurd the government's logic was and how unjust its actions and policies.

I agreed with Sparky, but the notion "for the greater good" weighed heavily on the decision to ultimately exclude the JLAs from what was already a legislative fight in which the odds were completely stacked against us. In the end, we decided to stick to our criterion for defining eligibility for reparations, which was limited to persons of Japanese ancestry who had been residing in the military's designated evacuation zone (the entire states of California, Oregon, and Washington, and the southern half of Arizona) on or before December 7, 1941, and/or those who had been affected by the orders emanating from EO 9066, including those who had been born in one of the government's concentration camps. These were the parameters we had decided on after realizing there was no other reasonable or equitable way to reconcile the strong, often emotional beliefs within the Japanese American community about who should or should not be included, such as the veterans versus the resisters, those who answered Yes versus the No-No Boys, the Renunciants, and so on. While this definition narrowly defined Japanese American eligibility, it also excluded the JLAs. When the JACL adopted this official definition of reparations eligibility, it accepted the exclusion of the JLAs only with the caveat that we would deal with that issue once the redress campaign was ended, regardless of the outcome.

When I was called back into the JACL fold in the late 1990s, I was surprised to learn that the JACL had done nothing about the JLA issue. Once the redress bill had passed, the JACL/LEC board took no actions to fulfill the organization's commitment to seek relief for the Japanese Latin Americans. When I learned that this obligation had been ignored, I agreed to represent the JACL as a consultant in the lawsuit *Mochizuki v. United States*.

The principal organization supporting the legal claim was the National Coalition for Redress/Reparations, and, as it became clear once I got involved, the JACL was little more than an observer. The *Mochizuki* suit sought $20,000 for each member of the class, plus a letter of apology from the president, and it cited the Civil Liberties Act of 1988 as the instrument that provided redress for Japanese Americans but excluded JLAs from consideration.

The case was resolved by a settlement in which the Justice Department accepted that the government had erred and agreed to a $5,000 payment to each plaintiff along with a presidential letter of apology. Those JLAs who accepted the settlement offer were dissatisfied with how little they got, but they also realized it was probably the best they could get. Those who didn't accept the offer continued to pursue other forms of remedy, but as of this writing, the matter has never been fully resolved. I am left wondering whether the outcome might have been different had the JACL pursued the issue soon after the passage of the redress bill, but that's a question that can never be answered.

HOW DO YOU FIX
SOMETHING SO BROKEN?

My involvement with the *Mochizuki* case and the broader concerns of the JLA issue reconnected me with the JACL only temporarily. I had turned my focus to areas of personal interest, such as the environment, civil rights, and especially public-policy issues relevant to Asian Americans. The organizations and players who took the lead on these efforts were far outside the reach of the JACL, which had no place in this new order forging the path for the future of the Asian American community. In that narrow period of time from the late 1980s to the beginning of the 1990s, it felt as if there had been tectonic shifts in the alignment of Asian American communities, a result of demographic changes in the population. Asian Americans were finding their political voice and, indeed, their political muscle. This felt nothing like the world before redress, and I couldn't help thinking the campaign had contributed in some ways to laying the foundation upon which Asian Americans were establishing their footing in the political arena.

In this new landscape, the JACL was, at least to me, most noticeable by its absence—its complete lack of presence despite its revered history as the oldest and largest Asian American civil rights organization in the country. Some Asian American leaders wondered if the JACL had seen its better days, and others blamed the organization's miscalculations for having virtually isolated it from the rest of Asian America.

Although I had been distant from it for some time, I still personally identified with, and was identified as part of, the JACL since that was where I had spent so much time in a high-profile position. I took no pleasure in the JACL's loss of prominence, in part because I knew what the JACL was capable of achieving for the community and for Asian Americans in general. It was unfortunate to hear about the JACL's problems rather than its achievements, but in the world of community and politics, the old question "What have you done for me lately?" was all that mattered, and the answer from the organization was, simply, not much.

The vacuum that the JACL had created by becoming a single-issue organization had been filled by other groups willing to take up issues including U.S.–Japan trade tensions, immigration, and all the other situations affecting different ethnic groups in the larger Asian American community. The prevailing view seemed to be that the JACL had disappeared in on itself and had not shown interest in being part of the wider community anymore. On the positive side of that absence, however, was that the myriad organizations that emerged to fill the vacancies the JACL had left undoubtedly strengthened the community. Besides, in my mind, such changes were inevitable and were only hastened by the JACL's preoccupation with its own issues. I had witnessed similar circumstances during my work in D.C., and I had seen it happen as well in Los Angeles, where I more recently had spent much of my time because it was emerging as the dynamic center and cutting edge of an Asian American community energized by a new generation of leaders.

It was during my work in Los Angeles that I came in contact with Alan Kumamoto, a skilled and highly regarded management consultant and also a name from the JACL's history in Los Angeles. He and I had long conversations about the JACL, and I was often surprised to learn how much he knew about the internal conflicts that had taken place throughout the redress campaign, as well as the problems that plagued the organization in the aftermath of the successful conclusion of redress. He obviously had connections with someone in the higher echelons of the organization, and that coupled with his reputation as one of the best Asian American management consultants led to his being selected to help "reinvent" the JACL. He was the perfect choice to take the JACL board through what would turn out to be grueling strategic planning sessions.

Alan convinced me to assist him with these planning sessions, during which he laid bare the choices past boards had made that he felt had contributed to the JACL's current predicament. His job would be to skillfully guide the JACL through a revival, working always to help the leadership discover the core value that would take them into the future.

I assisted him as he cajoled the board and led it through various exercises by which it might develop a new vision of itself. It was hard work, and we always rewarded ourselves with drinks before he left San Francisco to fly back to L.A. It was toward one of the last weekends of his sessions when he asked me over drinks, "You know what they're going to ask you, don't you?" I had no idea what he was talking about. "The person they're describing in there was you," he said, referring to a profile the board had created to define the type of person who could best lead the JACL into the next phase of its existence. It didn't matter if the board did ask because I had no interest at all in being dragged back into the organization.

Even apart from simply not wanting anything to do with the JACL, I was not looking to alter my life at that point. Things were good. I was thoroughly enjoying my work as a consultant and had developed a reputation that brought interesting projects to my door and allowed me to pick and choose my work. There was nothing about any of it that I would change. Having now also seen in the planning sessions the kinds of internal problems the JACL faced, I knew it would take a monumental effort to redirect the JACL's course, and I simply wasn't interested in being the one to do it. Looming over it all was the question Alan and I had first pondered over drinks after one of the especially long and challenging weekend sessions: How do you fix something so broken?

Alan was prescient in anticipating that the director would be removed during the planning session, and as he had predicted, Floyd Mori, a board member and an old friend, asked me if I would be willing to serve as an interim director while the board conducted a search for a permanent director. This might have felt like *déjà vu*, to be asked again to fill the director's position, but it wasn't. Whereas in 1981 I had been at least open to the idea, now, in 1999, I had zero inclination to take the position, even on a temporary basis. Floyd acknowledged he could not provide a single compelling reason why I should even consider the board's request, but he also seemed to understand, maybe even better than I, that even after everything that had happened, I still truly cared about the organization. We both knew that as flawed as the JACL might be and maybe had always been, it was an organization worth saving; despite its checkered past, it had accomplished so much for the community. Even though the JACL's decision to forgo all other responsibilities in order to focus solely on redress was part of what led to its later struggles, some argued that its single-minded efforts had been a necessary sacrifice to ensure the success of redress. And yet, once Ron Wakabayashi resigned as national director at the close of the campaign, the organization floundered, and many wondered if it could recover from its loss of credibility and status in the larger civil rights community it had abandoned. In the years I worked with Alan, we often used the *Titanic* as a metaphor for talking about the JACL: once you see the iceberg out there in the distance, it's already too late. The JACL hadn't yet sunk, but it was clearly listing.

Much had been lost, but not all, and the question for the JACL was never dire and existential: the organization *would* survive, we were sure of that. Despite ten years of oft-publicized internal turmoil and despite the alarming drop in membership, the sheer number of people loyal to the organization would ensure its continued presence in the community. But the question was what that presence would look like now that the organization had lost its place in the order of things that mattered.

FINDING OUR WAY BACK

September 1999 marked my return to the JACL in what I assumed would be a three-month period as the interim director, just long enough to get the organization shifted into its new direction. I was determined that the changes I made in that time, whatever they might be, would not be simply cosmetic but substantive. The JACL needed once again to master the art of making a difference.

Before we could manage that, however, I thought we had some image building to do, and with the JACL's national convention scheduled for June 2000, I called on contacts I had at the DOJ and was able to get U.S. Attorney General Janet Reno as the convention keynote speaker. As it is for most organizations, the prestige of the keynote speaker at our major annual event was a reflection of what we were as an organization, and you could not get anyone more politically important than Reno, except for the president. Also that year, the JACL board would honor Paul Akio Kawata, executive director of the New York City–based National Minority AIDS Council, one of the only Asian American gay rights organizations in the country. Kawata's recognition was particularly appropriate because the JACL had passed a resolution in 1994 in support of same-sex partnerships. After the ACLU, the JACL became the second national organization outside the gay community to take this public stand, and I thought it was important that the JACL celebrate the fact that it had taken the courageous and absolutely proper position while other organizations remained silent.

By April 2000, as the end of my interim period approached, I was asked by the board to continue as the director on a permanent basis. I felt obliged to stay at least through the convention in June because I was responsible for getting Janet Reno as our speaker and needed to see that through. Rather than extend my interim position by a few months, I decided to accept the director's position for two years, which I figured would provide the board time to find a new director and give me an opportunity to get the JACL back into the civil rights arena in meaningful ways.

That challenge began with the election in November 2000 of George W. Bush and his nomination of John Ashcroft as attorney general. Bush could not have made a worse choice to fill the country's top law enforcement position, considering that, while in the Senate, Ashcroft (R-Missouri) had voted against every civil rights bill that came across his desk. To express the JACL's objection to the nomination, I wrote a letter to the White House and we joined the chorus of civil rights organizations raising their voices in opposition. We didn't succeed, but it was still important that the JACL joined the civil rights coalition in this fight.

Also during this time, I reorganized the JACL's priorities and made the organization's hate crimes program the centerpiece of our civil rights agenda, a response to growing anti-Asian sentiment and the decades-long increase of hate crimes against Asians in America. While the redress campaign may have awakened the nation to the discrimination faced by Japanese Americans and others of Asian descent, there would always be people who would never accept us as equal or even as bona fide Americans. In their minds, we didn't look like what they insisted Americans should look like.

The JACL still had plenty of work to do, and I hoped that with some renewed leadership and focus we could make ourselves relevant and effective once more. The structural elements of the JACL that had made the JACL so effective in spearheading the redress campaign—that is, its regional and chapter components—were still in place and were largely responsible for maintaining the operational integrity of the organization. Chapters continued to work at the local level to challenge discrimination where they saw it and developed programs to enhance the JACL's presence as a social asset. The strength of the organization would always be its robust volunteer core, the foot soldiers, the rank and file who connected with the local communities. On the sturdiness of that foundation, I knew we could rebuild the JACL's national presence. Little did we know how soon we would be tested and how massive the implications would be.

7

9/11: LESSONS FROM THE PAST

(2001-2007)

ANOTHER DAY OF INFAMY

Tuesday morning began like any other New York City morning in September: the last of the summer storms had passed over the East Coast, leaving clear blue skies, the temperature moderate but with a hint of fall in the air. And then terrorists flew airplanes into the Twin Towers, and into the Pentagon (and a fourth crashed in a field in Pennsylvania), and as the skies turned dark with ash and smoke that day, so did the mood of America turn dark with fear and despair.

Sixty years after Pearl Harbor, we had been attacked once again on our own soil, and the parallels were striking: in one case, nearly twenty-five hundred sailors buried in the hulls of sunken navy ships, and on the other, approximately three thousand innocent victims buried under the smoldering rubble of collapsed buildings. In both instances, an ethnic population in America could be seen to share physical characteristics with the attackers and became the target of public backlash. ABC news anchor Peter Jennings was the first to report that the FBI had announced that the attacks had all the earmarks of Middle Eastern terrorists, and before the day was over, the pieces of this horrific day would start to fit together as, one by one, the hijackers were identified, all Arab, all Muslim. By day's end, that had become the storyline. Through all the anguish of the day, the question was how America would respond to this national tragedy brought on by a still-amorphous enemy. New words were being introduced into mainstream America's post-terrorism lexicon, words like *Islamist* and *jihadist* and *caliphate* and a group known as al-Qaeda. For many if not most Americans, the totality of the information collected about the attacks seemed to be reduced to one simple concept: we had been attacked by Arab Muslims.

As the initial shock wore off and turned into fear, one could sense the feeling of helplessness that grew with the realization that we were a nation vulnerable to attack. What did it all mean in terms of our safety and future? Everyone felt a need to do *something*, whether that meant to help assuage the pain of a national trauma or to retaliate. As the news reports continued through the following days and we got a clearer picture of who the terrorists were, I knew that the stunned silence would quickly turn to anger and there would be an ugly backlash. Arabs and Muslims in America would not be safe for a long time, and maybe never again; they would become the innocent victims of America's wrath toward a cowardly foreign enemy.

Japanese Americans understood this situation only too well, having been scapegoats for the actions of another foreign enemy. Like us after Pearl Harbor, the Arab and Muslim communities in America faced the discrimination and danger that came from being identified with those nineteen terrorists. The sense of *déjà vu* was palpable for us. I knew that America's Middle Eastern communities would be linked with the terrorists and would become targets of bigotry and hate and deceit, just as we had been after Pearl Harbor. Images of the planes exploding as they hit the towers of the World Trade Center would become as iconic as those of the USS *Shaw* exploding from the direct hit by a Japanese dive-bomber, and those two scenes, while separated by sixty years, would be forever connected as singular moments in our nation's history, connected by our collective sense of national tragedy.

For Japanese Americans, the events of this day evoked the memories of our lives in the days following Pearl Harbor and our own stories of wartime discrimination, and for us at the JACL, it thrust upon us a deeply felt sense of moral obligation to respond and intervene. We knew what was coming, and we would not let it happen again. Yes, we all felt the horror of the attacks and cried for the innocent dead, but to allow America and Americans to act again from a place of rage, and to do so at the expense of reason and justice, would only further damage this nation and its belief in the principles upon which it was built and for which millions of Americans have given their lives to ensure and protect. And so, before the dust began to settle over New York City, the Pentagon, and that lonely field in Pennsylvania, we began laying out our plans, drawing on our past experiences and everything we had learned during the redress campaign, in an effort to caution the nation's leaders, and its citizens, about what further horrors could come from fear and hate.

———

By late afternoon of the 11th, I had contacted each of the JACL's regional directors to talk briefly and set up a conference call to discuss our course of action. I wanted to assess what was happening in their areas around the country and to coordinate our activities. The entire nation was still in shock at that point, but I knew the reactions were coming, and when they did, we needed to be prepared. Much of the work of civil rights organizations is educating people about the issues and, in doing so, to hopefully inform responses that will prevent potentially volatile situations. In an atmosphere as incendiary as this, we knew we would be called upon to be both proactive and reactive as anti-Arab and anti-Muslim sentiments flared up around the country.

The JACL staff on the conference call were professionals who knew how to handle situations incited by racial hatred, but even so, 9/11 was unlike anything any of us had experienced in our daily work, and we knew the backlash was coming and that it would be as fierce and unforgiving as a dark tsunami sweeping across the land. Anyone who even slightly resembled a Middle Easterner would be vulnerable to bigotry and hate crimes, and it would take all our collective experience and knowledge to keep the ignorance and violence at bay. We didn't formulate a new action plan. We didn't have to. Our standard protocol was that I would work with the national media and the political leadership. The directors, who had years of experience battling the kind of rancid bigotry we were already hearing on talk radio, would work their regional areas and coordinate the work on the ground.

I would coordinate the JACL's national effort from the San Francisco headquarters and keep the regional directors informed of any actions being undertaken by the national organization. We would check in with each other periodically as time allowed, knowing that we would all be busy once we finished this call. The directors would work with their chapters to focus their efforts where they were needed and would handle all local media. All position papers and public statements released by the JACL would be sent to them before release in order to keep them abreast of the organization's official response to what we knew would be a rapidly changing situation. Bill Yoshino, in our Chicago office, would have the heaviest burden because the Midwest was not only a hotbed of hate radio and white supremacist groups but also home to the nation's largest Arab community: Dearborn, Michigan. It would be the most difficult area to manage, but Yoshino was also the most experienced regional director in the organization and was in charge of the JACL's hate crimes initiative and program.

As an organization, we would do our best to try to stay ahead of the situation across the country, although that seemed hardly possible. The challenge we faced was that the attack on the World Trade Center was not just an attack on New Yorkers or any specific group of people but an attack on America and everything it stood for. It was an attack on the *idea* of America, an attack on what we embraced as American idealism. Although we knew it was coming, we couldn't predict how and where the backlash would manifest, as it could happen virtually anywhere in the country, at any time, and in ways we might not even imagine.

On behalf of the JACL, I sent a press release to all the major media outlets in the country, cautioning our nation's leaders and the American people against reacting as some had following the attack on Pearl Harbor. The statement quoted from letters I had already sent to President George W. Bush, Attorney General John Ashcroft, and the leadership of the House and Senate. I shared the statement with my directors before releasing it and told them that, in light of the rapidly changing situation, I would exercise unilateral authority and take responsibility for our public actions, and I instructed them to implement all of their activities and efforts as needed. "You're the professionals," I told them. "You know what needs to be done."

――――――

I had drafted our official statement on the evening of the attacks, and within twenty-four hours of the first plane hitting the North Tower of the World Trade Center, had sent it to every major news outlet, both electronic and print, in the country, plus to all local and regional news outlets for whom we had email addresses. The release was essentially a warning against racial profiling as a reaction to the previous day's terrorist attacks, and we noted our alarm that Arab and Muslim people living in America had already been mistreated and accused as enemy sympathizers. I quoted myself as saying, "It is in times of national tragedies…that the character and will of the American public are tested, as well as the strength and value of the Constitution," and I quoted Floyd Mori, the JACL's president, urging Americans "not to make the same mistakes as a nation that were made in the hysteria of WWII following the attack at Pearl Harbor." I remember thinking as I wrote it that I needed to inform Floyd lest he get caught off guard, and that instinct proved wise when, within fifteen minutes of sending the press release, calls started coming in.

Once the phone calls started, our lines got flooded and reporters were put into a queue, since I was the only one at the headquarters who could respond to the media. (The other three people in the building were administrative staff.) The first call was from a reporter from the Associated Press who told me, "John, you were the first out of the gate. You even beat the ACLU." I responded that this wasn't some kind of contest or race, and that I had issued the statement at the earliest possible time because it was important that we spoke out. As the only community in the country that had experienced a circumstance with a similar kind of potential backlash, we knew it was important that we bring our voice into the chorus of those we hoped would join us in cautioning the government against repeating the mistakes of earlier generations. Throughout the redress campaign, I vowed that our effort was not for our benefit but was intended to ensure that no community in the future would face similar victimization, and now we were determined that the findings of the CWRIC would steer our current national leaders to consider their actions in light of our experience during World War II. I made it clear that the JACL would lead any protest against unjust treatment of Arab and Muslim Americans, including any legislative or legal actions in response to injustices similar to the ones we had suffered. "We will not allow racists and reactionaries to dictate a course of action based on race and other bogus factors, to once again render the Constitution meaningless," I insisted. "We are fully committed to ensuring that doesn't happen and will do whatever necessary to protect our friends in the Arab and Muslim communities."

Throughout the rest of the day, the JACL headquarters was flooded with calls from reporters interested in our perspective on 9/11, given our experience of wartime incarceration. I heard from Yoshino, who informed me that the chapters in his district were also being contacted by local media and needed directions about how to respond. What was our party line? We put together a quick action memorandum that provided guidance on talking to media, including not just what message we wanted to emphasize but also clarity on what we, as a national organization, were prepared to do (i.e., lawsuits, legislation, etc.) to challenge any actions by the Bush administration and local governing authorities should they abridge the rights of Middle Eastern Americans without cause. We would not allow a repetition of our wartime experiences to be visited upon others. We also directed our chapters to initiate contacts with local Arab and Muslim community leaders as well as local law enforcement, political leaders, and media sources. The point was to be proactive rather than reactive only after incidents occurred.

As I was fielding calls one after another, the AP reporter called again to ask me about the story going around that I had ordered JACL members to act as human shields for people belonging to groups that had received death threats! When we tracked down where the story had come from, it turned out that one of the leaders of the Afghan community in the Bay Area had said, in an interview with a local reporter, that in the face of the death threats they were getting, they felt comforted knowing that the local JACL chapter president's offer to "help protect you." That statement had been misinterpreted. I got several other calls from reporters throughout the country asking about similar versions of this story, and while I confirmed that, yes, we would support our Arab and Muslim friends and resist those who threatened to harm them, we had not made any official commitment to stand between attackers and victims. I admired the courage of our members who said they would put themselves at risk should it be necessary, but I wasn't sure that even this selfless act would stop a bigot out to retaliate. In fact, I worried that in the backlash that was starting to build, those intent on inflicting harm on the "other" would not distinguish between a Japanese American and a member of the Arab Muslim community: in their eyes, we were one and the same—the same enemy, separated only by the sixty years between attacks on America.

In the days following 9/11, every racial incident seemed to be a flash point. Wherever they occurred, or wherever we knew tensions were rising, our chapters, if they were in the area, got involved to try to resolve issues, often joining with other Japanese Americans there for the same purpose. Chapter leaders reported in periodically to keep headquarters advised about local goings-on; regional directors were busy investigating incidents wherever they occurred, sometimes over very broad areas; and nationally, we worked with the media and various organizations in the Arab and Muslim communities to try to keep them safe. Talking to the media was still a major part of my work, but I was also keeping tabs on how the Bush administration and Congress were responding to the attacks. When journalists reported that approximately two thousand individuals from the Arab and Muslim communities had been arrested immediately following the 9/11 attacks and were being detained in an undisclosed location, the JACL joined with numerous civil rights organizations to demand information about the detainees, namely who they were and why they were being held. The JACL's press statement about this situation recalled the FBI roundup of over two thousand Japanese American leaders within twenty-four hours of the Pearl Harbor attacks. I pointed out that the FBI sweep of Japanese Americans had been predicated on nothing more than their being prominent in the community, and now, unlike 1942, when our community was beset by confusion, we publicly criticized the roundup, which included asking questions about why the Bush administration refused to provide any information about those arrested after 9/11. Was this the same situation, the only criterion for the arrests that these people matched the profile of boogeymen?

No one knew, of course, how far the Bush administration would go in its mistreatment of Arabs and Muslims, but I vowed that if it turned out to be anything similar to our wartime treatment, I would lead the JACL in a lawsuit and/or legislative campaign to seek reparations as a condemnation of the government's actions. Of this I was adamant: we would not allow the leadership of the United States to even consider such a preposterous move, and if they somehow managed it anyway, we would not let them get away with it. We would not equivocate on this matter. We were fully committed and we would not budge.

The most important Japanese American in the country at this time was Norman Mineta, then the secretary of transportation and an insider on the Bush cabinet. I *knew*—I was absolutely confident—there was no way Norm would allow the president's cabinet to discuss taking action against Muslim Arab American communities without just cause. Mineta was without question the most influential and significant voice against the mass exclusion and detention of the Muslim Arab Americans, and as I thought about him sitting in cabinet meetings in the hours and days following the 9/11 attacks, I was reminded of a saying that it's important to be at the table not only for what you contribute but also for what will not be said in your presence. With Norm, it would take little more than a look to silence any cabinet colleagues who dared to propose the unthinkable.

It was Mineta who created a small storm of controversy in December when, on *60 Minutes*, reporter Steve Kroft asked him if he thought a "seventy-year-old white woman from Vero Beach, Florida" should be scrutinized in the same way as a "Muslim young man from Jersey City," to which Mineta answered, "I would hope so," standing firm against racial profiling. It was the only correct answer for those who believe in democratic principles enough to live by them and expect our government to adhere to them, but there were others who thought his response ignorant and even traitorous. In February 2002, right-wing pundit Ann Coulter wrote in response to the program that Mineta "wants America to suffer" and was "burning with hatred for America."

Mineta's influence over the Bush administration's actions vis-à-vis the Arab and Muslim communities following the 9/11 tragedy went back at least as far as the weekend he spent with President Bush at Camp David just before the attacks. Mineta talked with the president about his experience as an eleven-year-old boy who had been one of 120,000 Japanese Americans imprisoned after Pearl Harbor. That interaction came back around later when, during a cabinet meeting after the 9/11 attacks, the president at one point admonished cabinet members against any thought of a mass roundup, directing their attention to "my friend Norman here" and then retelling the story of Mineta's experience of wartime imprisonment. President Bush, Mineta says, was determined that his administration would not make the mistake FDR's administration had.

In comparison to the scale of things Mineta was involved with in those critical days, it felt like we at the JACL were on the ground putting out brush fires. While our local chapters were at work quelling racial tensions in whatever ways they could, I was focused on communicating with the media and finding out what congresspeople were saying and how much of that chatter reflected a reactionary sense of urgency to *do something*, regardless of consequences or of risking the integrity of our governing ideals. I heard in their words echoes of my days lobbying congressional members on redress, listening as they prided this nation on its decisive and, in their views, necessary action in the aftermath of Pearl Harbor. Now I was hearing it all once more in conversations after 9/11, with House members saying they thought the actions of FDR's EO 9066 were reasonable and needed to be undertaken again, the Constitution be damned. But now we had a caution against such actions: the federal commission's study and the Civil Liberties Act.

The press and news outlets made the connection between the post-9/11 atmosphere and the conditions that had led to our wartime incarceration. Unlike my experience during the redress campaign, when I had to educate the media about the government's actions against us and the fallacies behind the rationale for those policies, the current wave of journalists were well informed about the internment, an awareness I believe was the direct result of the redress campaign. Reporters I talked to referred specifically to sections of the CWRIC report, trying to dig deep into the parallels between our experience and the current situation, and for the most part I spent very little time getting people caught up on the relevant history. It changed the dialogue: audiences were primed to understand the folly of repeating such injustices, even despite their fears about the possibility of another terrorist attack.

Of course, there were still those who argued that we would never be safe unless we detained every Arab and Muslim in the country, and the bottom line for them was the same as it had been for us: racism. The people who advocated race-based imprisonment couldn't explain why such a policy was reasonable when it came to Arab and Muslim Americans but not, for example, when it came to young white men in the aftermath of Timothy McVeigh's 1995 bombing of the Alfred P. Murrah Federal Building in Oklahoma City. Why was it all right to violate the civil liberties of some Americans but not others? Did their whiteness somehow make it different? I reminded audiences that the same arguments that had been used to imprison Japanese Americans during World War II were no different than what they were advocating now. And if they argued that they weren't being racist, then should the government have rounded up all German Americans during World War II? Oh, they were different? Really? And why not white supremacist groups known to the FBI as terrorist organizations? How were they less a threat to our security than law-abiding Muslims who were as horrified by 9/11 as the rest of us were? Did people really think they all had suicide bombs under their clothing? Really? *Really?*

If the government has concrete proof that any Arabs or Muslims living in this country, or any other Americans—including white people —are involved in terrorist activities, then by all means they should be arrested. But if the government takes actions against someone based on nothing other than race or religious beliefs or imagined threats, then we are heading into dangerous and indefensible territory. If the Constitution was going to mean anything, I said over and over, make it mean something *now*, in this situation. If we were truly a nation built on democratic ideals and beliefs, *now* was the time to give real meaning to those beliefs. Otherwise, to hell with the Constitution. If we resort to what extremists demand, our democracy is reduced to a sham. We are a better nation than that, and it would be a tragedy if we let the kind of madness that determined our fates in 1942 be repeated. How could we be proud of our nation if we allowed this to happen again? What would it say about us?

If the days and months following 9/11 proved anything to me about the value of our work on the JACL redress campaign, it was that everything we had done to educate the public was paying dividends now. The subject of the wartime treatment of Japanese Americans had become inexorably a part of the post-9/11 debate on how we maintain national security in the face of potential threats from a segment of the population feared to be within our borders. As the government and the nation grappled with the task of ensuring the public's safety from future attacks, the internment story and the commission findings were raised as warnings against unreasoned reactions. Even so, politically conservative commentators used the internment as evidence that such policies did in fact work because look how EO 9066 had prevented Japanese Americans from committing sabotage and kept America safe within our borders. I found it the height of hypocrisy to hear commentators such as Michelle Malkin and Rush Limbaugh invoke their love of America and democracy while at the same time promoting positions that revealed how little they thought of the Constitution, it being nothing more than a worthless piece of paper when it came to keeping America safe. But safe from what? The hatred they were spewing and advocating were more of a threat to democracy than the people they were so quick to admonish and condemn.

It was also interesting to me to discover, in talking with members of Congress, mainly House members, that everything we had accomplished during the redress movement—the public education, the commission report, the Civil Liberties Act—was important in dissuading members from considering a wholesale roundup of Arabs and Muslims. I found it heartening that members of Congress who initially favored at least some actions against America's Arab and Muslim communities were later able to see the parallels with the expulsion and imprisonment of Japanese Americans.

It was also persuasive to inform them that the approximately $2 billion paid in reparations for the action against 120,000 Japanese Americans was nothing compared to the amount the government would owe if it enacted similar policies against the Arab and Muslim communities, which numbered more than a million. I also assured them that if they took such action, the JACL would be the first organization to urge our Arab American friends to seek redress and that we would join in their effort. I am convinced that without Norman Mineta's presence on the cabinet and without the redress campaign having been waged in the 1970s and '80s, the public outcry for revenge after 9/11 could have provoked policies that would have resulted in the imprisonment of a substantial number of people from this nation's Arab and Muslim population. Groups like the JACL, the ACLU, and many other civil rights organizations would have challenged such policies, but, in the tension wrought by fear, there's no telling just how far the public might have allowed the administration to go in those days following the terrorist attacks.

In the end, neither the administration nor Congress sought whole-sale detention as an option (despite some angry members who argued otherwise), and ultimately, I believe the conscience of an informed public made the difference.

It is difficult to know what specific factors contributed to the decisions that resulted in such a markedly different outcome in 2002 compared to 1942, but from my own personal experience, I do know that there was a far different awareness in the public conscience after 9/11 because so many Americans had been educated on the injustices of the WWII internment of Japanese Americans. We *had* learned from the past, and I saw again just how important our message to the public had been and how successful we had been in our mission to spread the truth. Without the redress effort forcing the nation to acknowledge its past mistakes, I am convinced the road the United States would have traveled after 9/11 could have led us to a dark and unforgiving place.

JOURNEY'S END

My experience in the years-long redress campaign and in the ferocious battles in the weeks that turned into months that turned into years after 9/11 taught me much about myself, about my community, and about America. When we embarked on this long road to redress, I'm not sure any of us really understood the true magnitude of what we sought to accomplish and ultimately how profound the journey would be. And certainly, I did not truly understand the significance of Senator Daniel Inouye's words when he told me that if I succeeded in guiding the JACL to the commission strategy and changed America's view about the internment, it would alter the course of American history. I understood the difficulty of the challenge when I set the initial effort of the campaign to educate and convince the American public, but I did not understand how meeting that challenge would, in fact, change the future.

The campaign was not without its struggles, and it definitely pushed me to my limit at times. For my part, it was like taking a long look into a mirror and having to decide what I was made of, what was important to me, what it all meant. In my role as the JACL's voice for the campaign, I faced a lot of opposition along the way—the outrage of the mainstream public for daring to insist that we had been the target of a racist policy that betrayed our rights as citizens; the admonition of our community elders at the dishonoring of our cultural values; the resistance of opposing forces within our own community; the fierce outrage at what was viewed as my betrayal in forcing a decision that some said sold out the community; the painful journey we took together to get us finally to the end of the path.

To an outsider, I'm sure it seemed like Japanese Americans were a cohesive and unified group that took each step as a part of a logical strategy that ultimately opened the doors to an inevitable conclusion. Would that it could have been so, that it could have been that easy. The truth is that we fought tooth and nail at each turn, fought for what we each thought was the right course, for what we each believed was our true purpose, fought because we lived through the terrible times of the war years and because we were the product of lifetimes lived in the community. We fought because we *were* community. And ultimately, what we each were fighting for was the preservation of that community: our sense of dignity, our sense of pride in who we are. In so doing, we demanded—and received—recognition of who we are as Americans. *Who we are as Americans.* That's what it all came down to, and not for just ourselves but for what it means for *anyone* to be an American. When we ask what it means to be American, we ask whether the Constitution actually does what it says it does. Do I retain my rights under the Constitution at all times, even when things are bad? Even if I look different than what someone says an American should look like? Do I retain my rights if I criticize this nation and its leaders, or speak out against governmental policies and actions that offend my sense of what's right and what's just?

At its heart, the redress campaign questioned the fundamental meaning of democratic idealism and, in answering that question, sought to ensure that those ideals were maintained for all Americans for all time. We were not fighting for what we lost but for what we could give to this nation. We never gave up, we never stopped clinging to our belief in America's potential for greatness, and in so doing we proved ourselves right.

It was never about the money. Money was just a tool we used to give meaning to the words. Throughout the campaign, I probably said over a thousand times that if we should succeed in getting compensation, I was certain that most of those who received reparations would not keep the money but donate it to charities, churches, or other nonprofits, or put the money into educational accounts for their grandchildren. And I was right. In the end, the vast majority of Japanese Americans who received monetary redress gave their money away. Personally, I always hoped to hear about some Nisei blowing his entire $20,000 in Las Vegas over a weekend and having a blast doing so! But that didn't happen, in part because I think there was a sense of solemnity to it all. As the first payments started being distributed in 1990, it wasn't the money anyone talked about but the letter of apology signed by President George H. W.

Bush. In stating that "we can never right the wrongs of the past," the president added that, as a nation, "we can take a clear stand for justice and recognize that serious injustices were done to Japanese Americans during WWII." Ultimately, it was these words that mattered most.

———

The redress campaign had an enormous impact on Japanese Americans at the most personal and profound levels, and in ways we could never have predicted when we began the long journey eighteen years before the signing of the Civil Liberties Act. Those young Sansei in Los Angeles in the 1960s who first demanded an honest reckoning with the issue of "camp" understood instinctively the need to purge the collective guilt and shame from the soul of the Japanese American community. The federal commission hearings became the mechanism that finally liberated us from the burdens we had carried in silence for so many years, and as sobering and emotionally raw as the testimonies were through each of the hearings, it was a process that provided the catharsis we neither wanted nor felt we needed. But, in fact, we did. And the effect on us as a community was as intense as it was immediate. The Nisei began talking about camp in public, at community events, around dinner tables, and learned to forgive one another for the choices they had made, the answers they had given to Questions 27 and 28, the things they had done to survive. Once the silence was broken and the reconciliation began, there was a collective healing in the community.

The effects of the redress campaign can still be seen today, some thirty years since the signing of the Civil Liberties Act of 1988. In Japanese American communities throughout the West Coast, there are Days of Remembrance events commemorating the signing of EO 9066, pilgrimages to the various camp sites, decennial events celebrating the signing of the redress bill, various exhibitions on the camps in cities throughout the country. Japanese Americans frequent classrooms, where they are invited to talk about their wartime experiences, and public events in the community always include reminders of the camps.

Perhaps the most important outcome for Japanese Americans is that we have left a legacy for future generations. It is a story about the failures of government but also a story of courage—the courage of people to fight against the nation's most powerful individuals and institutions, and the courage of powerful individuals and institutions to admit and then correct a past wrong, and to make different choices when fear and hate once again threaten to unseat the ideals upon which our nation was founded. Japanese Americans have given everyone a true lesson in democracy and left a rich and important legacy for all future generations.

In the 1950s, my father was one of only a handful of Nikkei (a person of Japanese heritage) living outside of Japan to be honored with an Order of the Rising Sun award, an acknowledgment of his cultural and community contributions. It was a rare recognition, especially for a Japanese American in those days, and it apparently was a great distinction. There was a buzz in the community about it, but whenever the parents of friends mentioned it to me, I brushed it aside as if it was no big deal. I was a teenager and still trying to unload the cultural baggage that had identified me as an enemy during the war, and it was perhaps unkind to my father, but he understood. It wasn't until much later that I understood the importance of the award: it was the third highest order bestowed by the Japanese government.

Almost thirty years later, two different Japan consuls general asked permission to submit my name for the same recognition for my work on the redress campaign, and several years after that a third consul general asked to submit my name for my post-9/11 work. As graciously as I knew how, I declined the offers because I felt such discomfort with the idea of being recognized by the Japanese government for my role in an issue that was so fundamentally American. To the one consul general with whom I could be the most honest, I explained that it would be hypocritical of me to accept recognition from Japan for work that had come about as a consequence of Japan's brutality during World War II.

"I'm proud of my Japanese heritage," I told him, "but more than anything, I'm an American and I don't ever want anyone to think differently."

I never had an opportunity to apologize to my father for not having taken his award more seriously. It never occurred to me until it was too late. He was given what in those days was a rare recognition for a magnificent cultural achievement, but in those postwar years he understood that my brothers and I, like all of us in my generation, were being pulled in a different direction. We were learning to live in a dichotomous world in which we struggled to be accepted as Americans, while at the same time we maintained pride in our cultural heritage. We lived with uncertainties and understood that this was how life had to be. In the world of our parents, we did not make demands. Our Japaneseness would not allow it.

Redress revealed who we were as Americans. It represented our demands that we be treated equally and, more importantly, that we be thought of as equal. It was our Americanness manifesting.

ACKNOWLEDGMENTS

Every book worth reading, I have been told, has benefitted from skillful editors. That being the case, I have been especially fortunate to have had two, Emmerich Anklam at Heyday, who not only edited content but also put up with my many questions and demands, and Lisa K. Marietta, whose word crafting has been incredible. I'm indebted to both for helping shape this book into what it is. My thanks also to Ashley Ingram at Heyday, who came up with the brilliant design for the book's cover image and the interior design as well.

As I did research for my manuscript, several people were generous with their time and assistance. I am particularly indebted to Janice Torbet, research specialist at the San Francisco Public Library, who was most helpful in tracking down specific documents crucial to my research. I'm also grateful to Tomiko Ismail at the JACL headquarters in San Francisco for her kindness in always responding promptly to my requests for information from the JACL's archival files. Special thanks to Susan Kamei, managing director at the Spatial Institute at the University of Southern California, for her assistance. Thanks also to Diane Yen-Mei Wong for her contributions in the early process of my writing this book. And one of the most useful resources for my research, since so much of my story is part of the JACL's history, has been the digital archives of the *Pacific Citizen*, whose archival collection goes back to the paper's first issue in October 1929.

My wife, Carol, read through specific parts of my manuscript when I've asked her opinion and has always been insightful and candid in her responses, sometimes leaving me disgruntled, but only because I knew she was right in her suggested changes. I'm thankful for all of those trying moments.

To my good friend Wendy Ruebman, special thanks for introducing me to Heyday publisher Steve Wasserman at one of her delightful lunches.

And finally, I wish to acknowledge the late Miles Myers, who always urged me to tell my story because it was, he would say, such an amazing and important story that said so much about America. His enthusiasm and sincerity inspired me.

INDEX

ABOUT THE AUTHOR

John Tateishi, born in Los Angeles, was incarcerated from ages three to six at Manzanar, one of America's ten World War II concentration camps. He studied English Literature at UC Berkeley and attended UC Davis for graduate studies. He played important roles in leading the campaign for Japanese American redress, and, as the director of the Japanese American Citizens League, he used the lessons of the campaign to help ensure that the rights of this nation's Arab and Muslim communities were protected after 9/11.